FAMILY INTERACTION
A dialogue between
Family Researchers and Family Therapists

Program Participants

Nathan W. Ackerman
Anonymous
Norman W. Bell
Ivan Boszormenyi-Nagy
Murray Bowen
Nathan B. Epstein
Antonio J. Ferreira
James L. Framo
Alfred S. Friedman
Jay Haley
Gerald Handel
Henry L. Lennard
George Levinger
Nathene Loveland
Robert MacGregor
Salvador Minuchin
Otto Pollak
Robert A. Ravich
David Reiss
Jules Riskin
David Rubinstein
Melvin Roman
Murray A. Straus
Fred L. Strodtbeck
James L. Titchener
Paul Watzlawick
John H. Weakland
Oscar R. Weiner
Carl A. Whitaker
Lyman C. Wynne

Family Interaction

A DIALOGUE BETWEEN

Family Researchers
and
Family Therapists

JAMES L. FRAMO
Editor

Springer Publishing Company, Inc., New York

International Standard Book Number: 0-8261-1211-0

Library of Congress Catalog Number: 77-188704

Printed in U.S.A.

This book is dedicated to Nathan W. Ackerman, the "grandfather" of family therapy and my friend, who died just before publication of these proceedings. (Ed.)

Program Participants

Nathan W. Ackerman, M.D. *Director of Professional Program, The Family Institute, New York, New York*

Norman W. Bell, Ph.D., *Professor of Sociology, Associate Professor of Psychiatry, University of Toronto, Head, Family Studies Section, Clarke Institute of Psychiatry*

Ivan Boszormenyi-Nagy, M.D., *Director, Family Psychiatry Division, Eastern Pennsylvania Psychiatric Institute, Philadelphia, Pennsylvania*

Murray Bowen, M.D., *Associate Clinical Professor of Psychiatry, Georgetown University School of Medicine, Washington, D.C.*

Nathan B. Epstein, M.D., *Professor and Chairman, Department of Psychiatry, McMaster University, Faculty of Medicine, Hamilton, Ontario, Canada*

Antonio J. Ferreira, M.D., *Research Associate, Mental Research Institute, Palo Alto, California*

James L. Framo, Ph.D., *Chief, Family Therapy and Training Unit, Jefferson Community Mental Health Center, and Associate Professor, Thomas Jefferson University, Philadelphia, Pennsylvania*

Alfred S. Friedman, Ph.D., *Director of Research, Philadelphia Psychiatric Center, Philadelphia, Pennsylvania*

Jay Haley, M.A., *Director of Family Research, Philadelphia Child Guidance Clinic, Philadelphia, Pennsylvania*

Gerald Handel, Ph.D., *Associate Professor of Sociology, Director, Social Research Laboratory, Department of Sociology, The City College of the City University of New York, New York*

Henry L. Lennard, Ph.D., *Associate Professor of Medical Sociology (Psychiatry) and Director, Family Study Station, Department of Psychiatry, University of California, San Francisco Medical Center, San Francisco, California*

George Levinger, Ph.D., *Professor of Psychology, University of Massachusetts, Amherst, Massachusetts*

Nathene Loveland, Ph.D., *Private Practice, Washington, D.C.*

Robert MacGregor, Ph.D., *Director, Team-Family Methods Training Program, Illinois Department of Mental Health, Chicago, Illinois*

Salvador Minuchin, M.D., *Director, Philadelphia Child Guidance Clinic, Philadelphia, Pennsylvania*

Otto Pollak, Ph.D., *Professor of Sociology, University of Pennsylvania, Philadelphia, Pennsylvania*

Robert A. Ravich, M.D., *Clinical Assistant Professor of Psychiatry, Cornell University Medical College, New York, New York*

David Reiss, M.D., *Chief, Section on Experimental Group and Family Studies, Adult Psychiatry Branch, National Institute of Mental Health, Bethesda, Maryland*

Jules Riskin, M.D., *Associate Director, Mental Research Institute, Palo Alto, California*

David Rubinstein, M.D., *Associate Professor of Psychiatry, Department of Psychiatry, Temple University Medical School, Philadelphia, Pennsylvania*

Melvin Roman, Ph.D., *Associate Professor of Psychiatry, Albert Einstein College of Medicine of Yeshiva University, Bronx, New York*

Murray A. Straus, Ph.D., *Professor of Sociology, Department of Sociology, University of New Hampshire, Durham, New Hampshire*

Fred L. Strodtbeck, Ph.D., *Professor of Social Psychology in Sociology and Psychology, The University of Chicago, Chicago, Illinois*

James L. Titchener, M.D., *Professor, Department of Psychiatry, University of Cincinnati College of Medicine, Cincinnati General Hospital, Cincinnati, Ohio*

Paul Watzlawick, Ph.D., *Research Associate, Mental Research Institute, Palo Alto, Clinical Instructor, Department of Psychiatry, Stanford University, Palo Alto, California*

John H. Weakland, *Research Associate and Associate Director, Brief Therapy Center, Mental Research Institute, Palo Alto, California*

Oscar R. Weiner, M.D., *Head, Family Therapy and Study Section, Department of Mental Health Sciences, Hahnemann Medical College, Philadelphia, Pennsylvania*

Carl A. Whitaker, M.D., *Professor of Psychiatry, University of Wisconsin Medical School, Madison, Wisconsin*

Lyman C. Wynne, M.D., Ph.D., *Chief, Adult Psychiatry Branch, National Institute of Mental Health, Bethesda, Maryland*

Foreword

This volume represents a wedding picture in which members of two families, clinicians and researchers, are seen in a joyous moment of trying to share their best with one another.

For years we have tried to reach out and bring together in meetings people who are leaders in both family therapy and family research. In 1964, Gerald H. Zuk and I planned our first conference on family systems and psychopathology (Zuk and Boszormenyi-Nagy, 1967).*Later, in 1967, I was an advisor in planning the conference from which this book was derived, a conference which was essentially James L. Framo's burden and accomplishment. The planners had to consider, in anticipation, the personal reactions of the two families of workers, of the individual members in each group, as well as the encounter between their published positions. The results show that Dr. Framo did a successful job in inducing a genuine encounter between family investigators and therapists.

At the time of the conference Dr. Framo was one of the senior members of the Family Psychiatry Division of The Eastern Pennsylvania Psychiatric Institute, one of the early sites for the study and treatment of families. When it came to responding to challenging tasks of integrating conceptual and human requirements of progress in the field of family dynamics, Jim Framo has always acted with vigor and integrity.

The Conference on Systematic Research on Family Interaction has been guided by the same ideals as the Division of Family Psychiatry at EPPI. From its earliest beginning the Division has aimed at a synthesis of the two exploding realms of knowledge about family relationships: clinical and conceptual. As we gradually encountered an increasing depth of unknown complexities and anxieties in dealing with families, we became increasingly

---

*Zuk, G. H. and Boszormenyi-Nagy, I. (Eds.) *Family therapy and disturbed families.* Palo Alto: Science and Behavior Books, 1967.

aware, also, of a need for a reliable conceptual gyroscope. We realized that significant progress in the clinical field can only be made if the clinician can grow theoretically and integrate new thought and evidence with his own, largely anthropomorphic, orientation to concepts.

We have begun to develop a "third ear" also toward the voice of the systematic observer. We have realized that behind many apparently cold intellectual efforts to fit hypotheses, findings, and statistical analyses into a formal schema there was the search for a deeper connection of personal meanings. We feel that somewhere, hopefully before infinity, the paths of the clinician and of the systematic observer must and will converge.

The test of the dialogue in a multidisciplinary meeting is in the openness of participants in stating ideas and, perhaps even more, in their courage in listening to the ideas of others and in responding to the other in depth, rather than tangentially. The clinician needs courage to see his pet formulations exposed to the cutting edge of formal definitions and operational requirements. The systematic research worker, on the other hand, needs courage to open himself to the subtle threat implicit in the exploration of the subjective, most personal aspects of family life which form the human understructure of observable group behavior. He will have to be open to the "gut reactions" evoked through the release of the deepest needs that exist in the human realm. Can the systematic research worker afford to open up and utilize insight into the private aspects of his own close relationships in the service of his inquiry as, ideally, the effective clinician should?

Attempting to integrate the realms of clinical theorizing and systematic scientific thinking is an enormous task, whether related to the individuals or the family as a whole. Systematic research on observable interaction and communication is often attractive enough reading but essentially it is not germane to what the clinician feels to be the essence of his problems. On the other hand, much of seemingly elegant "dynamic" clinical theorizing is based on patently undisciplined, prescientific manners of thinking.

What I personally hope and expect from systematic research in the family field is not masses of exact results before the main dimensions of close relationships are known but rather that more effort will be spent on a scientific inquiry about these very dimensions. I would like to ask each originator of a new major conceptual framework to assume the humble role of being a comparative linguist of the existing major conceptual idioms of the clinical field as well.

I believe that in order to grasp the substrate of what determines "healthy" and "pathogenic" relating, we have to go beyond observable behavior and communication as they occur in typical "experimental" situations. Many family clinicians put great faith in what occurs in their therapy sessions. They believe that they are more "active" because they manage to "shake up" the family during one hour of the week. The true measure of therapeutic force, however, is the extent to which the family members' lives are affected during the other 167 hours of the week. Only a small part of the totality of change of family life patterns is visible during the therapy hour. In contrast, in an experimental situation with a family, conclusions are drawn about the family on the basis of what occurred during the experiment itself. I think the essence of therapy is to affect life in its totality, and the therapist is merely a catalyst who is in touch with some level of relevant underlying patterning of family relationships. Perhaps if therapists learn about the experimenters' blind spots and *vice versa*, they can contribute to a "metalanguage" of close relationships, not merely of interactions.

I don't believe that we have to discard all the theoretical knowledge we have about individual motivation in order to achieve the foregoing. I wonder what answer any conference of the present sort can offer to the question of how to resolve the antithetical relationships between the subjective, idiosyncratic component of motivations, on the one hand, and the scientific requirements of "standardized tasks," on the other. I doubt that we will ever be able to quantify the subjective experience of individuals, but we might delineate objective ways of judging the degree of manifest evidence for love, loyalty, or confirmation among people. We may be able to narrow the inference gap without having to restrict systematic study to responses between hypothetical functions of robots instead of whole persons whose lives are, we know, meaningless without commitment to relationships.

In this age of information explosion and mushrooming scientific literature, I am impressed with the need for the experts being responsible for their field as a whole. No computer yet, and I am afraid in modern times no single encyclopedic mind, is likely to produce a balanced critical review of an entire field of inquiry. I often think that, ideally, every worker who has earned a reputation for any exciting and richly rewarding piece of research should be expected, and should be given financial support, to commit himself to reviewing a segment of the total field of his discipline.

In this regard, I believe that the group process of this conference was able to go one step further and produce a system of interactions which both created ideas and endeavored to integrate them into a meaningful relationship with the logic of science on the one hand and the logic of the sensitive and reacting person in relationship on the other. At any rate, I believe this was the highest expectation that we as family therapists and interactional theorists could have had from this conference. As to a goal for the design of future conferences of this type, I believe that what we need ultimately is a new conceptual language, but before that can be accomplished we needed a new open relatedness between our two fields and our two camps. At this conference we took the first step toward these goals.

Ivan Boszormenyi-Nagy, M.D.

Preface

In March, 1967, 29 nationally prominent family researchers, theoreticians, and family therapists met together for a two-day conference at the Eastern Pennsylvania Psychiatric Institute in Philadelphia, thus giving formal recognition to an emerging field of investigation—family interaction research —which focuses on the intimate context of human behavior. The conference captured an early point in time in the development of a field of study that will probably have a profound influence on how behavioral science research is likely to be done many years hence. The proceedings of the conference, recorded verbatim by a stenotypist, were converted into a book so that fellow scientists and clinicians could share the germinal ideas of this creative, new vantage point, from which man and society are viewed through the ways family members act upon one another. A brief survey of why and how the conference was organized, and this present volume shaped, will illustrate the uniqueness of the whole endeavor, and how, in many ways, it was a moving experience which had to be communicated to the professional community.

In the two decades preceding the conference, the practice of family therapy had yielded new concepts and knowledge about what goes on between people intimately involved with one another. Numerous conferences and workshops at professional conventions had been held by family clinicians where attempts were made to share clinical experiences, explicate aspects of family dynamics and therapy techniques, and develop concepts of family process and therapy. However, there had been a notable absence of conferences oriented around the systematization of this newly acquired knowledge. At the same time that family therapy was being developed by clinicians, some research-oriented family investigators (a select few of whom also did family therapy) began doing formal experiments with whole families in controlled situations. Most typically in these experiments, the families were presented with a standard problem or task to work out with each other as a group, the verbal interchanges were coded and scored according to some standardized method of categorizing behavior and feelings, and patterns and characteristics in different families were then compared. This unique kind of experimentation was a fundamental departure not only from traditional family research methods, which have relied largely on information *about* the family obtained from individually-administered questionnaires, but also from usual methods of psychological research wherein subjects respond to the

xiv   Preface

investigator rather than to each other.

The Editor designed this present conference out of the conviction that these two innovative but separate directions of family work needed to be brought together in order to develop better understanding of the intricacies of family process. It should not be necessary to point out that increased comprehension of how families work is not just for the benefit of abstract science. As all clinicians know who come daily into contact with the tragic, human consequences of disturbed family life—from murder through child abuse to intense conflict or alienation between marital partners or parents and children—the eventual practical implications of this research are far-reaching indeed.

The time, then, was propitious for a conference on systematic research on family interaction, with particular emphasis on transactional phenomena directly observed and measured when the family members interact together as a unit, either in an experimental setting or in the naturally developing family therapy situation. In planning such a conference, we conceptualized it as an attempt to explore some of the methodological and clinical considerations which need to be taken into account in planning research in the area of family interaction. The question was: How can we extract meaningful variables out of the clinical complexity which treatment of the family reveals, and how can these subjective concepts be put into operational form and creative experimental designs? The question of whether the private can be communicated and made public, in Bertrand Russell's sense, was a pertinent one. However, the conference was not planned as a therapy conference as such, or even as an evaluation of the treatment process or its results, although many clinical and therapy issues did come up during the proceedings. The focus was on identification of problems, basic issues, and strategy of family interaction research rather than the presentation of completed studies; the latter, however, as points of departure were not eliminated from discussion. A conference grant was applied for and awarded by the Clinical Research Branch of the National Institute of Mental Health (MH 12963-01).

A singular aspect of this conference was the decision to include both clinicians and research investigators. These two groups are rarely brought together, for it is commonly assumed that clinicians and researchers have insurmountable communication problems. The family therapist is most qualified to intuitively identify significant dimensions of complex family dynamics, just as the researcher is better suited to bring to bear upon family life variables his methodological sophistication and specialized techniques of measurement. In the Editor's judgment, the two groups need and can enrich each other, especially in this new direction of family investigation where exclusive concern with clinical matters of family therapy could lead to a loss of the early vision of this field.

All of the invited participants were carefully selected, on the basis of recommendation and search of the literature, as having made outstanding and pioneer contributions to the family field or to the area of interpersonal psychology.* Since a major aim of the conference was to increase the dialogue between family clinicians and researchers, experts in both areas were chosen on the basis of their being somewhat familiar with the work of the other group. In other words, the family therapists selected were the kinds of clinicians who, while they did not ordinarily undertake formal systematic studies with significance tests, were clinical investigators who conceptually examined what they were doing. (One can take the position, too, that the clinical method of psychotherapy, based on repetitive, controlled observation of data on multiple levels, and the reinforcing and discarding of evidence, is a legitimate research method in its own right.) The experimentally-oriented investigators were selected on the basis of their being acquainted with the developments in family therapy. There were, to be sure, several investigators who had experience with both family therapy and interaction research. The final choice of participants was the Editor's responsibility. Inasmuch as a working conference was the goal, the number of participants was restricted to 30, since it was thought that a group larger than that could not meaningfully interact. A number of distinguished family researchers and therapists, consequently, could not be included. A format whereby the group would be broken down into small workshop units would have permitted more professionals to attend, but the workshop format had the shortcoming of not enabling the group to be together the whole time. Because of the widespread interest in the conference, several hundred interested mental health professionals and students were invited to observe it; a few observed in the conference room itself, as space allowed, and a large audience in a nearby auditorium viewed the proceedings via closed circuit television.

Preparatory conference planning also included the Editor's arranging for all the participants to exchange summaries of their work and ideas so that valuable conference time would not have to be spent on these preliminaries. Each participant, then, prepared a ten-page summary, and, further, had to read 28 other summaries before attending the conference.

The Editor polled the participants for their ideas about the specific

---

*The following investigators, who had been invited to participate in the conference, were unable to attend: Drs. Robert Bales, Eric Berne, Frances Cheek, Wells Goodrich, Erving Goffman, Jules Henry, Rueben Hill, Theodore Lidz, Daniel Miller, Elliot Mishler, Alfred Scheflen, and Israel Zwerling.

kind of format that would be most productive; there was near unanimous agreement that the conference should *not* consist of a series of formal presentations of papers that bore no relationship to each other, and there was also consensus that large amounts of free time should be put aside for discussion. The following structure took shape from the suggestions of the participants as well as from the Editor's own thinking:

A period of two full days permitted eight sessions of three-and a-half hours each, and it was decided that seven half-hour position papers and a filmed family therapy session would be presented in order to stimulate discussion. Seven especially qualified experts were requested to prepare position papers on assigned topics dealing with broad, fundamental issues that were sequentially related and that unfolded from each other. The presenters were expected to cover their assigned topics in such a way as to spark discussion, but they could not be expected to be encyclopedic in the half hour allotted to them.

Each position paper was discussed by panels of three to five persons, and all participants were assigned to a panel on the basis of their expertise and interest in the area; each panel contained both family therapists and researchers. Two separate panels were selected to discuss Dr. Ackerman's filmed family therapy segment: a panel of researchers and a panel of clinicians. In addition to panel discussions, time was allotted for free discussion by all participants of issues raised by the position papers. Chairmen for each of the morning and afternoon sessions were selected from among the participants for the purpose of introducing speakers and guiding discussions. Some participants had requested that time be set aside in order to explore in detail several specific projects; there was interest in such questions as: why certain research decisions were made; what the consequences were of such decisions for the type of data collected; the problems faced in carrying out the research—in short, the kinds of information not ordinarily communicated in published reports. Accordingly, in the evening between the two days of the conference there were informal presentations of three projects: Dr. Robert A. Ravich talked on "The Interpersonal Behavior Game Test"; Dr. George Levinger discussed "Class Patterns in Marital Communication" and "Interpersonal Distance"; and Dr. Jules Riskin presented "Problems in the Selection of Families for Family Interaction Research." Unfortunately, considerations of space would not allow inclusion of these worthwhile presentations and the ensuing discussions in this volume. The final aspect of the organization of the conference was that two of the participants were requested to summarize their impressions of the conference; one summarized the trends developed during the proceedings, and the other discussed areas that had been neglected during the conference as well as his thoughts about the future direction of family interaction research.

These summaries were delivered off-the-cuff, without the benefit of previous reading of the position papers.

Following the conference itself, the Herculean task of editing the verbatim proceedings into a coherent and integrated book began. The position papers were all original compositions which had not been published elsewhere, and by themselves they would have constituted excellent chapters in a book. However, because of the fascinating interchanges that took place during discussions between these experts of different persuasions as they grappled with the issues, interchanges that resulted in rich, creative, and sometimes confusing ideas, the Editor was determined to make every effort to get the entire proceedings published. Dictating against this resolve was the precedent that conferences are rarely published; few books based on conferences succeed in transforming free discussion into readable material. Mr. Bernhard J. Springer of the Springer Publishing Company read the raw manuscript, became as convinced as the Editor that this conference was an exception to the rule, and offered to publish the book with the discussions included. This publication owes a great debt to the vision and confidence of Mr. Springer who, sadly, did not live to see the final product.

Numerous precautions were taken to avoid the errors of previously published conferences. The verbatim proceedings were reproduced and sent to all participants with instructions to do initial editing on their remarks, but to confine their alterations to clarification of wording and grammar so as to preserve the original intended meanings. Those who had prepared position papers were requested to put their chapters into finished written form with references, and to keep in mind the original subsequent discussions in adding any material or making revisions. When most of the preliminarily edited material was returned, it was collated into a master copy of material which still needed major surgery. The next safeguarding step that was made was to engage the services of someone to assist with the massive editing job who, not having been present at the conference, would be better able to assume the stance of the potential reader. Mrs. Lynn Hoffman, a talented person quite conversant with the family field,* agreed to help as an editorial consultant. We worked together for many hours, both in New York and at my home on weekends, going over every sentence in fine detail, deleting repetitions, condensing, clarifying statements, tightening up the verbal exchanges, and keeping just enough of the disorganization and humor so that the lifelike touch would not be lost. We adopted an editorial screen which extracted the nuggets of meaningful encounter, and attempted to eliminate all pointless, boring, or ambiguous material that did not flow in an

---

*See Haley, J. and Hoffman, L. *Techniques of family therapy.* New York: Basic Books, 1967.

understandable way. The aim in all of the editing was to communicate the substance and spontaneity of the conference in such a way that the printed word would not violate the spirit of the original spoken words. All the while we had to keep in mind the potential reader, who did not have the benefit of the nonverbal context of the statements or knowledge of the participants involved.

The editing on this volume was substantially complete by the fall of 1969, and the delay after that was due to the legal and ethical problems surrounding publication of one chapter which described a family therapist's attempts to free himself from his own family emotional system. We could have gone to press without this paper (titled in the text "Toward the Differentiation of a Self in One's Own Family"), but the Editor felt it was important enough to make every effort to have it included. After considering all of the sticky issues involved in this deeply personal treatise, the final decision was that the paper would have to be published anonymously. There is another reason why the Editor was not only willing to give this author more space, but even delayed publication of the entire book for several years: This rather remarkable chronicle may well become, in the Editor's judgment, a classic and a breakthrough in the history of psychiatry and the behavioral sciences. In many ways this paper is years ahead of its time in its profound implications, and the Editor is honored that the author selected this conference and publication for so courageous a document. His family, moreover, has made a lasting contribution to the study of human behavior.

The Editor wishes to acknowledge, further, the help and encouragement of numerous others in the organizing of the conference and the preparation of this book:

Dr. Ivan Boszormenyi-Nagy assisted in planning and organizing the original conference, participated in the selection of participants, determination of format, and the many other decisions that had to be made. His wise counsel, support, and encouragement are deeply appreciated. The memories of the twelve years I spent with Ivan Nagy at the Eastern Pennsylvania Psychiatric Institute, where I was privileged to participate in the development of one of the outstanding family therapy centers in the country, will always remain with me as the high point of my professional life.

Appreciation is expressed to Jay Haley for his suggestions and backing during the early phases of the conference.

Gratitude is expressed to Dr. William Phillips, Medical Director, and Dr. Richard Schultz, former Business Administrator, of the Eastern Pennsylvania Psychiatric Institute, for their help in arranging the hundreds of details in organizing the conference.

Thanks are expressed to Mr. Harold Russell of EPPI who organized the audio-taping and closed circuit televising of the conference.

To Miss Jean Leech, who typed the manuscript from my indecipherable sentences written in margins and between lines, go my many thanks.

Finally, and far from least, I wish to express my deep gratitude to the authors of the position papers and to all of the other participants in the conference for sharing their thoughts and selves for those memorable two days, as well as for all the work they have done in helping to make this publication possible. Behavioral scientists everywhere who are planning research in this area will now have the benefit of the thinking of these advanced investigators in this fascinating and challenging new field of family interaction research.

James L. Framo

Table of Contents

Introduction

This volume introduces one of the beginning steps in the systematization of a scientific revolution in the understanding of human behavior. Kuhn (1962, p. 91) has stated, "Scientific revolutions are here taken to be those non-cumulative developmental episodes in which an older paradigm is replaced in whole or in part by an incompatible new one." Academic psychology (with the exception of a few social psychologists) has traditionally studied man segmentally in terms of cognition, imagery, sensation, perception, affects, motives, and consciousness. Although clinical psychology and psychiatry try to deal with man as a whole person, these fields have, essentially, viewed individual behavior as occurring in a vacuum. By moving away from a model which postulates that disordered behavior stems from a central illness process in one person toward one which views deviant behavior as adaptive to its context, the family transactional approach represents a quantum leap forward so discontinuous from the past as to qualify as a scientific revolution.

Family therapy, created originally for practical clinical purposes, is not just another technique or form of treatment but a reconceptualization of the very basis from which to view human behavior. When family members were directly observed interacting with each other in a therapeutic setting (forbidden heretofore by professional and cultural taboos), phenomena began to be discovered that had never before been known to exist because the special microscope for their disclosure had not yet been invented. Clinically, for instance, mental health professionals for the first time were able to move beyond the point of sensing that the family had something to do with psychiatric conditions to having palpable evidence of *how* pathogenic relationship patterns and individual psychopathology were generated over time by such powerful forces as family myths, rules, alliances, distorted communication channels, and covert loyalty pressures. The

1

findings of family therapy challenged existing concepts about the very nature of emotional disorder, as well as beliefs that focused on "curing" a patient and returning him to the same unchanged environment. Instead, psychiatric symptoms came to be viewed as expressions of intimate relationship struggles, the *substance* of disturbed behavior could be seen as a system phenomenon, and therapy had to be reformulated as efforts aimed at changing contexts (Framo, 1970). As Ackerman states in this volume, the phenomenon of psychiatric breakdown now becomes redefined as a multiplicity of behaviors playing into one another, involving a number of persons interacting in a special way and reflecting a range of vulnerability patterns over time within an intimate group.

Increased knowledge about the special psychology of intimate relationships promises to have synergistic effects, not only on the etiology and treatment of psychiatric disturbances, but on other social and behavioral sciences as well. Wynne points out in this book that the family as the fundamental unit of society is the converging point of all four major conceptual systems of human behavior—culture, social structure, personality systems, and biological systems. Although, according to systems theory, all systems have the common properties of homeostasis, transaction, and communication of information, the blood ties and enduring emotional attachments between the people who make up a family give it a unique quality unlike that of any other social system. Aside from clinical questions, because the family occupies such an uncommon position, fulfills such important functions, and has such powerful influences, the study of basic family processes and interactions can decode and make intelligible many behaviors of individuals and groups in other social systems. A number of human problems may be reinterpreted in the light of depth understanding of family dynamics: there are extensions of family role assignments (the placator, the realist, the blamer) into other social relationships; we have clearer understanding of why people can be socially accomplished or successful at their work yet behave in an irrational or childish fashion when with their family; just as in a family where one person may carry psychic functions for another ("I will be your conscience if you will express my impulses"), so the interlocking of motivations increases as a function of the degree of emotional closeness between unrelated people; the person without a family is much more likely to turn the work situation or living situation of a school, commune, military post, or prison into a family one, with attendant love and hate, jealousy, and alliance behavior. Just as in a family a conflict between parents can be acted out between the children, so can unexpressed conflicts at the top level of management be transmitted to and expressed between employees at the lower levels of a business organization; the concept of triangulation, described by the anonymous author in this volume, which postulates that whenever two people get together they say something bad about a third party, is a ubiquitous interpersonal phenomenon, not restricted to the family; and, certainly, the phenomenon of scapegoating, seen most vividly in the family setting, is a mechanism as old as Man himself.

Prior to family therapy, nearly everything that science knew about relationships between people, or interpersonal psychology, was either based on inferences about the relationships obtained from individuals (e.g., traditional family research) or on direct observation and measurement of interaction between strangers (e.g., the area of small group research). There are two obvious shortcomings to these two methods: 1) there is often a wide discrepancy between how a person *says* he behaves with intimate others and how he actually behaves, and 2) small group research, or even conventional group therapy, deals with groups that have, as a group, no past history or likelihood of a future together. Research on the family has been undertaken by many disciplines and at numerous levels: sociologists have discussed the family in terms of role distribution or division of labor, psychoanalysts in terms of incestuous and oedipal strivings, demographers in statistical terms of population distribution, and anthropologists have focused on cross-cultural family patterns. Only the family therapists, however, have gained access to the essential, intrinsic, gut issues of family life. While the requirements of scientific theory require an objective, impersonal, descriptive language in order to delineate the formal characteristics of family organization, there are certain family experiences that go beyond words or scientism. For example, the intense satisfactions of family living, the joy of belonging, the pleasure over being the chosen one, or the bliss during the togetherness phase of symbiosis are counterbalanced by the human tragedies of dehumanization, rejection, persecution, disappointments, hypocrisy, and conspiracies of silence which can occur in family life. Carl Whitaker once said in this connection that the family is the place where you're dealing with life and death voltages.

On the other hand, systematic researchers would argue that, while clinicians can provide vital information and inspiration for the formulation of hypotheses via hunches and impressions, opinions are still opinions, unable to be proven or refuted by any scientific standard. According to these investigators, although there are controversies over whether science should be problem or method oriented, and how science should be defined, there is general agreement that observations must be organized into theory, that theories should be operationally stated and put in the form of testable hypotheses, and that variables should be manipulated by certain rules so as to permit the data to confirm or disprove the hypotheses by other than personal means. Only in this way, the researchers state, can laws of broad applicability be abstracted from the individual instance. The clinicians dispute this thesis, saying that problems are defined by researchers in terms that are most convenient to research, and that experimentalists, in their quest for scientific objectivity, end up measuring pallid, trivial variables and distill all humanity from their investigations. Arguments about different models of Man and the methodology associated with them have been going on for a long time (e.g., behaviorism vs. phenomenology in the study of individuals). These issues are no less pertinent in the field of family interaction research which, in addition to the subjective-objective dimension, has its own distinctive philosophical and methodological problems. Behavior of the family as an aggregate unit or system is more than the sum of the behaviors of its individual members. In interaction research the focus is on circular, reciprocal feedbacks of behaviors which have to take into account the behaviors of others. Moreover, when the investigator attempts to re-create typical, repetitive interchanges which family members have toward each other, and devises a test situation which promotes group coping in face-to-face interaction, he is departing from traditional research which attempts to eliminate or hold constant variability and context.

The foregoing sets the stage for the kinds of concerns dealt with in this book. The proceedings of the conference from which this book was derived offer the family researcher, theoretician, or clinician an unparalleled opportunity to become informed about where the experts are in this developing new field. More to the point of this volume, the informal dialogue between family researchers and family therapists, in the sections between chapters of this book, contains the kind of unguarded comments, doubts, marginal thoughts, debates, and frank confessions of scientists that rarely find their way into print. During the planning phases of the conference, we had no way of predicting how this group of investigators would interact with each other. There was some concern about how the group process would affect the purposes of the conference. Most of the family therapists had a history of relationship with each other, and comments sprinkled throughout the conference give hints about some of the dynamics of the "family" of family therapists. The reader is afforded a glimpse into some of the inner workings of this group of well-known professionals. Some of the family therapists and family researchers had had prior contact with each other, but most had never met before. Since all of the participants had established reputations in their fields, there were bound to be some clashes as strong convictions were exposed and as various stances were taken by colleagues to force modification of treasured ideas. What finally did happen is contained in this volume—a running account of the interpersonal by-play between these experienced specialists as they struggled to deal with exceedingly complex issues. The editing of the proceedings, while adhering to the principle of organized communication, was also aimed at retaining the raw, lifelike quality of the exchanges in order to impart the ring of authenticity present at the original conference. One will find in these pages, thus, an account of the sparks that flew between "hard" and "soft" researchers and how this controversy got diminished by the end of the conference; the struggle between Straus, Handel, Reiss and others over the "true" nature of science; Ackerman's and Whitaker's pleas to the rigorous scientists to join the clinicians in a common endeavor; Bowen's wry, deadpan efforts to deal with the system of the group itself; the surprise of the clinicians when they discovered that a phenomenon they knew well had been studied systematically in another field; the discussion between Wynne, Bell, MacGregor, Rubinstein, and Ferreira over whether the family always behaves as a system; Wynne's questioning of Haley's assumptions about the limits of interaction research; the bridges that Levinger tried to establish between the researchers and clinicians; the interchanges between Ravich, Titchener, Strodtbeck, Ferreira, and Levinger on whether two- and three-person groups are essentially different; the shock effect on the group process of the anonymous paper; the differences between Lennard and MacGregor over coding of interaction; and Whitaker's puncturing of intellectualism with humor throughout the conference.

It should give some comfort to the beginning researcher that the field of family interaction research is not a set one with an established body of knowledge and known limits. It would be difficult, for instance, for a student to take an examination on this book for a catalogue of facts. Rather, the value of this book lies in the insights it gives into the usually private process of incubation of ideas, the disagreements, and the puzzlements that always accompany creative conceptualizing. The ferment reflects the healthy state of confusion that characterizes the early stages of any new field of investigation. Instead of being presented with slick, finished reports of research that leave out the misgivings an investigator has about his procedures or findings, the reader can participate in the *process* of research. The clinically oriented investigator, moreover, can partake of the thinking of distinguished family therapists as they labor to organize their clinical data. Those family therapists, family sociologists, interaction researchers, social psychologists, family experimentalists, and other behavioral scientists interested in studying intimate relationships systematically can become aware of the present status of this fascinating new area. If, as some say, the family is a dying institution, the practical implications of this work are far-reaching indeed—perhaps ultimately tied in with man's survival.

REFERENCES

Framo, J. L. Symptoms from a family transactional viewpoint. In Ackerman, N. W. (Ed.) *Family therapy in transition*. International Psychiatry Clinics, Vol. 7, No. 4, Boston: Little, Brown & Co., 1970.

Kuhn, T. S. *The structure of scientific revolutions*. Chicago: Univ. of Chicago Press, 1962.

Charge to the Conference

Dr. James L. Framo: It is a pleasure to welcome you to this national conference on a new area of research which has such exciting promise for understanding what goes on between people closely related to one another. The full title of this conference is "Methodological and Clinical Considerations Involved in Systematic Research on Family Interaction and Dynamics."

Before I go on to state my view of the philosophy and goals of this conference, I would like to tell you a little bit about the history of its development from idea to fruition. Two more or less independent movements have been occurring in the family field over the past decade or so. (I am eliminating from consideration at this time the voluminous traditional work and research done on the family by sociologists, anthropologists, and others.)

In reformulating concepts about the very nature of emotional disturbances and its treatment, the family therapy movement, a tour de force breakthrough, really, has yielded a mass of undigested information about the transactional nature of intimate relationships. Family therapy is not just a modality of treatment but a philosophy which offers a wholly new theoretical model for thinking about psychopathology, contexts, and systems. Another movement in recent years in the field of family has been the proliferation of systematic studies on family interaction in the laboratory. This endeavor has proceeded somewhat independently of the family therapy movement. It is a unique kind of research which, in general, relies on observation and measurement of the family members' responses to each other rather than to the investigator.

The specific idea that precipitated this conference was that these two movements should not go their separate ways. If they did, it would be somewhat analogous to what happened when psychoanalysis and academic psychology lost touch with each other in dealing with the same phenomena. How can the newly acquired knowledge about family interaction, relationships, and dynamics which family therapy has given us be systematized and made more a part of the scientific arena? I am not sure if the reverse is true, whether systematic research ever really affects clinical practice. I doubt it.

With the idea, then, that clinical variables can be systematized in a meaningful way so that in the process of translation to operations not too much of the dynamic complexity is lost, I conceived of a conference composed of hard and soft family researchers, what William James called the tender and the tough-minded. I mentioned the idea to Ivan Nagy, who endorsed it and worked along with me, and then in the summer of 1965 I wrote to Jay Haley and he and I kicked the ideas around in a few letters about the purposes and rationale, the kinds of participants, etc. I am grateful to Jay for his help in those days.

I applied for an NIMH grant for the conference, conceptualizing it as a preliminary free-wheeling one consisting of a spontaneous free interchange of ideas. The idea was that the field was so new that we should try to identify the problems and discuss research strategy. This goal, we thought, could not be reached by the presentation of a series of disconnected papers. The Review Committee deferred their decision and the conference had to be postponed because they felt that problem areas should be more defined beforehand and more structure introduced. I won't go into the vicissitudes of our negotiations with NIMH, but the philosophy of the conference eventuated into a kind of compromise which, actually, I realize now, will probably be more productive.

As the program is now planned, a series of seven position papers will be presented, and their main purpose will be to spark discussion among panel members. Time has been set aside also for free discussion among all participants. The topics of these position papers and their sequence were carefully planned so as to sample the major systematic and clinical issues and tap the various levels of family interaction research. We have maintained our goal of aiming toward that which is basic, fundamental, and general, building on what is known and leading toward that which is even more unknown. The primary focus of the conference is on clarifying problem areas, exchanging viewpoints, and developing research outlooks, and not on therapy as such, which has to do with bringing about change in people.

Much advance planning has gone into this conference. For example, in the preceding months all the participants shared with each other summaries of their work so that they would be somewhat familiar with

each other's thinking and background before they met here. As I understand it, in a prior, smaller conference held on this topic in Boston, the
participants ran into difficulty because they had to acquaint each other
with what they were doing, and by the time they did that, it was time to
go home.

We are fortunate, indeed, to have such distinguished participants
present at this conference. The group is composed of family therapists,
research sociologists, research clinical psychologists, research psychiatrists,
family theoreticians, and family experimentalists. All were carefully chosen
as being somewhat familiar with each other's domain. We are hoping to
develop a flow back and forth between clinical and methodological
concepts so that each discipline, faction, and person will be stimulated into
seeing the problems of the other. This conference is an experiment in
whether professionals with diverse premises, approaches, and language can
create dialogue without communicating past each other.

I would like to spend a moment on this latter point because I think it
is important. In 1946, I heard a phrase in a lecture by the philosopher
T.V. Smith from the University of Chicago, which has always stuck with
me. He spoke of how, in art, one must expand the imagination and how, in
science, one must contract the imagination. In 1955, Carl Rogers, in his
thoughtful article, "Persons or Science," described how, as a therapist, he
immersed himself in the therapeutic experience and reached "the height of
personal subjectivity in a mutual process of becoming."* The therapy
experience has an incommunicable validity and reality which goes beyond
objective, consensually shared truth. As a scientist, however, one has to
determine how one knows what one knows so that a body of organized and
communicable, replicable knowledge can be built up. In science, we need
theory to organize and make sense out of our observations, and we need to
follow agreed-upon rules of investigation so that relationships between
events can be described and manipulated and predicted with the highest
degree of probability. We need science, in short, to prevent self-deception.
Ideally, this is the way the scientific method should work, but the method
of science is executed by people. I refer here not only to behavioral
scientists re-proving the obvious and the superficial, but also to experimenter bias, examined in the work of Rosenthal,** and the social

---

*Rogers, C. R. Persons or science? A philosophical question. *American Psychologist*, 1955,
10, 267-278.

**Rosenthal, R. *Experimental effects in behavioral research.* New York: Appleton-Century-
Crofts, 1966.

psychology of the experiment itself, examined by Martin Orne,* which casts into doubt, really, many research findings.

Despite these reservations about research, I would like to mention a few methodological issues of family interaction research that I hope will be touched upon during the next couple of days:

Do we have a right to assume that a family's style of interaction as it occurs either in the laboratory or in the therapist's office is a reliable sample of that family's characteristic behavior in the home? Don't we need to know the demand characteristics of the setting?

We know clinically that the display of certain transactional behaviors of an individual or a group depends on who is actually physically present: a man, for example, will be a different person and will behave differently when he is 1) with his wife alone, 2) with his wife and children, 3) when his mother or father or therapist is added to the group, and so on. Can we systematically vary the permutations of various combinations of intimate others in order to observe the various kinds of behaviors that are elicited?

How do we handle the problem of disguise of motives in communications? *Why* do people have to double-bind? What lies behind manifest, latent, and meta-communication? In doing family interaction research, what do we need to know about the wider context within which the family is embedded? How do we go about determining what categories to use in classifying family behavior over time, and what should we sample?

How do we develop concepts that embrace not only the individual, with his levels of consciousness, internal motivations and fantasies, and inner and outer worlds, but behavior with experience, the other with the self, and the transactional relationships between people? Can we develop methods that will reveal the deeper levels of family relationships? Will we be able to move beyond the simplistic typology of normal and abnormal families and study family *processes?*

Can we use the methods and findings of small group research, done with strangers, and apply them to intimate relationships that have a past history together and a future?

Can we move beyond studies of leadership, decision-making, power, dominance, and cohesiveness, borrowed from the small group discipline?

Is the interjection of controversy the only way to experimentally stimulate family interaction in the laboratory? Can we, for example,

---

*Orne, M.T. On the social psychology of the psychology experiment: With particular reference to demand characteristics and their implications. *American Psychologist,* 1962, *17,* 776-783.

stimulate affiliative, supportive, loving, or mourning responses of the family members to each other?

What is the influence of the observer and our observational devices—movies, tape recorder, one-way mirror—upon the processes under study?

Can the questionnaire method of family research be utilized innovatively in the light of new knowledge about family transactional behavior that family therapy has given us?

I might mention that, in this random sample of methodological issues, quantification itself is not a problem. Statistical techniques are available to correlate and test the significance of differences in anything that can be classified or counted. The question is, rather, *what* to quantify so that human meaning is not lost. Gill has labeled this problem as the dilemma between the significant and the exact.

You have probably all heard the joke about the drunk who was walking around the light pole looking on the ground for something he had lost, and how, when somebody came along and asked if he could help look, the drunk said, "I didn't lose it here; I lost it up the alley, but the light is better here." Well, I am now going to take a little trip up the clinical alley, in the dark, where the pay dirt is, I feel. I will change my hat to that of the clinician, and raise a few questions that seem to me to be worthy of systematic investigation:

Can we understand more about the mechanisms of transpersonal motivational systems? How is it that, if you are brave, I can allow myself to be scared? If you are responsible, I can be irresponsible? If you are frugal, I can spend? If my wife takes the soft line with the children I can take the hard line?

Why do we reserve for our family the best and the worst that is in us? Why is it especially difficult to be kind to those we love? How is it that we show our greatest cruelty toward our family intimates, yet for them we will make our greatest sacrifices? Why is it that family members can hurt and frustrate us the most, and why can they give us the kinds of gratification for which no price is too high to pay?

Why do we have a different psychology when we are with our families? How is it that one person can be a functional failure outside and give his family a lot, while another gives to the whole world and lets his family down?

Are ties of blood tighter than legal marital ties when it comes to a showdown? What do we know about mutual projection in marriage, where each partner believes that what he does is only in reaction to his mate's behavior? ("How can you feel affectionate toward someone who is always critical toward you? Is it that *I* can't love or that my mate is unlovable?")

When someone with whom I am deeply connected becomes irratio-nal, how do I know whether he or she is really irrational or whether I am producing the irrational response?

How much do you owe yourself and how much do you owe others? How can I meet the other's needs and wishes without sacrificing myself as a person with my own individuality? What is mature selfishness?

How necessary for survival are some shared myths? Should reality always be king? *Whose* reality?

How does one deal with the deceit, lies, disappointments, hypocrisy, and injustices which seem to be an inevitable part of family life?

Why do we show different sides of ourselves to different people? Why are certain responses pulled from us only by certain people under certain conditions? (One sibling to the other: "I can't understand how you can say Mom was cruel. She was never that to me.")

Isn't it true that one of the most painful, rockbottom things people learn in any form of psychotherapy is that, in the final analysis, you can only change for yourself? That you cannot wait for somebody else to change first? That you cannot change *for* somebody else.

Is it better to help a son work things out with his father in his real presence or with images of father with a professional therapist?

Can we ever understand the *why* of emotional enslavement? What is there about the power of the emotional system of a family that even intensive psychoanalysis will not always enable one to break free from it? How does one free oneself of one's family fossil remains from previous generations?

Can we overemphasize hostility in the family? Statistic: in 36 per cent of the 696 homicides in New York City in 1965, the victim and murderer were related to each other. Nationwide, 28 per cent of all law officers killed in the line of duty were killed responding to family fights. And in the first family, Cain slew Abel.

Can we overemphasize love in the family? Have you noticed how people will do anything so that their parents will not suffer? Or is it that they will do anything to make them suffer? But what wrenches the heart more than a death in the family?

Can we ever really be better parents than our parents were? What did we really want from our parents? What do we *really* want from our children?

Questions like these are representative of the preoccupations of those of us who work with families, not only because we had to struggle with these dilemmas in our own families, but also because riddles like these keep us awake at night.

Now to some procedural details. Inasmuch as this is a working conference, only the participants of the conference itself are to take part in the free discussions. We recognize the frustration that is likely to arise in the observing audience, and we recognize that opinions of members of the audience are valuable, but this is the way the conference was organized. We do have some distinguished visitors from all over the country observing the conference, both in this room and in the Auditorium via closed circuit TV. There is a visitor who came all the way from Milan, Italy,* and one from Greece.**

The chairman for each section of the program has been requested not to allow imbalance in participation and to moderate in such a way that strong personal feelings and narcissism will not be any greater than they have to be.

Finally, it is my hope that in the years to come we will recognize the value of having gotten together for these two days. Now let us begin!

*Dr. Mara Selvini Palazzoli

**Dr. George Vassiliou

Critical Overview of Present Status of Family Interaction Research

JAY HALEY

Chairman Norman W. Bell: I am sure all the participants and many of the observers here admire Dr. Framo and Dr. Nagy on two counts. One is their courage in bringing such a diverse group together and attempting to get them interacting at a significant level about things on which there can be quite violent disagreement. I think we ought to congratulate them, too, and give them a straight A for getting this conference organized. Dr. Framo and Dr. Nagy have persisted more than most of us would be willing to do.

To move on to this morning's program, the position paper, titled, "Critical Overview of Present Status of Family Interaction Research," is being given by Mr. Jay Haley. If there is one person in the country in the field of family research and family therapy who needs no introduction, it probably is Jay Haley, our gadfly supreme, master of many skills, with honors too numerous to mention. I will confine myself to mentioning the most recent—his appointment as President of the International Society for Communications Analysis. Jay!

Mr. Jay Haley: It is nice to see so many familiar faces in the room and I think we should all be grateful to Dr. Framo and Dr. Nagy. A lot of us talk about arranging meetings but these fellows actually arranged one and went through with the tremendous amount of organizational work that is involved.

I am supposed to do a critical overview of the present status of interaction research in half an hour, and I think this is impossible. The

13

most I can hope to do is skim over the field and list many of the research studies and try to deal with some of the issues we face.

This review will necessarily reflect my own views or biases, and I will try to say things that people can disagree with so that we can have some discussion. If I say anything that is disagreeable, I want you to realize I am doing it as a duty, not because I prefer doing it.

A new way of looking at and explaining the behavior of human beings appeared in the world when it was suggested that a person exhibiting psychiatric symptoms could be described as someone adapting to a unique family context. To determine whether the intimate relationships of psychiatric patients were different from those of "normal" people, research investigators began to bring members of families together to study them responding to one another. These investigations have been continuing for ten years and there is a growing body of literature on procedures for observing and testing the patterns of ongoing relationships. Most of this work is preliminary and exploratory. Many investigators have tried out new tests and measurements upon whatever samples of families were convenient, planning to take more care in their procedures when they had a better understanding of the nature of the methodological problems. Despite the preliminary nature of the work that has been done, is there evidence at this time to support the idea that the family, rather than the inner nature of the individual, is the locus of psychopathology and the unit which should be treated in therapy? More important, what can one consider as "evidence" in this new field of family research? The investigations done in the area of the family-and-psychiatry will be reviewed here to examine the evidence and to illustrate some of the methodological problems that arise when one attempts to answer such questions.

The family orientation in psychiatry does not merely suggest a revision of past psychological theory; it raises a basic question about the *unit* that should be studied and treated. Previous psychiatric and psychological theories were based upon several assumptions: it was assumed that the unit of study was the individual, that symptomatic behavior was irrational and socially maladaptive, and that if individuals appeared to differ from one another the difference must lie within them rather than in their social situation, since all people are responding to essentially the same environment. The family view, in its extreme form, has proposed that the unit of study should be the social context of the individual, that symptomatic behavior is adaptive to that context, and that if individuals appear to differ from one another it is because the situations they are responding to are different. From this view, the difference between "normal" people and individuals with psychiatric problems would be a difference in the current family situation (and treatment situation) in which the person is imbedded. It is the examination of this larger context which is the focus of family research.

The study of the intimate interpersonal context of a person has relevance beyond questions about why people behave as they do. For the practice of psychiatry, there is extremely practical significance in this study. If families containing a psychiatric patient are different from other families, the argument is supported that the social context in which a patient lives must change before he can change. The entire orientation of therapeutic intervention hinges upon this question.

Although there are many aspects of the family research field, the focus of family investigations that is most pertinent to psychiatry and clinical psychology can be presented in terms of several questions:

1. Are families that contain a member who is "abnormal" in a psychiatric sense different from families in which all members are "normal"?

2. Is the family that has a member with one type of abnormality different from a family with a member of another type? For example, is the family with a schizophrenic member different from the family with a delinquent, a hysteric, or a phobic?

3. Is one part of a family different from another part? For example, is the parental relationship with an "identified patient" different from the relationship with his sibling, or are parental relations with extended kin different in important ways among families?

4. Has a family changed into a different system after individual or family therapy?

These questions about differences involve classifying families into types, which would seem to be the approach most commonly taken in current family research. An alternative view is that families in a particular culture and class are all of the same type from a psychiatric view but appear different if one examines them at different stages of development. For example, every marriage may typically include periods of disturbance which take the form of symptoms in a family member (Warkentin & Whitaker, 1966). An "abnormal" family would then only be different from a "normal" family because it was observed at a different point in time in the progress of the marriage and/or the family had happened upon a referral route which defined it as "abnormal."

To the clinician who is treating whole families, it is "obvious" that the family in the session with him is abnormal and differs significantly from normal families. Yet the clinician cannot really know whether the interpersonal action he is treating also occurs in families where no members exhibit symptoms. He also does not know whether it is the act of intervening with treatment which disrupts a person or a family and provokes the behavior that he is observing. Since there is no examination of normal individuals or families in clinical training, therapists do not have a normal base line which permits them to judge the presence, or degree, of psychopathology. Although many of the ideas in family research were generated by clinical observations, research is a necessary corrective for illusions generated in that setting. Investigators who began their inquiries with family therapy not only believed that the abnormal family was grossly different from other families, but they also assumed that it would be a simple matter to demonstrate that difference. One would merely bring in samples of families and look at them. It has not proven to be that simple; questions began to arise about what samples would be brought into what settings to look at what variables in what ways under what conditions. This review examines ways of dealing with these problems.

Research Approaches

The study of families of psychiatric patients has culminated in three general types of published papers: the theoretical paper offering concepts, the article discussing a possible method of testing concepts, and the paper fully reporting a piece of accomplished research. Only the latter type of publication will be emphasized in this review.

Until quite recently the most common paper in the family field was the theoretical paper, with ideas drawn from logic or clinical impressions, which dealt with the nature of families or of a particular type of family. Most of the papers that attempted to relate "personality" to the family, and that were published in the mid-1950's during the first flush of ideas about psychiatry and the family, were theory papers. Suggestions about the presence in families of "pseudo-mutuality" (Wynne, Ryckoff, Day & Hirsch, 1958), "emotional divorce" (Bowen, 1960), the "double-bind" (Bateson, Jackson, Haley & Weakland, 1956), and "homeostasis" (Jackson, 1957) were proposed. Similar papers continue to appear. Many of these ideas are derived from individual interviews with family members and others from conjoint family therapy or preliminary family testing. I will not attempt to document the theoretical ideas since what is being offered is not evidence but speculation which might ultimately lead to the gathering of evidence. Reviews of the ideas proposed, with little or no emphasis upon methodology for testing the ideas, have been offered by Meissner (1964), Mishler & Waxler (1965), Frank (1965), and Handel (1965).

Little specific investigation of these early ideas has been done by investigators working out research methods. Instead, they have tested derivatives of them or premises about people based upon them. Among the many approaches used, it would seem there are now at least four general ways of conceptualizing a family for purposes of family research.

1. Families are studied in terms of the character of individual members with an emphasis upon personality and affect. For example, it is suggested that normal families have members who are less hostile, aggressive, dependent, immature, and so on, than abnormal families.

2. An emphasis is put upon family structure, and particularly on whether the family members fulfill their roles properly. For example, it is said that in normal families the father has a more dominant position than the mother while in abnormal families the reverse is the case.

3. An emphasis is put upon the processes in the interchange between family members: a measurement of interaction. Within this communications approach it is said that normal families communicate more clearly, exhibit less conflict and discord, have fewer disagreements, have more stable coalition patterns, and shift to different patterns of behavior if the setting requires.

4. An emphasis is put upon the family as a working group which produces a kind of outcome in a task. This view appears more related to information theory and it is said that normal families must cooperate and transmit information better since they get a task done more quickly and efficiently and with less "noise."

Within these different approaches, it is becoming assumed that the more severe the individual psychopathology the more the family's behavior will deviate from normal family behavior as defined by the investigator's conceptual framework.

For most investigators in family research the basic problem has been to devise a way to measure how family members *typically* behave with each other. This problem is unique; most previous research has focused upon the ideology of individuals, the response of individuals to a test stimulus, or the responses of strangers to each other in small group research (Halcy, 1962).

Faced with the problem of studying typical family behavior, investigators have proceeded in several different ways. Each approach has its merits as well as difficulties. One of the more common methods has been to ask family members about their family life. This is accomplished either with individual interviews, with questionnaires, or with check-list inquiries about interpersonal life given to individuals. With this approach, which sociologists tend to prefer, one can collect data from large samples. One need not take the trouble to bring family members together for study. The chief defect of the method is that there is little reason to believe family members will, or can, report how they typically behave with one another. The method assumes that untrained people, who have a built-in bias, can be participant observers. Additionally, the data are by definition responses to an investigator, an outsider, rather than the responses, which are the focus of observational family research, of one family member to another. Although many "facts" about families can be obtained by self-report, the kind of variables of interest to the investigator of psychiatry and the family do not seem measurable in this way. The revolution in the field occurred when family members were brought together and observed dealing with one another. Once he has observed that interchange, the investigator loses his enthusiasm for asking family members their opinions about the family. In this review, the considerable literature on the self-report method will not be discussed.

Studies where family members are brought together and examined while dealing with each other include observation of "spontaneous" conversation and of experimental procedures which limit the communication of family members. The merit of the observation approach is that it allows family members to behave in more unrestricted ways so their behavior is more typical. However, the measurement must be the subjective judgement of the observer with the probability that he is likely to project his ideas into the complex interchange. The experimental approach provides more rigorous measurement, but family behavior must be restricted in order to obtain these measures and typical behavior may thus be distorted.

Observational Studies

When family members are brought together for observation and testing, they can be studied either with 1) an observer participating in the action he is examining or 2) with the observer absent from the group. In the latter case he either examines the family through a one-way screen or works with film or tape recordings at his leisure.

Participant Observation

For the psychiatric study of the family, the primary type of participant observation has been family therapy where the therapist joins the family members in the interchange. This type of study is mentioned here only to dismiss it as a source of *evidence* about differences between types of families, as valuable as family therapy might be for therapeutic purposes or as a means of gathering ideas. One cannot put a control group of "normal" families into family therapy for comparison, and when contrasting two types of abnormality, such as schizophrenia and delinquency, one cannot assume that the therapist remains the same with both families so that they face a standard stimulus. Equally important, when a therapist is influencing a family to change, he cannot simultaneously be examining how they typically behave without his influence. One has only to listen to different family therapists talk about supposedly similar types of families to realize that families tend to deliver the kinds of behavior the therapist expects and provokes when he is working with them intensely over periods of time. This is analogous to the familiar observation that patients in Freudian analysis dream in appropriate Freudian symbolism while those in Jungian analysis have dreams that corroborate the Jungian theories. In addition, the family is in a context where someone is trying to change the ways the members typically behave with each other. The effect of this therapeutic context is not known, but presumably it generates behavior, such as resistance to change, which does not occur in contexts, such as those for observing "normal" families, designed for observation only. Despite its value as a way of gaining impressions about families that can revolutionize a therapist's ideas about psychopathology and change, family therapy cannot provide an adequate sample, a standard context, reliable measurements, statistical results, or controlled replication.

The research type of participant observation is one where the investigator makes observations without attempting to bring about change. Typically, this takes place in the home with the observer participating in family life for a period of time. Anthropological types of observation are of this kind (Henry, 1966; Laing & Esterson, 1964), but they do not include adequate samples or control groups. One of the best examples of the method available, as well as one of the earliest observational family studies, was done by Behrens and Goldfarb (1958). An observer entered the homes of 20 families with a schizophrenic child and 10 "normal" homes. Family behavior was summarized using a set of categories such as "support and cooperation," "warmth and affection," "appropriate demands," and so forth. Significant differences were found between the two groups in all categories except in the physical aspects of the home. The investigators used this method with a conscious awareness of its limitations, for, by its nature, there was opportunity for considerable bias. When the observer entered a home, he knew which type of family he would find, and one can assume that his responses to the members were affected by that knowledge. Additionally, since this method depends upon the observer's judgement, there is always the possibility that he will see what supports his hypotheses and overlook what does not. In this particular study, there was not the protection which is often used with this method; the observer did not have categories set up in advance. He first visited the homes and made his observations and notes, and from these he devised a set of categories that showed the two groups of families to be different. The possibility of replicating a study done in this way is small, and the results seem best interpreted as indicative.

Non-Participant Observation

The bulk of the research on families observed as groups takes place in the laboratory where the family members are exposed to some type of stimuli and their behavior is observed and categorized. Most of the published papers using this method are preliminary reports which do not offer evidence based upon comparisons with control groups; they describe a method of testing that is still being developed. Usually an illustration, often only an anecdote, is used to show the research method. No attempt is made to offer an adequate sample. Typically, these papers report ongoing research by describing the stimulus material used to test the family and they offer a description of the ways the behavior of family members will ultimately be coded.

Examples of these preliminary studies that do not use control groups can be listed. A number of investigations have used some form of questionnaire or verbal stimulus for the family to talk about and have offered possible ways of categorizing the family conversation (Drechsler & Shapiro, 1963; Jackson, Riskin & Satir, 1961; Riskin, 1963, 1964; Schulman, Shoemaker & Moelis, 1962; Stabenau, Tupin, Werner & Pollin, 1965; Terrill, 1963; Titchener, D'Zmura, Golden & Emerson, 1963; Watzlawick, 1966). Similar studies have used the Rorschach as a stimulus for a whole family conversation (Levy & Epstein, 1963; Loveland, 1963), and new pictures have been created for family testing (Minuchin & Montalvo, 1966). An experimental game for married couples has been described (Ravich, Deutsch & Brown, 1966), a button pushing test has been used with families of retarded readers (Miller & Westman, 1966), the Wechsler Bellevue has been used with couples (Bauman & Roman, 1966), and a comparison has been made of self-report data and observation on a small sample (Levinger, 1963).*

Granting the ingenuity of many of these procedures, these studies are not intended to offer evidence about differences between types of families.

Comparisons Using Control Groups

The published papers which offer theory, method, and results are the final culmination of investigations. These papers report studies which use control groups, provide standard contexts in which families are placed, use measurements meant to be reliable, and include a sufficiently large sample to talk with some confidence about differences. The studies will be reviewed here in terms of the questions posed and the reliability of the answers found.**

Rater Judgment Studies

First there will be a review of studies where a rater made judgments about differences between a type of family and a control group, and then the more experimental studies will be examined. There have been five rater judgment studies contrasting normal and abnormal families and six studies contrasting families with different kinds of abnormality.

Normal Families Contrasted with Abnormal Families

Of the five studies contrasting normal and abnormal families, four of them compared the family of the schizophrenic with a control group. All of them used some form of questionnaire as a stimulus for the family conversation. The judges listened to tape recordings and classified differences according to a coding system. The summaries offered here are brief, and the reader is referred to the articles themselves for a more complete description of the investigations and other findings.

---

*Studies that have not compared "normal" vs "abnormal" families but are examinations of conjoint family and couple behavior are the work of Strodtbeck (1951), one of the earliest family investigators, and the conflict-inducing procedures of Goodrich (1963).

**This review does not include theses which have not been summarized and published. For example, an interactional study was done by Arthur Bodin, Ph.D., which was a doctoral thesis submitted in 1966 to the State University of New York at Buffalo. It is called "Family Interaction, Coalition, Disagreement, and Compromise in Problem, Normal, and Synthetic Family Triads."

1. One of the larger samples used, a group of 67 families with a
schizophrenic member and 56 normal families, was examined by
Cheek (1964, 1965) with a focus on the characteristics of fathers and
mothers. The mothers of schizophrenics were found to be more
dominating than mothers of normals, and the fathers were more
passive than normal fathers. The family conversations were analyzed
with a variation of the Bales categories.

2. Caputo (1963) contrasted the parents of 20 schizophrenics
and 20 parents of normal children in a conversation about items o˜
The Parent Attitude Inventory. The children were not included in
the conversation. The Bales categories were used, and the investigator concludes the data "do not lend support to the maternal
dominance, paternal passivity contention held by many investigators
in this area." He found that the schizophrenic's parents displayed
more discord than did the parents of normal children.

3. Another comparison of parents without children present was
conducted by Garmezy, Farina, and Rodnick (1960). The sample
consisted of 18 parents with sons who were schizophrenic and 12
with sons who had TB. Various problem situations were discussed by
the parental pairs, and raters judged categories focusing on dominance and conflict. A sharing of dominance was found in the normal
group and not in the schizophrenic group. The schizophrenics were
divided into Poor and Good premorbids, and only the former were
found to be different from the normal group.

These three studies deal with the individual characteristics of the
family members and the dominance structure in the family. The results are
mixed, with the Cheek study finding a difference related to maternal
dominance and the Caputo study not finding it. Caputo found more
discord between the parents of schizophrenics than between normal
parents and Garmezy only found this difference with the Poor premorbid
schizophrenic's parents. Only the Cheek study was a family study in the
sense that parents as well as a child were in the testing room. Since it is
commonly assumed by family therapists that families of schizophrenics are
grossly different from normal families in that they show more maternal
dominance and conflict, it is surprising that the differences found in these
studies are not more grossly apparent.

4. A somewhat different approach was taken by Lennard,
Beaulieu, and Embrey (1965), who interviewed 10 families with a
schizophrenic child and 19 families with normal children in conversations concerning family life. These investigators focused upon the

number of communications and to whom they were directed as judged by raters. Based on this study, the schizophrenic is said to communicate less with father while the mother communicates more to him. Mothers and fathers talk less with each other than do those in the normal group. Mothers of schizophrenics are more intrusive and they label the feelings, experiences and thoughts of their schizophrenic children more than the normals do.

5. Studies using rater judgment on some of the variables and not on others was reported in several papers by Ferreira and Winter (1965), Ferreira, Winter, and Poindexter (1966), and Winter, Ferreira, and Olson (1965). Their sample included families with schizophrenic offspring as well as families whose children revealed a range of other abnormalities. Fifty normal and 75 abnormal families were tested. The family members were first isolated and asked to fill out a questionnaire. They then discussed together all the items (rather than just the items on which they disagreed as in the Revealed Differences procedure). Each family was also asked to make up a story that would connect sets of three TAT cards. The rater judgment aspect of this study included the finding that the normals stated their likes and dislikes more clearly and talked differently about the TAT stories.

6. Forty abnormal families and 40 normal families, each consisting of parents and one child, were studied discussing the neutral questionnaire of Ferreiria and Winter. The measure was the sequence of audible sounds in the family conversation. This sequence was planned to be measured automatically, but at this stage most of the data were examined by a rater listening to tape recordings. The families were found to follow repetitive patterns, with the normal families participating more equally in the conversations than the abnormal families (Haley, 1964).

Different Types of Abnormal Families

Whether families with different kinds of patients differ from each other has been investigated with the rater judgment procedure. The Ferreira-Winter study previously described (Ferreira & Winter, 1965; Ferreira et al, 1966; Winter et al, 1965) dealt with this question, and their findings indicated that the more extreme disorders, such as schizophrenia, were more extreme on their measurements than milder problems. Five other rater judgment studies dealt with this area and one study contrasted parental behavior with a schizophrenic and with his sibling.

1. Three reports focused upon the families of two supposedly different kinds of schizophrenics: those with a Good and those with a Poor premorbid history (Farina, 1960; Garmezy, 1960; Farina & Dunham, 1963). The procedures used in the last paper listed illustrate the method. Family members were exposed individually to a set of hypothetical problem situations and were then brought together to reach a joint resolution as a group. The conversation was analyzed with categories related to dominance and conflict in the family. Two judges were used. The fathers were found to be more dominant in the Good premorbid families and the mothers more dominant in the Poor premorbid group. More conflict was also found in the Poor premorbid families. The sample consisted of 10 Good and 8 Poor premorbid families.*

2. A study that used all Poor premorbid schizophrenics sought to find differences in families of male and female schizophrenic patients (Baxter, Arthur, Flood & Hedgepeth, 1962). Family conversations were about household activities, financial situations, and social activities; two judges scored conflict categories. Differences in amount of conflict were not found, but there was more conflict between the parents if the child was male, and the child was more involved in family conflict if female.

3. A study used excerpts from family therapy sessions to contrast families with a schizophrenic child from those with a neurotic child (Morris & Wynne, 1965). In the sample were 12 families; 4 neurotic and 8 schizophrenic. A judge listened to parental conversations and predicted whether the offspring were amorphous schizophrenics, fragmented schizophrenics, or neurotics. The procedure was similar in theory and approach to the same group's study of parental response to the Rorschach test (Singer & Wynne, 1963; Wynne & Singer, 1965). In this case the focus was upon an idea or theme proposed by the therapist rather than upon an inkblot. The study was largely a comparison of individual responses by

---

*The studies which assume there are two types of schizophrenics, those with a good social history and those with a poor one, also assume that the information about the history is accurate. This assumption can be questioned since the history is often drawn from hospital records which vary enormously in their accuracy and completeness and are based largely upon the self report of a family member at the time of admission. When contrasting family types in this way, it can be argued that the findings are circular. The more conflict in the family, the more likely that the family member who describes the patient at time of admission will emphasize his past inadequacies. Therefore the Poor premorbids will be found to have families in which there is more conflict.

mothers and fathers with the table of categories not including items which involved an exchange between the two parents.

4. Finally, a study contrasted the relationship of parents with their schizophrenic child and with his sibling in 24 families. First the members were tested individually with the Wechsler-Bellevue. Then one child was sent from the room and the remaining triad was given one form of the Wechsler subtest and were asked to formulate a response acceptable to the entire group. The measurements were a combination of the individual and the group intelligence score, and a Bales analysis of the conversation, both coded blindly by two raters. Fathers and mothers were found to be equally dominant, the group was as efficient with the patient present as with his sibling, and patients were more supportive of the parents than was the sibling. Parental discord was greater when the patient was present than it was with the sibling present (Sharan [Singer] Schlomo, 1966).

In summary, these studies are the published reports which contrast a type of family with a control group by the use of rater judgment. There are two questions which can be raised about the rater procedure: Is it used properly, and should it be used at all? Looking over these reports, it would seem evident that proper care was not taken by many of those who used the method. We are asked to believe that an abnormal family is different from a normal family because someone listened to a tape recording of the conversations and found a different frequency of occurrence of some type of behavior. The results are said to be more sound if two people reach the same conclusions.

In many of the studies reported it is difficult to determine whether more than one rater was used. In others, it is clear that the only rater was the investigator. Of the comparisons of normal controls and abnormal families, only the Ferreira-Winter study reports rater reliability figures. More important, only the Ferreira-Winter study reports whether the rater's judgment was made "blind" in that he did not know the type of family he was judging. The studies contrasting Good and Poor premorbid schizophrenics and male and female schizophrenics report this type of information.

Several of the studies reviewed here would appear to consist of one judge with full knowledge of the hypotheses he was testing listening to tape recordings with full knowledge of the kind of family he was judging. Unless categories of judgment are set up in advance, there is no protection against bias when the method is used in that way. If the method is to be used, one should at least expect more than one judge to be involved, together with a report that compares their judgments. One should also expect the judges to listen "blind," since the data are so complex that a judge can always find substantiation for his ideas somewhere in the family conversation.

Granting that human judgment is of excellent use in gathering ideas and that it is a necessary preliminary step in research, the question can still be raised as to whether a judge's findings are reliable as evidence. Even if three or four judges report that they all saw the same thing (which is not the case in the research described here), the reliability is not necessarily increased. If one uses more than one judge, he finds that those with different backgrounds see and hear different things. One can achieve meaningful reliability only if the judges are trained to see the data in the same way. Paradoxically, however, reliability is not increased because of independent observations; the observers having been trained to view the data similarly, have just been collapsed back into one judge.

Raters may disagree because they are not equally well trained as observers. For example, one rater may say that mother is "agreeing" with a statement by father. Another may note that mother's voice had an ironical inflection, or that mother turned away as she made her verbal statement, and therefore this rater would not classify her response in the "agree" category. Who is to say which rater is correct? When family members are talking together they communicate with body movement, vocal intonation, and verbal statements which have an almost infinite number of subtle meanings. Slow motion films of family conversations reveal a world of communication by body movement which is sufficiently complex to be almost uncategorizable. Added to that, and qualifying the meaning of every movement, is vocal intonation—tone, rhythm, inflection, timing, and so on. In addition, the verbal statements exchanged qualify themselves as well as the body movement and vocal intonations. To say that one thing is happening in a family, such as "disagreement," is to take an axe to a cobweb. A rater accustomed to the subtle intonations of voice, or a rater who has devoted years to the significance of body movements, will observe behavior which is not even noticed by the average rater. Yet the method depends upon a human being judging that something happened or did not happen in a family interchange. Also, it is not necessarily a comfort to believe that there is so much redundance in behavior that crude estimates will suffice. Patterns may be repeated in various ways and with different types of behavior, but there is always the question of whether an observer is seeing patterns in the data or structuring that complexity in line with the expected findings. Finally, the use of human observers means depending upon instruments which have opinions and moral biases about families. As Gregory Bateson once put it, "The probe we stick into human material always has another end which sticks into us."

Some people in family research have argued that for gross differences one can use crude categories and depend on rater judgment, accepting "quick and dirty" results. Yet the results which have been published by those with this view indicate that the differences are not that crude and gross; even if they were, such an approach can hardly be considered more reliable than the judgment of a good clinician.

After observing a considerable number of "normal" families in testing situations, this writer lost his confidence in his ability, and the ability of other people, to determine what type of family was conversing by listening to a tape recording of a family conversation—or even whether it was a "normal" family or a family with a psychotic child. To test this question, a rudimentary attempt was made to determine whether experienced family therapists and research people could tell one type of family from another by listening to a tape recording of brief family interchanges. In this study there was absolute insurance that the judgments were made "blind." From a collection of family conversations, a selection was made of six families with a child who had been diagnosed schizophrenic, six families with a delinquent child who had been incarcerated, and six families who were "normal." The latter were selected randomly from a high school directory and reported no therapy or arrests. These families all discussed the same subject matter in a standard interview—the choice of color of their next automobile. Parents and one child (the abnormal one in the abnormal groups) discussed this neutral subject matter for about two minutes, with the conversation ranging from amiable discussion to argument. These 18 two-minute segments were randomized on a tape recording. Four family research groups in the country were asked to listen to the tape recording and estimate which kind of family was conversing. Of the 40 experienced family people tested, none guessed better than chance, even though as a group these people reported having treated over two thousand families. One research group which did do better than chance was asked to take the test again, and they did not succeed any better than the other groups on the second try. A group of laymen were also asked to listen and make their guesses; they did slightly better than experienced family people but did not do better than chance (Haley, in press). This was hardly a crucial experiment since the subject matter was neutral, the excerpts were short, and the listeners heard the conversations only once straight through. Still, until someone demonstrates that investigators can do better with less neutral subject matter and longer excerpts, it would seem indicated that those who use the rater judgment method should take care that judgments are made "blind" when raters listen to tape recordings.

Experimental Studies

Additional attempts have been made to differentiate normal and abnormal families by using a method which might be called "experimental" to contrast it with the rater judgment studies. In this procedure a variable is not necessarily controlled, but the results are obtained by measurement of some act rather than by human judgment about whether something happened. Another way to put it is to say that in the rater judgment studies the data is simplified *after* it is collected. The judge listens to a tape recording (he cannot judge body movement), or he reads a transcript (he can judge neither body movement nor vocal intonation). Conversely, in the "experimental" studies the data is simplified in advance. An arrangement is made whereby the communication among family members is limited so that measurements can be made.

There have been six studies which contrasted a sample of abnormal families with a normal control group by making measurements which do not involve human judgment about what happened.

1. Ferreira (1963) tested "25 normal and 30 pathologic" families with a simple procedure in which the family members in separate rooms were asked to color a number of flags on pieces of cardboard. They were then asked to "throw away, i.e., to reject" the flags of the other family members which they didn't like for any reason. Additionally, they were asked to guess how many of their own flags would be thrown away by other members of the family. Differences were found between the normal and abnormal families when a frequency count was made of the number of flags rejected and the estimates of the number to be rejected by other family members.

2. In the Ferreira-Winter studies previously described (Ferreira & Winter, 1965; Ferreira et al, 1966; Winter et al, 1965) and an earlier Ferreira study (1963), the family members filled out a questionnaire of neutral items separately and then were brought together to reach agreement on the items. Differences were found between normal and abnormal families in the number of items the family members chose in common without consulting each other. In this "spontaneous agreement" measurement, the normal families chose more items in common than the abnormal families. Additionally, the normal families took less time to complete the task of reaching agreement when talking together. Another measure made in the study was "choice fulfillment." Of the choices made individually by family members, how many of those choices became the family

choice when the members talked together? The choice fulfillment was higher for the normal than for the abnormal families.

3. An experimental game (Haley, 1962) was devised to test the hypothesis that families with a schizophrenic member had more difficulty maintaining coalitions than normal families. The game involved three family members pressing buttons. When any two members pressed each other's buttons, they ran up a score together. Differences were found between a group of 30 families with a schizophrenic child and 30 normal families.

4. A sample of 50 normal and 50 abnormal families consisting of parents with two children present discussed Ferreira's neutral questionnaire (Haley, 1967a). This was a continuation of the study which previously tested only parents and one child (Haley, 1964)(See page 22). With two children present, including the problem child in the abnormal group, the measure was again the sequence of audible sounds. The sounds were transmitted from throat microphones directly to an analyzer which totalled the frequency with which each family member spoke after another. Both the normal and abnormal families followed repetitive patterns but the normals did not participate more equally than the abnormals, as they did in the previous study when only one child was present. (A sample of Japanese-speaking families tested in this way with one child present differed from the American group [Haley, 1967b].) Parents talked after the problem child in ways different from the ways in which they talked after his sibling. The normals took significantly less time to reach agreement.

5. A limited communication network was arranged where family members had to reach agreement on items of the neutral Ferreira questionnaire while talking from separate rooms over an intercommunication network (Haley, 1967c). The network was so arranged that only two of the three persons could talk at a time. A sample of 23 abnormal families and 21 normal families, each composed of parents and one child, were placed in this setting. Each member had to press a button to talk to one of the other two family members. When two were talking, the third could not hear or be heard. Yet all three members had to reach agreement to complete the task. The sequence of audible sounds as well as the frequency of button pushing were both counted as part of the measure of "who speaks *to* whom." In the abnormal group, the fathers were the most frequent button pushers and so "managed" the task more than the presumably "dominating" abnormal mothers. There were no significant differences between normal and abnormal families either in

sequence of audible sounds or in frequency patterns of button pushing. The only differences between the two groups were in the length of time to complete the task and in the amount of talking and button pushing required to complete it. Since it seemed possible that the neutral subject matter around which the discussion centered might not be bringing out differences, an additional sample of 15 abnormal families and 10 normal families was placed in the same setting while talking about a questionnaire dealing with family problems. They had to reach agreement on ways to resolve simple problems which come up in families. Again, there were no differences between the normal and abnormal groups except in amount of time to complete the task, amount of button pushing, and number of speeches.

6. A sample of 20 normal families, 12 schizophrenic families and 12 families with nonschizophrenic abnormal children was tested to determine the amount and kind of conflict in the parents' communication to their children (Haley, 1968). To test the hypothesis that parents communicate to their schizophrenic children in conflicting ways, the parents were asked to instruct their children in a task from a separate room. The achievement of the children in the task was measured. Since the instructions were tape recorded, matched samples of normal children could listen to the instructions of a group of parents of schizophrenics to determine whether they could follow the instructions more successfully than the schizophrenic children. The indications were that parents of schizophrenics do not communicate in more conflicting ways than parents of normal children when the measurement is the success of a child in following their instructions in a laboratory setting.

These "experimental" studies illustrate part of the dilemma of family research. What one is attempting to measure is typical family behavior. Presumably, the more the members of a family are allowed to deal with one another naturally and spontaneously, the more typical would be their behavior. However, the measurement in such a situation can only be the judgment of an observer with all the risk of his subjective bias. To obtain more rigorous measurement, the behavior of family members must be restricted, yet such restriction quite possibly changes the family behavior so that it is no longer typical. The most one can say is that contrasting groups of families behaved similarly or differently in the same setting.

Inferences from Individual Testing

One study requires a special category in this review since it does not include bringing the family members together and yet it is not the usual self-report study. Margaret Singer and Lyman Wynne have been doing a series of studies in which they test family members individually with Rorschach and TAT tests. From a blind reading of the individual test protocols, they differentiated the parents of 20 autistic children from the parents of 20 neurotic children (Singer & Wynne, 1963). Recently they published an extensive report of a new study describing their theoretical approach as well as their methods and results (Singer & Wynne, 1965; Wynne & Singer, 1963.) Members of 35 families were tested, including 20 families with a young adult schizophrenic offspring, nine with a borderline schizophrenic offspring, and six with a severely neurotic young adult. Hospitalization for psychiatric evaluation and treatment had been in-dicated for all of the ill offspring. Verbatim transcripts included "questions and asides made both by the subject and the tester." The projective "response" alone was not enough. The task was to predict the diagnosis of the patients blindly from the protocols of the other family members and then blindly to match the patients with the appropriate parents. Of 20 patients who were diagnosed schizophrenic, 17 were correctly identified from the test protocols of the other family members. All but two of the patients in each of the borderline and nonschizophrenic groups were correctly predicted.

If one accepts the premise that thought disorders and cognitive dysfunctions exist in schizophrenic individuals, it is reasonable to use projective test protocols to make such evaluations. However, while arguing for the value of these kinds of data, the authors appear to use projective test stimuli largely as a device for provoking conversations which they then analyze. The analyses do not seem to emphasize ways of thinking as much as they do ways of communicating. What the person sees in the inkblot does not seem to be the focus as much as whether what the person says to the tester is amorphous, vague, fragmented, shifting in levels of abstraction, and so on. In this sense it is a procedure where a test devised for an intrapsychic portrait is used as a transactional test. Looking at the study from a transactional orientation, it seems an unusual way to gather these kinds of data. An assumption of the study is that the transactional field in which a child developed and currently lives is important to his psychopathology; this is why a major goal is to determine how families differ from one another. It would seem to follow logically that the investigators would directly examine the interpersonal field of the offspring, the family. Yet instead of examining how the parents communicate with each other and making predictions about type of offspring, the study examines how each parent communicates with an outsider, a psychological tester. From that behavior they infer how the parents must communicate with each other and then infer the type of offspring. A more direct way of making such predictions would seem to be directly to observe father and mother communicating with each other. (This group also studied total family interaction over Rorschach stimuli but they have not yet reported results contrasting families of schizophrenics with controls.) Such direct observation would eliminate the question of whether, in this study, one psychologist is communicating with another through a Rorschach interview. The chief merit of the Wynne-Singer study is its emphasis upon relating symptomatic behavior in the individual to patterns in the family, a connection which is not often made in family research.

The studies reviewed here have been presented in bare outline and the reader is referred to the original reports themselves for details. A few of the methodological weaknesses can be reviewed.

Sample: A major weakness of most of the studies is the nature and size of the sample studied. Many of these reports do not describe the sampling method and typically the contrast groups are quite small. The experienced family tester has often found that results appeared good with a few families but disappeared with larger groups. When individual diagnosis, which is the basis upon which abnormal families are often selected, is doubtful, the sample needs to be large. To say that ten families adequately represent the total population of families containing a schizophrenic is unreasonable. Yet we don't know how much more representative a sample of fifty families would be. When matching contrasting groups of families, we do not yet know what variables are important—the social class of the family, the length of marriage, the number, sex and position of the children, the frequency of previous marriages, amount of contact with extended kin, or any number of other factors. Many of these studies do not state the criteria of the sampling, and it is significant that no paper has been devoted to the problem of drawing representative family samples from total populations.

Standard Context: When contrasting two groups of families, it is necessary to place them in the same context if one wishes to contrast the behavior. Many of the studies reported here do not describe the situation of the family; others assume that the context for contrasted groups is the same when it might not be. How families are recruited as well as the instructions given them define the context for the family. Serious questions can be raised as to whether families who are brought to the laboratory because they have an "abnormal" member are in the same context as families that volunteer because all the members are "normal." For example, when the parents of a schizophrenic are asked to come in with their child for testing, this request may seem to be an accusation that they have contributed to driving their child insane. Since the accusation is not specific, the parents do not know what they might do or say to prove their innocence of this undefined crime, and they may feel like characters in a Kafka trial scene. The parents may communicate in vague and amorphous ways because they do not know what statement might prove their guilt, or they may turn upon each other and insist that it is the other who is really at fault. Studying their interaction, the observer could see peculiar and conflictual interaction and conclude that this mystifying atmosphere in the family is the setting in which the child was raised, without considering that it might be the context of observation which provokes this type of behavior. Many family investigators still deal with the family as they once did with the individual; as if it exists independent of a relationship with others, including the observer.

As another example, we have contradictory descriptions by clinicians and testers which might be explained by the influence of context. Typically clinicians report that abnormal families have a father who is withdrawn and passive. Yet family testing with these families often show the father to be an active organizer of the family in the test task. This discrepancy might be because, when a therapist intrudes in a family, the father withdraws and lets him take charge, while, when in the testing room without an intruder, the father becomes active. Since family therapists and interviewers often don't include themselves in the field of observation, they can conclude that the father is a withdrawn type of person without noticing that their intrusion provokes this behavior.

When testing families of schizophrenics, the accusational context is of utmost importance. One of the studies reported here offers a way to handle this problem. The Wynne-Singer investigation used contrasting groups of families where hospitalization was recommended in all cases, so with illness in the picture for the entire sample of families, presumably the accusational context would then be the same. Another example of a way of ameliorating this problem would be to select families because they all live on a particular block or because they all have a child in a particular class in school. The families would then enter the test situation for reasons independent of the presence of abnormality, and later the family backgrounds could be examined to select the contrasting groups.

Experimenter Bias: A problem inseparable from the question of providing a standard context is that of experimenter bias where the experimenter who knows the type of family being tested might "engineer" the members to behave according to the hypothesis being tested.*

Most family investigators leave the tester out of the room, but typically the person who instructs the family knows both the hypotheses of the study and the type of family being tested. Only one of the studies described here reports a procedure to avoid experimenter bias, and such influence was not found (Haley, in press). From a family orientation, the question of experimenter bias is not merely one of influencing a subject, it is the discovery that all test responses are interpersonal. An assumption basic to family research is that one cannot have a response that is not in relationship to another person.

Conclusion

Psychotherapy with individuals developed without many of the questions now being asked in family research. For example, it was assumed that if a person sought psychiatric treatment he was different from a "normal" person and that this difference was a stable character or personality trait. The therapist usually contrasted the patient with an ideal normal person. Only recently has the question been raised whether patients differ from "normals" only in that they happened upon referral routes which brought them into therapy.** In the family field this question was raised early, and patient families have been contrasted with normal controls.

A puzzling question is why the "disturbed" family appears so grossly malfunctioning to the therapist treating the family, while in the testing situation it is difficult to demonstrate that the family is different from a normal control. Possibly normal families are also disturbed, and possibly a clinician has an exaggerated view of problems. It is also possible that therapy deals with more subtle and complex factors than research can focus upon. However, we should keep in mind that the usual testing

---

*Cf. Rosenthal, R. On the social psychology of the psychological experiment: The experimenter's hypothesis as unintended determinant of experimental results. *American Science,* 1963, *51,* 268-283. See also Rosenthal, R. The effect of the experimenter on the results of psychological research. In Maher, B. (ed.), *Progress in experimental personality research.* New York: Academic Press, Vol. 1, 1964, and the same author's Experimental outcome-orientation and the results of the psychological experiment. *Psychological Bulletin,* 1964, *61,* 405-412.

**Cf. Scheff, T. J. *Being mentally ill: A sociological theory.* Chicago: Aldine, 1966; and Becker, E. *The revolution in psychiatry,* Glencoe, Ill.: Free Press, 1964.

situation is quite different from the therapy situation. If psychopathology in the family is a product of the ways the family meshes with the outside world, then the most common procedure in family research—leaving the tester out of the room and encouraging the family members to deal only with each other—would minimize the differences between normal and abnormal families. An outsider intervening in the family, as in therapy, would bring out the difference. It is also possible that the clinician is largely influenced by his own internal responses; the way the family makes *him* feel is the basis for his judgment about its abnormality. If this is so, the kind of testing described here would not reveal differences any more than it would pick up abnormal fluctuations in family development over time.

There seems to be a conceptual gap between the traditional idea of individual symptoms and the measurements typically used in family research. Even if the parents of a schizophrenic or delinquent child were more hostile than parents of normal children, even if the mothers were more dominant, the conflict in the family greater, or the family more inefficient in doing a task, still how is this related to the symptomatic behavior of the child? Individual symptoms were conceived originally as unrelated to other people, and a basic problem for family research is to relate such symptoms to the processes between people. A redefinition of symptoms is necessary to make this step. The symptoms must be translated into interpersonal terms and the function of that particular type of interpersonal behavior demonstrated in a family. Perhaps the next step in family research will be away from bringing samples of supposedly different families into the laboratory and observing them, and more toward testing a quite specific hypothesis with an experimental procedure designed for just that purpose.

If we accept the findings of the research reported here, and assuming it is sound, evidence is accumulating to support the idea that family with a patient member is different from an "average" family. As *individuals,* the family members do not appear different according to the usual character and personality criteria. Similarly, evidence is slight that family *structure,* when conceived in terms of role assignment or dominance, is different in normal and abnormal families. On *process* measurements there is some indication of difference: abnormal families appear to have more conflict, to have different coalition patterns, and to show more inflexibility in repeating patterns of behavior. The most sound findings would seem to be in the *outcome* area; when faced with a task on which they must cooperate, abnormal family members seem to communicate their preferences less successfully, require more activity and take longer to get the task done. The findings in this area seem most affected by the testing context, and appear most difficult to relate to specific symptoms of the individual.

However, if we judge the exploratory research done to date by severe methodological criteria, one can only conclude that the evidence for a difference between the normal family and a family containing a patient is no more than indicative. This does not mean that schizophrenia is not produced by a type of family, nor does it mean that a family with a schizophrenic is grossly different from the average family. It means that sufficient reliable evidence of a difference has yet to be provided. The methodology for providing that evidence is still being devised.

REFERENCES

Bateson, G., Jackson, D., Haley, J., & Weakland, J. Toward a theory of schizophrenia. *Behavioral Science,* 1956, *1,* 251-264.

Bauman, G., & Roman, M. Interaction testing in the study of marital dominance and its dynamics. *Family Process,* 1966, *5,* 230-242.

Baxter, J. C., Arthur, S., Flood, C., & Hedgepath, B. Conflict patterns in the families of schizophrenics. *Journal of Nervous and Mental Diseases,* 1962, *135,* 419-424.

Behrens, M. L., & Goldfarb, W. A study of patterns of interaction of families of schizophrenic children in residential treatment. *American Journal of Orthopsychiatry,* 1958, *28,* 300-312.

Bowen, M. Family concept of schizophrenia. In D. D. Jackson (Ed.), *The etiology of schizophrenia.* New York: Basic Books, 1960.

Caputo, D. V. The parents of the schizophrenic. *Family Process,* 1963, *2,* 339-356.

Cheek, F. E. The father of the schizophrenic, the function of a peripheral role. *Archives of General Psychiatry,* 1965, *13,* 336-345,

Cheek, F. E. The "schizophrenogenic mother" in word and deed. *Family Process,* 1964, *3,* 155-177.

Drechsler, R. J., & Shapiro, M. I. Two methods of analysis of family diagnostic data. *Family Process,* 1963, *2,* 367-379.

Farina, A. Patterns of role dominance and conflict in parents of schizophrenic patients. *Journal of Abnormal and Social Psychology,* 1960, *61,* 31-38.

Farina, A., & Dunham, R. M. Measurement of family relationships and their effects. *Archives of General Psychiatry,* 1963, *9,* 64-73.

Ferreira, A. J. Decision-making in normal and pathologic families. *Archives of General Psychiatry*, 1963, *8,* 68-73.

Ferreira, A. J. Rejection and expectancy of rejection in families. *Family Process*, 1963, *2,* 235-244.

Ferreira, A. J., & Winter, W. D. Family interaction and decision making. *Archives of General Psychiatry*, 1965, *13,* 214-223.

Ferreira, A. J., Winter, W. D., & Poindexter, E. J. Some interactional variables in normal and abnormal families. *Family Process,,* 1966, *5,* 60-75.

Frank, G. H. The role of the family in the development of psychopathology. *Psychological Bulletin,* 1965, *64,* 191-205.

Garmezy, N., Farina, A., & Rodnick, E. H. The structured situation test: A method for studying family interaction in schizophrenia. *American Journal of Orthopsychiatry*, 1960, *30,* 445-451.

Goodrich, D. W., & Boomer, D. S. Experimental assessment of modes of conflict resolution. *Family Process*, 1963, *2,* 15-24.

Haley, J. Family experiments: A new type of experimentation. *Family Process*, 1962, *1,* 265-293.

Haley, J. Research on family patterns: An instrument measurement. *Family Process*, 1964, *3,* 41-65.

Haley, J. Speech sequences of normal and abnormal families with two children present. *Family Process*, 1967, *1,* 81-97. (a)

Haley, J. Cross-cultural experimentation: An initial attempt. *Human Organization,* 1967, *3,* 110-117. (b)

Haley, J. Experiment with abnormal families. *Archives of General Psychiatry*, 1967, *17,* 53-63. (c)

Haley, J. Testing parental instructions of schizophrenic and normal children: A pilot study. *Journal of Abnormal Psychology*, 1968, *73,* 559-565.

Haley, J. Estimating differences between types of families. Kansas Symposium on Family Therapy, in press.

Handel, G. Psychological study of whole families. *Psychological Bulletin,* 1965, *63,* 19-41.

Henry, J. The study of families by naturalistic observation. In I. M. Cohen

(Ed.), *Family structure, dynamics and therapy. Psychiatric Reports of the American Psychiatric Association,* 1966, *20,* 95-104.

Jackson, D. D. The question of family homeostasis. *Psychiatric Quarterly Supplement,* Part I, 1957, *31,* 79-90.

Jackson, D. D., Riskin, J., & Satir, V. A method of analysis of a family interview. *Archives of General Psychiatry,* 1961, *5,* 321-339.

Laing, R. D., & Esterson, A. *Families of schizophrenics. Sanity, madness and the family.* Vol. I. London: Tavistock, 1964.

Lennard, H. L., Beaulieu, M. R., & Embrey, M. G. Interaction in families with a schizophrenic child. *Archives of General Psychiatry,* 1965, *12,* 166-183.

Levinger, G. Supplementary methods in family research. *Family Process,* 1963, *2,* 357-366.

Levy, J., & Epstein, N. An application of the Rorschach test in family interaction. *Family Process,* 1963, *2,* 187-215.

Loveland, N. T. The family Rorschach: A new method for studying family interaction. *Family Process,* 1963, *2,* 187-215.

Meissner, W. W. Thinking about the family—psychiatric aspects. *Family Process,* 1964, *3,* 1-40.

Miller, D. R., & Westman, J. C. Family teamwork and psychotherapy. *Family Process,* 1966, *5,* 49-59.

Minuchin, S., & Montalvo, B. An approach for diagnosis of low socio-economic families. In I. M. Cohen (Ed.), *Family structure, dynamics and therapy. Psychiatric Reports of the American Psychiatric Association,* 1966, *20,* 163-174.

Mishler, E. G., & Waxler, N. E. Family interaction processes and schizophrenia: A review of current theories. *Merrill Palmer Quarterly,* 1965, *2,* 269-315.

Morris, G. O., & Wynne, L. C. Schizophrenic offspring and parental styles of communication: Predictive study using family therapy excerpts. *Psychiatry,* 1965, *28,* 19-44.

Ravich, R. A., Deutsch, M., & Brown, B. An experimental study of marital discord and decision-making. In I. M. Cohen (Ed.), *Family structure, dynamics and therapy. Psychiatric Reports of the American Psychiatric Association,* 1966, *20,* 91-94.

Riskin, J. Family interaction scales: A preliminary report. *Archives of General Psychiatry*, 1964, *11*, 484-494.

Riskin, J. Methodology for studying family interaction. *Archives of General Psychiatry*, 1963, *8*, 343-348.

Schulman, R. E., Schoemaker, D. J., & Moelis, I. Laboratory measurement of parental behavior. *Journal of Consulting Psychology*, 1962, *26*, 109-114.

Sharan (Singer) Shlomo. Family interaction with schizophrenics and their siblings. *Journal of Abnormal Psychology*, 1966, *71*, 345-353.

Singer, M. T., & Wynne, L. C. Differentiating characteristics of parents of childhood schizophrenics, childhood neurotics, and young adult schizophrenics. *American Journal of Psychiatry*, 1963, *120*, 234-243.

Singer, M. T., & Wynne, L. C. Thought disorder and family relations of schizophrenics, III. Methodology using projective techniques, IV. Results. *Archives of General Psychiatry*, 1965, *12*, 187-212.

Stabenau, J. R., Tupin, J., Werner, M. M., & Pollin, W. A comparative study of families of schizophrenics, delinquents and normals. *Psychiatry*, 1965, *28*, 45-59.

Strodtbeck, E. L. Husband-wife interaction over revealed differences. *American Sociological Review*, 1951, *16*, 468-473.

Terrill, J. A method for studying family communication. *Family Process*, 1963, *2*, 95-120.

Titchener, J. L., D'Zmura, T., Golden, M., & Emerson, R. Family transaction and derivation of individuality. *Family Process*, 1963, *2*, 95-120.

Warkentin, J., & Whitaker, C. Serial impasses in marriage. In I. M. Cohen (Ed.), *Family structure, dynamics and therapy. Psychiatric Reports of the American Psychiatric Association*, 1966, *20*, 73-77.

Watzlawick, P. A structured family interview. *Family Process*, 1966, *5*, 256-271.

Waxler, N. E., & Mishler, E. G. Scoring and reliability problems in interaction process analysis: A methodological note. *Sociometry*, 1966, *29*, 28-40.

Winter, W. D., Ferreira, A. J., & Olson, J. L. Story sequence analysis of family TATs. *Journal of Projective Techniques and Personality Assessment*, 1965, *29*, 392-297.

Wynne, L. C., Ryckoff, I. M., Day, J., & Hirsch, S. I. Pseudo-mutuality in
the family relations of schizophrenics. *Psychiatry*, 1958, *21*, 205-220.

Wynne, L. C., & Singer, M. T. Thought disorder and family relations of
schizophrenics: I. A research strategy, II. A classification of forms of
thinking. *Archives of General Psychiatry*, 1963, *9*, 191-206.

DISCUSSION

Chairman Bell: Thank you very much, Jay, for a very comprehensive
and stimulating paper. If this paper doesn't raise the hackles of a few
people around the table, I will be very surprised and rather disappointed,
yet I think we do have this problem. When one refers to the preface in Dr.
Zuk's and Dr. Nagy's book, which was based on the last conference in this
room, one sees a statement that goes something like this: "It became
obvious during the conference that there were not yet shared conceptual
systems which allowed people to discuss things in an orderly way."* I think
Jay has tried to lay out some of the problems to make that orderly
discussion a little more possible.

One of the perils of discussions at meetings of learned people is that
discussants give papers which they would like to have given, anyway. I
hope we can cut that down and have a more free-wheeling kind of
discussion. To get things going, though, perhaps we could give the
discussants the alternative of making a brief introductory statement in
reaction to Jay's paper. Dr. Friedman, would you like to say a few words?

Dr. Alfred S. Friedman: I think this is a great beginning. Naturally, I
like Jay's paper because he has said most of the things that I agree with. If
I pick one or two points to slightly disagree with to start off the discussion,
it is only because that is my duty.

I think Jay could have given a little more emphasis to the need for at
least two types of control groups, both the normal and the various
pathological control groups. If you get a difference between normal families
and so-called schizophrenic families, you don't know whether the difference
you get is specific to schizophrenia or whether it is just some general noise
in a family which is less normal or less well functioning. Studies like
Wynne and Singer's—there's also one by Seymour Fisher—comparing
normal, neurotic and schizophrenic families, have an advantage because if
you get a difference between the normal and schizophrenic, you want to

---

*G. H. Zuk and I. Boszormenyi-Nagy (eds.), *Family therapy and disturbed families.* Palo
Alto: Science and Behavior Books, 1967.

find out whether the same difference exists between a neurotic and a schizophrenic.

Any one of us could draw up a list of ten more pages of required controls to do exact research with families in addition to what Jay already spelled out. I have drawn up such a list recently in a proposal, so I know he wasn't being overly strict or rigorous. I will just mention one of those other controls and that is the male-female. With this control you not only have to have whole families but you have to control for the structure of the family. You need an older brother and a younger sister in one family, and an older sister and a younger brother in another family, and you have to balance these and control positioning of siblings, and so on.

I want to get later into this question of whether we have to throw out rater judgments completely, as Jay implied, and whether we can't raise some of the same questions about the experimental approach because of the findings on experimenter bias.

Dr. George Levinger: I, too, find it a pleasure to discuss Mr. Haley's paper. It is a thoughtful and informed review. It is critical, but at the same time sympathetic.

As is proper for a beginning talk at this sort of beginning conference, it raises more questions than it can answer. I find it, therefore, very productive. I would like to reinforce some points having to do with methodology and also several concerned with theory.

In the area of methodology, the paper has raised the following problems:

> *How* is evidence gathered in family research?
>
> *Who* gathers it? Remember that the measuring instruments are human observers, and that the probe sticks in us as well as in the subjects of our study.
>
> *Where* is it gathered? In the laboratory, in the home, or elsewhere? And *how?*

It seems to me that the artificiality issue that Haley pointed up was rather interestingly resolved by him. Instead of trying to reduce the artificiality of research, we might actually *increase* it, by putting people in contact with intercoms rather than face to face. This procedure might have fascinating consequences. There also are alternatives to introducing artificiality of this sort. For example, Murray Straus has a notion of what he calls "the totally absorbing situation," where you get a group of people so excited with what they are doing that they forget they are being observed. (Perhaps we can do this here at this conference. We are being observed, too, by the videotape cameras.)

Another interesting issue of methodology was Haley's point that a group of experts—and laymen, too—were willing to try to differentiate between abnormal and normal families on the basis of hearing merely a two-minute sample of the interaction. What does this say about the state of our field, particularly when we discover that these judges were rather unsuccessful? To me, the issue of how we resolve methodological problems is to obtain a more sophisticated understanding of how a variety of observers, a variety of research approaches, and a variety of methods can triangulate what is going on.

A second issue is theoretical, and here I can only briefly allude to something that will surely come up later in the conference. This has to do with the problem of studying the "abnormal" vs. the "normal." As a research and social psychologist, I deplore the emphasis of so many research studies which keep on trying to investigate typologies—differences between normal and abnormal "types" of families. I think there are certain alternatives to this emphasis which I hope we can discuss later.

Dr. Lyman C. Wynne: My first reaction to Mr. Haley's paper is that he has stated many things which have previously been commented on, mostly in bathrooms and corridors and places like that, and are not usually said in public this way. I think they badly needed saying and I am exceedingly delighted to hear him raise some vexing questions about the adequacy of essentially all family studies.

My second reaction is that I should leave the meeting immediately and get back to work. (Laughter) However, I would like to warn against a possible danger, which is one side of what I feel, that maybe it is hopeless to get back to work. This, I think, would be a very unfortunate interpretation to give to Mr. Haley's comments. One unfortunate reaction people may have, especially clinicians, is to feel that the methodologic problems, the problems of controls, the problems of specifying the context of the experiment or the context of the observations, including the observer's effect on the interaction, together with numerous other issues, all make systematic research impossible. I think this is a fear that certainly is not necessary to act upon. Even though no study, in itself, is going to cope with all the various complex issues, we can, nevertheless, deal with certain aspects of these issues fruitfully and get on with the job without being nihilistic.

Turning to the content of Mr. Haley's paper, I believe it should be recognized that the stimulus value of the paper derives at least in part from the fact that it is *not* a balanced overview of the field under consideration but, rather, a highly selective and partisan view of the portion of the field in which Mr. Haley is interested. He expresses a frank preference for experimental methods which, I think, most family researchers do regard as full of promise, but a promise that is yet to be empirically fulfilled. In contrast, he tends to dismiss rater-judgment methods with, as I see it, insufficient consideration of their potentialities. Mr. Haley describes at some length the "study" he conducted a few years ago in which bits and pieces of taped family interaction were given global judgments by a number of family therapists around the country. As a participant, I regarded the "study" as a spoof, an amusing effort to deflate those who were overinclined to make snap judgments about families on the basis of minimal information. Surely, however, this "research" cannot be seriously presented as an evaluation of rater-judgment methods in general. The raters were "blind," to be sure, but that is a necessary, not sufficient, feature of the rater-judgment approach, and, actually, is the most simplistic aspect of the various conditions necessary for sound rater-judgment research. There was no effort at all to specify criteria for making the judgments; there was no way at all of evaluating the sources of disagreement. For these and other reasons, the results are not interpretable. Giving raters the task of making global diagnostic judgments as their sole function is too primitive a research procedure to deserve continuing mention in public meetings or professional publications. The study which Mr. Haley reports in this paper was nothing more than an amusing diversion; the fact that he gives it such prominence suggests to me that he was not interested in making a serious critique of the rater-judgment method. There is no requirement, of course, that he should be interested, but I hope that others do not thereby dismiss their own consideration of variations of these methods.

Similarly, Mr. Haley rather cavalierly dismisses all self-report methods. He selects for criticism the least meaningful versions of self-report methods and speaks as if these comments were equally valid for all varieties of self-report studies. For example, he fails to mention the use of self-report methods in the numerous variations of the Q-Sort Technique. Also, there are the procedures, such as Laing's Interpersonal Perception Method, which compare what one family member says about himself with what other family members *think* he is saying about himself.* Although I have not yet used these methods in my own research, I believe they provide promising combinations with interaction research and should not, at the present date, at least, be rejected on the emotional grounds given by Mr. Haley, namely, that the immediate impact upon investigators of observing family interaction directly arouses their enthusiasm. I am not impressed

---

*Laing, R. D., Phillipson, H. & Lee, A. R. *Interpersonal Perception,* New York: Springer, 1966.

that the sense of richness of observable data has been, as yet, very fully translated into empirical research methods and data. Indeed, some self-report methods may provide *better* ways of discovering how family members *typically* behave with each other than brief samples of communication data which are so unduly subject to the particular stimulus and interaction conditions. In contrast, some of the self-report data give material relevant to longer-term samples of behavior and of the kind of relationships which the family members *typically* have with one another because of their particular perceptions and misperceptions of one another, particularly in the degree of "fit" which the perceptions of one have with another. This is closely related to a long tradition of work on role-expectations in sociology and social psychology in which the picture of the family as a social subsystem is characteristically built up from individually obtained data, but which does *not* depend upon what *each individual* knows about his family. I don't feel that the shortcomings of how certain methods have been applied justifies a blanket dismissal of methods which may still make a contribution.

In my experience, it is extremely hard work to select and apply research procedures with sound methodologic precautions to the complex groups called families, who are always immersed in even more complex social matrices, including the research and treatment setting itself. Despite those well-known difficulties, there are a number of studies which could have been much more meaningful if more attention had been given to only one or two methodologic details. I feel that we need to converge on issues and concepts with a variety of methods in order to develop "constant validity," rather than limit ourselves to data interpretable only within the frame of reference of an inevitably special method. Thus, experimental work with families directly interacting with one another can best be regarded as a useful approach—but by no means the *only* approach with promising potentialities.

Chairman Bell: Well, panel members, we have built Jay up here, patting him on the back, and then we've slipped a knife or two into him. One of the very beginning questions that I thought Dr. Wynne was alluding to is, How appropriate is it to apply the technically sophisticated research methodological techniques in this field? If we say that we are in a beginning stage of accumulating knowledge and that therefore we should wait a while, we may be ducking some important issues and compromising the future. Do any of you want to give your feelings about this question?

Dr. Friedman: I go along with Haley's comment that we can do both at the same time. When Jay got down to listing the experimental studies that have met scientific tests, we find that most came out of one place— Palo Alto. This is kind of a challenge to the rest of us. If there is one office in the country that is doing the scientific work, all the rest of us can still be developing ideas and using our imagination. Both approaches can be done simultaneously.

Dr. Levinger: When I was talking about the conceptual problem of "typology," I was attempting to suggest something like this: Let's take an example of research on schizophrenia. Most of the research that is done on families with a schizophrenic member (usually a child of a given age) is concerned with describing the interaction between the members. I can readily recall very few instances—and maybe this is just my own ignorance—in which the researcher also relates these interactions to some underlying theory of individual schizophrenic behavior. For example, how often have family researchers considered individual psychological variables such as the tendency of a schizophrenic to respond with great impasse to certain kinds of conflict situations or his being more confusingly aroused by standard situations in which other people tend to be more quickly responsive?

To what extent, then, can these studies focus in on the arousal component of the interaction situation and manipulate this variable systematically to get at some of these problems experimentally instead of just providing good techniques for evoking disagreements? Maybe we can conceive of "disagreement" as a kind of arousal. At a theoretical level this might be done very explicitly. This all goes back to the issue: What are the concepts of family theory and family research? What conceptual structure can we use in talking to each other? How are we going to communicate if we are going to link our research approaches?

Chairman Bell: Jay, do you have any further thoughts?

Mr. Haley: I think it would be a good idea to open it up. Perhaps the clinicians would have some comments.

Dr. Wynne: I would like to address myself to one issue which is of a clinical nature. In your comments about the use of self-reports and the problems of using family therapy for developing systematic evidence, it does seem to me that there is a good deal of consideration that needs to be given to ways of systematically making use of subjective experience and self-reports as one variety of data.

You mentioned Gregory Bateson's speaking of the probe into the situation, of which one end is in the observer. If there is always a transactional process between the experimenter and the family—and this is true even when they are in another room, because you have set a transactional process going by inviting them to come and join you—attention needs to be given to what this probe feels like to the person who is feeling one end of it. We don't know that the two ends of the probe are shaped similarly, if their action is similar, but we can get some further idea about the transactional interchange by making use of the subjective experience of both therapists and researchers as further leads. Whether this, then, is simply a way of suggesting hypotheses or whether such data can be used more systematically, I think is a vexing but important question that I hope we can include in the discussion.

Chairman Bell: May I join the panel and put in two brief remarks? First, it seems to me very curious that there has not been more systematic accretion of research techniques. In any academic field, first somebody invents a technique, then somebody else comes along and tries to replicate it systematically, and then somebody else comes along to manipulate one variable at a time. For some reason family research very seldom does this. Fred Strodtbeck's "Revealed Difference" technique is very widely used, but when you look at it, different items are used and in different ways; sometimes a method of tape-recording is used and sometimes a method of direct observation. The variety of the specifics of the technique almost destroys the comparability, and I wonder if one of our tasks isn't to get to the business of systematically replicating and extending methodologies.

The other comment is one which Jay did not mention, and that is the possibility of taking some of the key variables involved and finding out ways of investigating them epidemiologically, taking a total population. Can we get a random sample of a total population and a survey kind of method, see various combinations of family members together and find out something about the way they interact? It seems to me we have really overlooked the possibilities of getting formal knowledge about what goes on in a total population.

I will now open the discussion to all of the participants around the table.

Dr. Murray Bowen: I have one question for Jay. Do you have any comments about how one diagnoses a normal family?

Mr. Haley: Sure. A normal family is any family that hasn't come to community attention for a problem. That's the best we can do.

Dr. Carl A. Whitaker: A normal family is any family just like mine.

Mr. Haley: Gee, I don't believe that.

Dr. Whitaker: That's what you get for living in my house. (Laughter)

Mr. Haley: The difficulty is that if you send a clinician out to make a judgment of normality, he never finds normality. He is trained to discover abnormality and he has never seen normality. Most people use some criterion like "randomly selected average family." The criterion we use is that no member of the family has been in therapy or been arrested. If they have ever been in therapy or arrested, they are abnormal.

Dr. David Rubinstein: Perhaps one of the difficulties we are having about standardizing research procedures in families is that we are not yet agreed on what the real family is, or what kind of family we are talking about. As I understand it, the family is a completely different level of integration; it isn't just the sum of its members. Can we, from this conference, get some ideas of what the family system is, so that we can know what it is we are researching?

Mr. Haley: A major point is that we haven't even, in our research, decided what the unit is. We shifted to two and then we went to three, and then we got to four with a sibling in, and then there was the argument that the extended family was very important, and it keeps getting bigger, particularly when you start including the context in which the family is being treated or observed. I don't think there is any general agreement, by any means, on what a family is, in the sense of what should be looked at.

Mr. John H. Weakland: I would like to make a comment that puts together a couple of things that were said by Dr. Levinger and Dr. Wynne. Dr. Levinger said that there is too much concern about typology, and the main typology we get involved in over and over again is abnormal versus normal. This is a natural consequence of the close ties of the whole field with the family therapy business, but it seems to me that what we should really be aiming at is to use what we know and can find out about abnormal families to work toward a more general picture of the nature of the family as such, without emphasizing the distinction between normal and abnormal. It hasn't been done in the sense that is comparable to what Dr. Wynne said about Jay's presentation.

In other words, we are trying to bring things about the family's personal world out of where they are only privately known and privately spoken of into the open discussion of science. It seems to me that is what we are really about at the broadest level. Of course, it is also the hardest problem.

Dr. Jules Riskin: I wonder if Jay would comment on the problem of reliability versus triviality. It seems to me that he prefers machine judgments because they are more reliable than observer judgments and can be used with reproducible results. So far, it seems to me that machine judgments have been made and have not been significant. We have been weighing people by machines, and I'm not sure this tells us much about families.

Mr. Haley: This is a problem, as it has been in all psychological research. Clinicians usually feel that psychologists measure that which is irrelevant at the expense of that which is important, and I think the problem is how to find a measurement that is reliable and isn't trivial. One factor is that most clinicians feel that nothing the family members do with each other is trivial.

There is some interesting work developing which involves reliable

measures of nontrivial matters. An example is the work of Dan Miller in
Michigan. He hasn't reported on findings with control groups as yet, but
his measure is a button-pushing type. He deals with families who have 12-
or 13-years-olds who are severely retarded readers. He brings parents and
child together and they face some buttons and are asked to guess which
button to push to receive a reward. The family members think they are
making a choice, but actually the buttons are rigged so that someone in
the control room can make any family member right or wrong in his choice
of button. Miller will arrange it so that whichever button the child chooses
is right and whichever buttons the parents choose are wrong. He is testing
whether the parents can acknowledge that their nonreading child can be
right about something. In many of these families, the parents don't follow
the child's choice even though he is right every time and they are always
wrong.

Another variation is to have any family member be consistently
correct in his choice over a series of trials, and then make a shift and have
that person wrong and someone else right. The researchers want to see
whether the family is flexible enough to allow a shift to accepting the
choice of someone else. There is some evidence that the normal family will
shift to another member when one begins to be wrong, whereas in the
abnormal family they follow the one who has been doing it right for a long
time after he starts being wrong time after time.

This kind of measurement is objective in the sense that you get a
measure of who pushes what button. I don't think it is necessarily trivial. I
think, too, the sequence of speech isn't necessarily trivial. We have to
assume that the sequence in which family members talk to each other, at
least from our observations in family therapy, is relevant to the patterns of
behavior in the family. I am a little uncomfortable about having a rater
determine who is talking because I think it is very hard to tell this when
you listen to the tape. I prefer machine measurement.

I would agree that the question of triviality exists, but there is also a
question as to whether many of the things that clinicians think are
important are not necessarily so ambiguous that they are part of mythol-
ogy which can't be tested. If you do try to frame some idea so that it can
be tested and it doesn't come out, then it is said to be trivial because by
the very process of measuring it the phenomenon has changed. But this is a
problem that you are going to face in any field of research.

Dr. Robert MacGregor: Certainly, Jay, the raters can get together and
be measured on the accuracy with which they can predict who is trying to
talk to whom. Regardless of who a family member looked at, or to whom
he addressed himself, you can get some measure of agreement. It seems to
me it would be necessary to have this procedure to supplement the Miller

study you just cited. It could well be that Dad never pushes Mother's button, because at home or in the therapy situation Dad only speaks to Mother through Johnnie. This kind of indirect communication can't be picked up by button-pushing.

Mr. Haley: It can in some cases. Father may say to Son, "You call mother and talk to her and then call me back." They will talk through the child. But this is a basic dilemma. If you want a more reliable measurement, you have to restrict the complexity of the communication.

I think the rater judgment procedure is as restrictive as the experimental, because by the time you transcribe the interchange and somebody reads the transcript, then he has to guess who spoke to whom, and who responded. Watching through a window, as I have often done, doesn't make it any easier to tell who is speaking to whom because of the way people talk via each other. Who is speaking to whom is a complicated judgment to make, and we have to rely on crude measures, but even working on this mechanical level has many merits for many purposes. I see it as a preliminary step to doing something more. This is a complex problem.

Chairman Bell: These are important issues, they are issues which we can disregard but can't avoid, and I am sure they are going to come up time and time again throughout this conference. I hope that we will come back to these issues and also return to the people who have given position papers.

Methodological Problems in Family
Interaction Research

NATHAN B. EPSTEIN, JOHN J. SIGAL, VIVIAN RAKOFF

Chairman Bell: The second position paper on this program is by Dr. Nathan
Epstein, with coauthors Drs. John J. Sigal and Vivian Rakoff. It is
entitled, "Methodological Problems in Family Interaction Research."

Dr. Nathan B. Epstein: After listening to Jay's paper, I felt that if we
had followed some of his criteria, we probably wouldn't be here today. I
am reporting on clinical research in which therapists are actively involved,
and in which we heavily use the rater method of observation and coding.
However, this research is just one part of a program of studies going on in
our unit in which my coauthors, Dr. Sigal and Dr. Rakoff, have
collaborated.

Rather than undertaking to cover methodological problems in the
whole area of interaction research, I will deal almost exclusively with
problems arising specifically from one aspect of our research project,
namely, the attempt to do interaction research on families in treatment. I
must say I came into this from the other end. I was involved in a study
that went on for about eight years which dealt with so-called "normal"
families. We found that we couldn't really use the term, so we called them
"nonclinical families," and that project sort of funneled into this one,
where we tried to get into the clinical end of things and see whether we
could squeeze any meaningful and rigorous findings out of the clinical
work which we were doing.

Our aim was to test certain hypotheses that are currently accepted
implicitly or explicitly about family functioning and families in treatment.

50

Rabkin (1965) has given an overview of methodological problems encountered in many other areas of family research but he has touched only rather lightly on this particular one. Now, as I believe Dr. Framo said at the beginning of the conference, past experience suggests that therapy will go on being done regardless of what is turned up by the laboratory research. The position taken here is that clinical research, such as the systematic study of families in treatment, has its place alongside research of a more basic descriptive or experimental nature and will have at least as great an impact on therapeutic practice.

We feel it would be fruitful to offer the problems we have encountered in our work for discussion, since others engaged in this field are likely to come up with similar ones. We have achieved some measures of success in solving some of the problems; we are painfully aware that many others remain to be solved.

First, however, we will present you with an overview of our therapy research project. Because of the great upsurge of interest in conjoint family therapy on this continent and elsewhere, and the paucity of systematic descriptions and assessment of the technique, it was felt by our group that we should mount a research program aimed at: a) systematically describing the actual techniques utilized within our setting and, b) studying the course of therapy and the variables affecting process and outcome.

During a pilot study we developed and refined a series of questionnaires. We then offered treatment to the first families that presented themselves at our clinic. In order to be part of the research sample they had to meet the following criteria: the identified patient had to be at least eight years old, so that he could be tested on our battery of psychological tests, and not so psychotic that verbal communication was impossible; the family had to be sufficiently fluent in English for treatment to be carried on in that language; and the mother and father had to be living together with their children. The family had to attend at least two conjoint therapy sessions. It was intended that the actual therapeutic phase of the research program extend over a period of roughly twelve months. The research sample consisted of twenty families.

The questionnaires developed during the pilot study were utilized at specific stages of this study. A first diagnostic and prognostic questionnaire called the Screening Interview Questionnaire, was filled in by the research group immediately following the initial intensive interview of the whole family. The interactional functioning of the family and the intrapersonal functioning of its members were described and predictions made as to changes anticipated as a result of the treatment. Our intention was to test the accuracy of our initial critical impressions by comparing our prognostications against the later developments.

During the course of therapy, the Therapy Questionnaire was filled in by the family therapist in collaboration with his supervisor after the second therapy session, after the sixth session, and after every sixth session thereafter. The Therapy Questionnaire dealt with the behavior of the family in therapy—the therapeutic problems encountered, how they were dealt with, the family's reaction, and changes that occurred (for better or for worse) in various aspects of the functioning of the family and its members.

Other questionnaires covered the following situations: modifications in the therapeutic procedure, such as building into the situation of individual therapy the treatment of dyads, etc.; transfer of families to another therapist; and termination of treatment for whatever reason or the end of the research period, whichever occurred first.

At the end of the research, the families were rescreened by the original screening team. The status of the family's functioning at the time of the rescreening was noted and recorded. Special note was taken of the functioning in the specific areas of the original predictions.

A feature common to all the questionnaires mentioned was that they called for a description of the family under the headings of the Family Category Schema which had been developed by myself, Dr. Rakoff, and Dr. Sigal, and the other members of the research team of our hospital. This Category Schema was an extension of the work done by myself and William Westley as part of our eight-year McGill Human Development Study dealing with nontreatment families, which I talked about at the beginning of this paper (Epstein & Westley, 1969).

The categories were designed in an attempt to describe important aspects of the structure and functioning of any family and to permit a systematic comparison of families with one another. In our therapy research study, the screening team made predictions concerning anticipated change under each of these Category Schema headings, the therapist noted changes as they occurred, and, at the end, the screening team compared predictions with outcome.

Apart from these reports and questionnaires, other information was obtained by various techniques:

1. Social workers did an intake interview, and home visits before and after therapy. Their observations were recorded under predetermined headings arrived at as a result of our experience during the pilot study.

2. A sociological research assistant administered questionnaires covering various sociological variables, such as division of labor, patterns of authority, uses of leisure time, etc., before and after

therapy. Some of these variables were extensions of the McGill Human Development Study.

    3. Individual psychiatric histories and individual health questionnaires of the various members of the family were completed by the therapist.

    4. Psychologists administered a specially devised battery of psychological tests, including the following:

> a. Perceptual tests—tests designed to measure the effect of the presence of family members on perceptual thresholds of neutral and affective stimuli.
>
> b. The Family Interaction Test, which is a TAT-like test.
>
> c. The Figure Placement Test, which is a MAPS-like test.
>
> d. The Family Rorschach Test—the standard Rorschach Test with instructions adapted to permit administration to the family and a scoring system devised to get at family interaction.

The FIT and the FPT were given to almost all families and the Family Rorschach Test to five families before and after treatment.

Recordings were made of actual therapeutic sessions at the second, sixth and every sixth therapy session thereafter. We attempted to codify these taped sessions into basic transactional variables, using a system based upon a much modified version of the Dollard and Auld model for scoring individual psychotherapeutic interviews. We hope to be able to relate the coding of the transactional variables to the clinical progress and change of the families.

In the course of screening families who presented for therapy at the beginning of the research program, four families had been accepted for treatment but decided not to return after the initial screening. At the end of the research therapy period these four families were called back in and were given another diagnostic interview. The findings were recorded on the screening interview questionnaire in the same way as at the time of the initial screening and the data were used as a means of checking the reliability of our observations and predictions.

In yet another aspect of our program, the research group attempted to develop effective diagnostic procedures of family transactions. These included the psychological tests mentioned earlier and a series of questionnaires based on the Family Category Schema.

Now I would like to turn to methodological problems. One study, recently completed, will illustrate the use made of records kept by the therapists. At predetermined intervals during the course of therapy, therapists were asked to describe the patterns of collaboration of the families they were treating. Trial runs on a questionnaire used in a preliminary study suggested that closed-end questions would best satisfy our purposes. However, we felt some provision should be made for therapists to give their impressions of the family in treatment free of an externally imposed structure. Accordingly, the question on collaboration was worded so as to permit a therapist considerable freedom in his description of a family's course in treatment. Probably as a result of our approach to conjoint family therapy, all therapists, in their description of these patterns of collaboration, made some mention of the interaction and emotional involvement of the various members of the families they were treating.

Interaction and change in interaction, as seen by the therapist in the early treatment sessions, were examined as possible predictors of the eventual success or failure of the treatment. The therapist's responses were coded by categories, each of which was assigned a weight. The category Resistant Family Unit was given a weight of 0; Passivity, a weight of 1, Reluctance and/or Passive Relating, 2, Cooperation But No Active Engagement, 3, Sharing Responsibility for Participation with no explicit content, 4, and Active Engagement, 5.

The families were independently rated for improvement in a number of areas of family functioning some fourteen months after treatment began. Interjudge reliabilities were high on both sets of ratings. The initial patterns of interaction were then compared with the amount of change in family and individual functioning in the search for early prognostic indicators. (Complete details of this particular study will be found in Sigal, Rakoff, & Epstein, 1967.)

The results were embarrassing in view of the current attitude about the importance of fostering interaction in family therapy.

1. Comparing outcome and interaction, the results were as follows:

a. No relationship was found between outcome and interaction at any of the three points during the first twelve sessions of treatment.

b. Very high interactors during the first two sessions were found only in the good result group (this is what we would expect on the basis of previous observations); however, not all of those with good results were very high interactors. Furthermore, in later sessions the relationship between high interaction and good outcome did not hold.

c. Five of the six early dropout families (i.e., those who

attended at least one session beyond the screening interview) had interaction scores below the median in the first
two sessions, but the sixth had the highest interaction
score in the whole sample. However, a low interaction
score was not a predictor of early dropout.

2. Comparing outcome and *change* in interaction, the results
were as follows:

a. There was a general increase in the amount of interaction in the course of treatment but *it bore no relationship to
outcome.*

b. There was a suggestion that low change in interaction
over twelve sessions is predictive of poor outcome. This
must be a tentative observation pending examination of a
larger sample, as it is only based on two poor outcome
families. (The other poor outcome families were no longer
in treatment by the twelfth session.)

There are many difficulties in interpreting the meaning of these
results but this study is illustrative of what might be done even with the
clinical information providing the recording is adequately done.

In carrying out the study just described, some problems had already
been encountered. For example, in evaluating outcome, one family was
particularly well integrated at the time of reevaluation and we were
amazed at the level of functioning of the girl who had been grossly
delinquent at the beginning of treatment. Several weeks later, however, the
girl had once more become delinquent. There was a marked change in the
parents' handling of the girl compared to when they came into treatment,
but as a family their functioning had not radically altered. The problem,
then, is that the behavior at the time at which the crucial observation is
made may not be representative of long-term behavior. Experimenters have
a similar problem, for example, in knowing to what degree test or test-
situation behavior is representative of natural-situation behavior.

This brings us to a second difficulty encountered by almost anyone
involved in attempting to describe families, namely, that there is no
vocabulary available to describe the family's interactional functionings as
a unit apart from a description of the functioning of individuals or of
dyads. What do we mean when we say, "The family is a healthy family"?
Or, "The family made a decision," or what-have-you?

In one section of our Family Category Schema we talk about family
psychopathology. It is one of the categories we have constructed. There, we
arbitrarily state that for a type of psychopathology to be labeled a family
psychopathological area, the pathology has to be present in at least the two

parents and one child. Such a solution is something less than satisfactory, and sometimes totally inadequate.

The absence of a vocabulary not only hinders our diagnostic and descriptive capacities, but from the research point of view, perhaps more importantly, it hampers our capacity to construct closed-end questions. The importance of the closed-end question in this field became only too obvious to us when we attempted to examine answers given to us by different therapists to open-end inquiries. Their language was often so various that it was like comparing apples and oranges when we tried to relate their answers to the same question. A more consistent language would have obviated this difficulty to a great extent. However, a system of terminology implies a unified theoretical model which in fact does not exist.

Another problem, common to any research in psychotherapy, is to relate the amount of change to the total change possible. Judgment of degree of improvement must be relative to the base line used and the amount of change possible. These factors vary a great deal from one family to the next. For example, in one of our more successfully treated families, a very schizoid man was finally able to smile in appreciation of something his wife would do for him, or smile at his children. In this family, such a slight change produced very considerable effects, whereas the identical change in another family might pass relatively unnoticed and be of little significance.

It was in attempting to code transcripts of family interviews that we came up against the greatest difficulties.* The first problem that confronted us was the problem of time sampling. (Actually, unofficially, the first and perhaps the greatest problem is getting secretaries who are capable of transcribing these things satisfactorily. I had visions of seeing a whole research program go down the drain because we weren't able to get this satisfactorily in hand at the beginning.) It became obvious that the task of coding an entire interview was an almost impossible one because it was so time-consuming. In addition, there was the methodological problem of comparing interviews of unequal length. We thought that taking some fixed proportion of a total interview would cope with the problems of interviews of unequal length. That is, we would be comparing equal parts of one interview with equal parts of another.

We had to find which segment of the interview would be most representative of the total interview. The question that arises here is

---

*Miss R. Spector and Dr. Herta Guttman have been the two members of our team with primary responsibility for this aspect of the project.

whether different things happen at different times in the interview and whether we would not be better off taking several time samples through an interview than taking one large one at any given point in the interview. There is already some evidence in the literature (Guze & Mensh, 1959; Riecken, 1960) that, in fact, different things do happen at different points in an interview. The Scylla to the Charybdis of taking too long a time sample was the danger of taking too short a time sample, one that would not represent a sample of anything that went on in the family. We started out bravely to find the most suitable time sample of our interviews by comparing segments of an interview with the total interview. Our intention was to take that segment that correlated highest with the total inverview.

The scores we used for comparison purposes were based on a coding system in which we scored the amount of emergency (E), welfare (W), and affectively neutral (N) statements made by each of the participants in the session. A bit further on we will talk about the difficulties we encountered in arriving at a satisfactory interactional system for coding family interviews. On the basis of comparing the total amount of emergency emotion expressed by all members in the session in relation to the sum of emergency and welfare emotions expressed, we obtained the following results:

>Comparing the two halves of the session the correlation was + .64
>
>Comparing the middle third and the whole session the correlation was + .77
>
>Comparing the end sixths with the total the correlation was + .93
>
>Comparing the second and the fifth sixths with the total the correlation was + .85

Thus, it seems that a combination of the first and last sixths could be taken as most representative of the total score for this particular score.

Difficulties were encountered in the next comparison. We compared the emergency emotion expressed by any given person in relation to the total emergency emotion expressed in the two halves of any given session. The correlations here were all uniformly low and nonsignificant. This suggested that for the score of emergency emotions of a given person in relation to the total E, the two halves of a session were not comparable and the appropriate time segment representing each of the two halves would have to be found.

Obviously, establishing the best time sample for each of these scores was going to be a very time-consuming job. In addition, there was the knotty problem of comparing sessions of differing lengths. Here, reality intruded and we had to start turning out results because our grant was expiring, so we put aside this part of the project for a while and carried on in the following way:

On the assumption that there might be an initial warming-up period in any session, and in order to sidestep the problem of comparing sessions of uneven lengths, we decided to take as our time sample the 20 minutes of any session that followed after the first 15 minutes of the session—that is, the segment from the 15th to the 35th minute of any given session. Of course, here we left unanswered the questions of coping with different rhythms of evolution in any given session, between families and between therapists.

Next we come to the problem of the coding system itself. We do not want to go into the details of how we arrived at the coding system that we are using. Suffice it to say that we started with the Dollard and Auld system, trying to adapt it to indicate family interaction, and we found that the reliabilities were very low in detecting the nuances of conscious and unconscious expression and the great variety of emotions which Dollard and Auld suggest may be coded reliably. When we read the literature and get the reports of these various coding systems that anybody can get wonderful results with, we kind of have the feeling that something happens to the systems by the time they cross the border, because when they come up to Canada we don't get the same results.

We decided to settle grossly for emergency and welfare emotions and to try to score *to whom* the statement was directed, which is a To-score, and *about whom* the person spoke, the Re-score. Here, our findings agree with the statement made by Jay earlier, that the *about whom* is very difficult. Interscorer agreement concerning *to whom* a message was directed was satisfactory, in the neighborhood of 90 percent. The agreement among judges was lower but still satisfactory (in the neighborhood of 75 percent) when the judges had to rate the affect associated with the message. However, when the judges had to rate *about whom* a person was speaking, the reliabilities became quite unsatisfactory, falling in the neighborhood of 55 percent, that is, the judges disagreed on about half the scores in this category.

These latter data were examined for two possible sources of disagreement. The first source concerned who was being talked about, and the second, disagreements on the affect, taking only those statements that the judges agreed on with respect to "about whom" the speaker was speaking. The reliabilities in scoring affect were comparable to those in the "to whom the person was speaking" category, that is, in the neighborhood of 90 percent. We tried to salvage the remainder of the Re-scores in the following way: We examined the ratio of E to W (that is, emergency to welfare) for the units on which the coders agreed on the person referred to and for the units on which the coders disagreed on the person referred to. We reasoned that if the ratio did not differ significantly in the two groups, then we might still use the Re-scores in the area of affective expression even though they might not be reliable in identifying the person concerned.

In fact, there was a very marked difference in the ratios in the Re-groups and we therefore had to conclude that we could not score in a reliable manner "about whom" a given speaker was speaking. Modification of our scoring rules may raise the reliability to the point where this information can be scored satisfactorily. Until this reliability is established, clinicians and experimenters trying to infer the direction of indirect messages had better take heed, and those trying to make second or third order inferences about unconscious messages had better be even more cautious.

Another question common to anyone doing research that entails coding of responses and assessing the reliability of coding is whether variations in interjudge reliability from one family or setting to another is the result of poor reliability of the coding system or a result of differing levels of ambiguity of the material being coded. In the case of scoring family interaction, if the variations and reliability from one family to another are due to characteristics of the family rather than to characteristics of the coding system, then we may have a valuable indicator of one aspect of family functioning, that is, its ambiguity.

We proposed that an analysis of variance would answer this question and, in fact, we carried out such a procedure on material derived from three judges coding four families. The between-pairs-of-judges variance was significant, while the between-families variance was not. Fluctuations in interjudge agreement did not parallel differences in families. We were, therefore, forced to conclude that fluctuations in interjudge agreement could not be used as a measure of the ambiguity of the interaction or communication process within the family.

We know of no one who has explicitly recognized the next problem, although it is a very obvious one. Studying "family interaction" is as meaningless as studying the results of psychotherapy on "clinic patients." Both treat as homogeneous categories which are in fact heterogeneous. One major source of heterogeneity in family interaction is the age of the children. For example, in our project we thought of applying Haley's (1964) method of measuring deviation from equal participation in family interaction to our data. We immediately ran up against the problem of the participation of young children in family interaction.

It was a relatively simple matter to count the number of times each person spoke after each other person, but while this was being done it became obvious that these participations were not of equal value. A child of four or a child of six might be pursuing his own particular interests—for example, asking for a drink of water or for a lollipop—intervening in the exchange between the parents and an adolescent child. Some group therapists might argue that, on a deep unconscious level, he may be pursuing a solution to the problems being discussed by the parents and the older sibling, but more often than not that seems to be an unlikely possibility.

In the absence of normative data on the extent and kind of participation to be expected by children of various ages in various types of family constellations, we are at a loss to know how to interpret a noncontent interactional score when all family members are not at least consciously working toward the solution of a given problem. Even given satisfactory experimental conditions, a satisfactory measure for one age group may not be satisfactory for another. This problem becomes acute if we wish to do longitudinal studies of the evolution of family interaction beginning at the age of verbalization, let alone at the birth of the first child.

Before concluding, a point mentioned earlier should be expanded. If we are not to fall into the trap of assuming that families form a homogeneous group and, from this assumption, launch upon "studies of family functioning," and if we wish to limit ourselves to studying the functioning of specific kinds of families, what means are we to use to identify these specific kinds of families?

Methods that have been used in the past have been to resort to the diagnosis of one member of the family. For example, families of schizophrenic patients are compared with families of delinquents, neurotics and normal children. This, however, is not selecting a *type of family* but, rather, selecting a family of a *type of patient.* We are here running into the danger of confounding individual psychology with family psychology. To this problem, we have no clear solution. However, such methods as the Family Category Schema or the Interpersonal Check List, and a number of others that have been reported in the literature as adaptable for use in the family, may hold some promise.

In summary, then, our research and that of others have shown us many negative things and few sure ones. Most distressing is the fact that many of our strongly held implicit assumptions, such as the importance of interaction as an indicator of therapeutic progress (referred to above), have not held up under critical examination.

Finally, we are still left with the problem of finding the crucial diagnostic indicators of family functioning, without which we cannot construct a fixed, workable model and vocabulary.

REFERENCES

Epstein, N. B., & Westley, W. A. *Silent Majority*. San Francisco: Jossey-Bass, 1969.

Guze, S. B., & Mensh, I. N. An analysis of some features of the interview with the Interaction Chronograph. *Journal of Abnormal Social Psychology*, 1959, *58*, 269-271.

Haley, J. Research on family patterns: An instrument measurement. *Family Process*, 1964, *3*, 41-65.

Rabkin, L. Y. The patient's family: Research methods. *Family Process*, 1965, *4*, 105-132.

Riecken, H. W. Social psychology. In P. R. Farnsworth and Q. McNemar (Eds.), *Annual review of psychology*. Palo Alto: Annual Reviews, Inc., 1960, *11*, 479-510.

Sigal, J. J., Rakoff, V., & Epstein, N. B. Indicators of therapeutic outcome in conjoint family therapy. *Family Process*, 1967, *6*, 215-266.

DISCUSSION

Chairman Bell: We will now carry on with the panel discussion of Dr. Epstein's most interesting paper. Dr. Epstein is as aware as anyone, I think, of the methodological problems we face and he is not one of those who has lain down and said, "I can't do anything." He has really taken a very hard look at what can be done. His paper provides a very interesting case example of research in this field.

May I call on the panel members serially for brief comments?

Dr. Robert A. Ravich: I didn't have an opportunity to see the paper that Dr. Epstein presented beforehand, so I have to confine my remarks to several general points that I think are illustrated by his talk.

It seems to me that little notice has been taken of the extreme difference that exists between studying any group composed of two individuals as opposed to a group of three or four individuals. We often speak of small groups of two, three, or four as if they were similar. But the difference between a group of two and a group of three is enormous. The sociologist Georg Simmel (1858-1918) clearly expressed this when he wrote:

"The difference between the dyad and larger groups consists in the fact that the dyad has a different relation to each of its two elements than have larger groups to their members. Although, for the outsider, the group consisting of two may function as an autonomous superindividual unit, it usually does not do so for its participants. Rather, each of the two feels himself confronted only by the other, not by the collectivity above him (i.e., the dyad). The social structure here rests immediately on the one and on the other of the two, and *the secession of either would destroy the whole.* The dyad, therefore, does not attain that super-personal life which the individual feels to be independent of himself. *As soon, however, as there is an association of three, a group continues to exist even in case one of the members drops out.*"*

Simmel's major point was that the group of two is subject to obliteration as a social entity by the removal of one, whereas the existence of the group of three is not subject to the same threat. One person can be removed and a social group still exists.

I think this is a pivotal point. I certainly find it to be so in therapy, as well as in research. Research on families may in some ways be beyond our capacity at the present time because the significance of the profound differences between dyads and triads has not been recognized and appreciated.

Another point that is little understood, except to some extent by communications people, is the question of the interface, that area that lies between two individuals or two systems. Unless that is structured, and fairly rigidly structured so that the variables are limited, there are tremendous difficulties that beset the researcher from the outset. Dr. Epstein's paper illustrates this in several ways. He describes the difficulty of knowing who is talking to whom and about whom, and that unless you structure your questionnaire to the therapist very tightly, you wind up getting so many different kinds of responses that you are confronted with the impossible task of comparing oranges with apples.

Finally, I want to raise a question as to whether the family or a dyad within the family is not such a different and perhaps more complex unit that it is a kind of laziness to resort to individual personality tests or rating scales and merely adapt them to these other units. In my opinion we must develop whole new categories of tests if we are to be able to comprehend family processes for research and therapeutic purposes.

Dr. Antonio J. Ferreira: Since I have kept one foot in family therapy

---

*In K. H. Wolff (Ed.), *The sociology of Georg Simmel.* New York: Free Press Paperback, 1964, p. 123.

and another foot in family research, I must say that I feel very sympathetic and very appreciative of Dr. Epstein's efforts to bring well-structured, well-organized research into the chaotic field of therapy. Dr. Epstein was faced with a problem that we have already commented upon, namely, what to study. What are the variables? This is a problem that I don't think we are even close to solving. But should we have solved it—and some of us, including myself, feel that here and there we are beginning to sense some variables that are worth studying—we would still have to investigate whether those variables were critically capable of telling us if some changes had taken place in a given family in the course of therapy and/or time.

It is quite conceivable, for instance, that we may be able to measure "something" in a family at a given time, and yet, later on, in terms of that variable, we may find no appreciable change in the measurement, despite some obvious clinical improvement. In other words, that clinical improvement may not be reflected immediately, at least on that variable.

I had the opportunity of testing some twenty normal families and twenty abnormal families six months apart, in terms of five variables that had appeared to differentiate normal from abnormal families. The retest six months later revealed that both groups of families, normal and abnormal, scored essentially at the same level on all of those variables. The test and retest correlation was quite high for a thing of this kind, something in the neighborhood of .6. Apparently, then, six months of family therapy did not change the abnormal families on those variables, though it might have done so clinically. So, the question I would like to raise in this connection is this: Had we been able to detect some worthwhile variables, what guarantee would we have that, if an improvement took place, that improvement would be reflected in those variables when we came to study the family at a later date?

Dr. MacGregor: I am very pleased to be a soft researcher—I think some of us are defined as soft researchers in this context. I was little disappointed to see our free-spirited Jay Haley join the police force. At the last meeting in this room, it was only the anthropologists who were telling us, "You can't do this and you can't do that."* I see researchers like Dr. Epstein looking at the very valuable data that are accumulated, some of it by machinery, some of it by people, and doing things with it.

It seems to me that we are raising some false issues. Murray Straus has stressed the importance of getting the family involved around

---

*Conference on family process and psychopathology: perspectives of the social scientist and clinician, Eastern Pennsylvania Psychiatric Institute, Philadelphia, Pa., October 9 - 11, 1964, organized by Dr. Gerald H. Zuk and Dr. Ivan Boszormenyi-Nagy.

something important to them, not a task that they are given just to do something together. When they are responding meaningfully, you have some valuable data coming out.

You can say, "This is terribly complex," but anything in the human realm is complex. You have to ask simple enough questions, and there are ways to do this. One obvious way is to code a great deal of the material. When you select your coding method, you need to have a great many categories because, obviously, some people will be overrepresented and some will be underrepresented. You need the kind of categories that can be condensed to give fair representations so that what you get, if you are looking for a family attitude, is a family attitude and not just one kid's propaganda. There are ways of handling that problem too, if you can define it. If you can show that the youngster came by his propaganda honestly through the family, then you can lump that together with data from your other family members. I don't like the counsel of despair or the thought that we have to leave this rich clinical material and set up artificial experimental situations.

In regard to testing methods, I think the *a priori* methods of examining can be useful, and I speak here in favor of standard psychological tests just because they are standard. The most important thing that is standard about them is generally that the examiner is standardized in his use of them. Small differences mean a great deal to him. The long check list forms are the same when applied to each family member or to the whole family. Some standardized test data can also be taped. People say a lot of data is lost when you use audiotape, and when video-tape was introduced, many researchers turned off the sound to study the expressive movements. This may not be such a problem. We can still take an audio tape, get clear on what it does and doesn't have in it, code it, and study the reliabilities of the coders.

It seems to me that all this business of worrying about what you lose is like the superego type of professor of statistics who tells you that you have to have reliabilities in the nineties. You don't have to have reliabilities in the ninetics to test some things. You only have to have that level of reliability that gets an answer to your question.

Dr. Riskin: I suppose I am also on the soft side, although I have a bias toward being on the hard side, and with that bias I would like to raise a few points that focus on methodological problems.

One point alluded to by Dr. Ravich, was the question of whether individual questionnaires are valid. There is some sort of implicit assumption that if you add together a bunch of individual questionnaires you are going to come up with a whole. I am not sure that the whole is the sum of the parts in this situation.

I would like to hear a few more comments by Dr. Epstein about the rater bias. Did the raters know what kinds of families were being interviewed, what kinds of pathologies, what kinds of expectations?

This question of predicting is a particularly tough one, I think, because often predictions can be made in such a way that it is impossible, really, to confirm or disconfirm them. I would think it important to discuss quite explicitly the nature of the prediction and whether you can confirm it or not. Such a degree of precision may not even be possible in this kind of work at this time.

Dr. Epstein raised the issue of how to deal with young children in the interview situation. In our study, we have also used kids as young as five or six, and the way the family deals with the child is one variable that you can use. The family may ignore the child and let him pull the microphone apart or they can handle him in various other ways, all of which may be meaningful.

Chairman Bell: I would like to make one comment, a potshot at Nathan Epstein here, and then unfortunately, I have to close off this discussion for this morning due to lack of time.

I was shocked, Nathan, to hear you mention that we don't have languages for describing groups. This is what sociologists have been about; indeed, you are using many of these terms yourself when you talk about such things as division of labor. You may not find them very compatible because they grow out of other kinds of issues, but Georg Simmel has a very elaborate language for groups. Fred Strodtbeck has given us much on this, as has Murray Straus. Maybe that was just a slip.

Dr. Epstein: No, it was not a slip at all. I still hold to this opinion. When you are talking about division of labor, you are talking about who is assigned a piece of labor in the family. You are still talking about individuals, and this is what we are trying to avoid. We don't say that a family works hard or a family doesn't work hard. We say that members A, B, C and D of the family work hard, or A and B work hard and the others are lazy, and various things of that sort. So far, I haven't found anyone who has a language to describe more than the one.

Chairman Bell: I hope we can come back to this point. In the remaining minutes, would you like to say a word in response to any of the discussants?

Dr. Epstein: Yes. I deplore a little bit the trend of the meeting where it seems to be polarizing between the soft and the hard. I think this is unfortunate, because, particularly at our stage of development in this field of research, I don't think we are in a position to take sides. We are all looking, we are all groping, and we are all trying to find a handle to get hold of these tough problems. Whether answers come from the soft side or the hard side is irrelevant.

(Friday Morning Session Adjourned)

Some Basic Issues in Interaction Research

PAUL WATZLAWICK

Chairman Antonio J. Ferreira: Greetings. I hope you are all set to continue this morning's discussion, which I feel was a very promising one.

Just to refresh your memories, the morning ended with a bit of interchange as to whether or not we are soft and hard researchers, and if so, who is what. I guess we should admit that some of us are really more like a five-minute egg, by which I mean we are neither soft nor hard.

To start with, Dr. Paul Watzlawick is going to present his paper to us, "Some Basic Issues in Interaction Research." Dr. Watzlawick requires no introduction, I am sure. He is always very explicit in his thoughts; however, should he not be, let me make a plug for him. His book, *Pragmatics of Human Communication,** was recently published, and I am sure it contains all the things he is going to try to tell you today. Dr. Paul Watzlawick!

Dr. Paul Watzlawick: I find myself in the most unusual position of taking a more radical stand than Jay. I am somewhat encouraged in doing this by some of the opinions that were expressed this morning. What I would like to talk about has more to do with questions than answers. In fact, I have relatively few answers to give, and some of the questions that I would like to raise have already been raised this morning.

I would like to point out, however, that I have been engaged in a project that contains all the things that I am going to question. I am the perpetrator of one of the many structured family interviews that are being

---

*New York: W. W. Norton, 1967.

used to elicit particular types of behavior, particular communication patterns in families.

In spite of this, I want to raise the question of whether anything we are doing at the present moment (as far as I know, I should say) really does justice to the complexity of the phenomena that we are trying to observe. In this connection, several of the speakers and discussants this morning have stated the need for a more or less comprehensive theory of family interaction. I would like to push this a little further and would say we need a theory of interaction in general, not necessarily of families but of the kinds of organisms and physical environments that we are exposed to.

This paper will describe an approach to the study of human interaction that is based on the assumption that *communication* is synonymous with what is observable in such interaction. That is, communication is seen not as just the vehicle, not as just the manifestation, but as a better conception of what is often loosely gathered under the rubric "interaction."

We have, of course, no complete or formal theory. We will, rather, present what appear to be very simple and obvious premises which, *followed through to their necessary conclusions,* seem to yield a fundamentally new and quite productive outlook.

Before I continue, however, some general comments about the "obviousness" of these points should be made. First of all, it is often the intimately important, especially in our own behavior, which is overlooked or difficult to see, precisely because it is, like breathing, largely out of awareness until drawn to our attention. Second, and more important, while few would flatly exclude in theory the ubiquity and importance of the social context, actual research and application too frequently stop at lip service, so that involvement with a particular (monadic) subject of investigation results, in practice, in the neglect of the interactional perspective. That is, communicational factors are often regarded as random, or potentially excludable, sources of variance. This problem arises both in the definition of *what* is to be studied and—since the behavioral sciences are ultimately self-reflexive and all research by humans on other humans is social—to the strategy and analysis of *how* the data are studied; that is, to methodology as well as to content. In either case, even when the interactional context is thus, in effect, ignored, it does not go away; there always remains a valid *communicational* interpretation of the data. The latter is, unfortunately, often in conflict, or at least difficult to integrate with the investigator's intended, more monadic interpretation (e.g., Jackson & Haley, 1963; Rosenthal, 1966). Third, and perhaps most important, these basic notions may be obvious, yet they still are neither systematized into an adequate theory of communication, nor consistently utilized in research.

The question then is, what sort of theory would this be? What would be some of the characteristics of such a theory? I do not believe that in order to arrive at a theory one first has to look at the facts, necessarily. I think that physical science provides fairly clear evidence that it is possible to go the deductive way—it need not be inductive— and in support of this point I quote what Einstein has said: "We now realize with special clarity how much in error were those nineteenth century scientists who believed that a theory could be derived inductively from the facts." This, of course, is a very extreme opposite position to the one that says one has to look at the phenomena first and then try to make a theory. Needless to say, one has to look at the phenomena first, but the question is, How much does this procedure interfere with the possibility of formulating theories about facts that we are, ourselves, exposed to all the time, anyway?

The basic contention of my paper is that, in the behavioral sciences, we are obviously up against something which linguists and semanticists are up against, and which has largely been systematized in those two fields. Let me simply quote Whorf (1956) who, talking about linguistics, said, "Scientific linguists have long understood that the ability to speak a language fluently does not necessarily confer a linguistic knowledge of it, that is to say, understanding of its background phenomena and its systematic process and structure, any more than ability to play a good game of billiards confers or requires any knowledge of the laws of mechanics that operate on the billiard table."

I think all of us who behave and who communicate and who go about the daily business of living are, obviously, observing some kind of a structure or code of behavior that varies enormously from culture to culture, from subculture to subculture, and from family to family. My contention is that, just as there is in the logical syntax of language or in semantics, there must also be a structure, a code governing human behavior in general. I would like to look at this in my own work on the most basic level, and ask, for example, Is family communication any different from other communication? Is communication in one particular kind of family different from communication in the family that corresponds to a different diagnostic category?

I would also suggest that we take into account that all interaction is a process in which the occurrence of one event invariably influences the occurrence of future events. We have to deal with a stochastic process, another phenomenon widely studied in information and communication theories. Heraclitus was aware of this when he stated that nobody can step into the same river twice for the first time.

There is a basic question I would like to ask: An organism that is provided with a central nervous system and a brain like ours and that lives in a physical universe like ours obviously has certain possibilities of communication and not others. What are the basic laws of such an interaction, then? What I have in mind is the idea of a calculus that, like a logical calculus, pervades human communication. Just to explain a little bit what I mean by this calculus and by the idea of the axioms of such a calculus, let me point to what I think are some basic characteristics of interaction. They are by no means my discoveries. They have been formulated in various ways by other people, especially by those in the Bateson Project in Palo Alto.

For one thing, we must realize that the scope of "communication" is by no means limited to verbal productions. Communications are exchanged through many channels and combinations of these channels, and certainly also through the context in which an interaction takes place. Indeed, it can be summarily stated that *all* behavior, not only the use of words, is communication (which is not the same as saying that behavior is *only* communication), and since there is no such thing as nonbehavior, it is impossible *not* to communicate. Recent animal studies show, for instance, that certain monkeys will seat themselves during their rest periods in a forest clearing so that no animal looks at any other, and all stare straight ahead into the forest. They do this not only to keep watch but also for the purpose of resting. They seem to find it necessary to avoid even the communication inherent in a glance, very much as a man in a waiting room may stare at the floor if he wants to be left alone by other persons present. Not looking at others is tantamount to saying, "Leave me alone," and is normally understood as such.

All behavior has an effect as communication, an often very powerful effect which may be one of the most proven assertions of social science—though not always deliberately proven. That is, it is quite common that experiments with a variety of independent variables, including pharmacological agents, show significant changes in human behavior which are, however, not replicable *with that variable.* However, the original effect did in fact occur, and is usually construed as a "placebo" effect. We concur with those who interpret each such case as a demonstration of powerful though as yet unspecified communicational effects.

In our present state of knowledge, we have no final evidence as to whether all behavior is really completely free of "noise" in the information-theoretical sense. However, to date, explorations of the problem of noise (randomness) versus redundancy (order, patterning) in behavior-seen-as-communication have consistently shown an almost unbelievable degree of order and structure behind their protean manifestations. It becomes more and more plausible that communication in the widest sense is at least as rule-governed as natural language is determined by its grammar and syntax (Scheflen, 1965; Pittenger, 1960). As in learning a natural language, the ability to communicate is based on the acquisition of a very abstract structure or code which is never formalized and, in this sense, is never truly conscious.

The suggestion that there is virtually no sender-originated noise in human communication almost immediately raises the related issues of "conscious," "intentional," or "successful" communication. Many communicational events are routinely excluded from, or differently classified within, theory based on a simpler "information" model because they were either not *intended* to be communication or did not succeed in communicating what was intended. To take an extreme position, one which rests precariously on the edge of infinite regress, any measure of intention is, ultimately, garnered in a communicational setting. Thus, I may *say* that I did not (consciously) intend to ignore you, or you may yourself label my behavior in this manner. But this labelling procedure is no more and no less than further information in our ongoing communication. This, of course, has nothing to do with whether the unconscious really exists or whether people really have intentions. Seen as *labels of the participants,* such information is only communication—valid as such but not complete.

The issue of unsuccessful (and, therefore, implicitly meaningless) or successful communication obviously rests in part on the judgment of the participant or observer. To take an extreme counter-example, verbal or nonverbal nonsense is communicative. Information, especially at the relationship level (discussed immediately below) *is* conveyed to the receiver; this point has been especially well taken in regard to schizophrenic behavior (Haley, 1959), which may be seen *positively* as meaningful, rather than as gibberish outside the pale of human communication.

Another point that could be made is that no matter who communicates with whom, or under what circumstances, the communication has at least two levels, even leaving out the context in which this interaction occurs. The first is the level on which content is transmitted, that is to say, the level which communicates information. At the same time, there is invariably another level, a level on which the relationship between the two communicants is defined. While one or the other level may have greater relative importance in any given piece of communication, communications composed of only one or the other are impossible, just as in computer work a computer not only needs data (information) but also instructions as to what to do with the data in order to carry out the particular computation.

The relationship aspect as well as the content aspect is an ever-present property of human communication. To exemplify, if woman A points to woman B's necklace and asks, "Are those real pearls?" the content of her question is a request for information about an object, but at the same time she also gives—indeed, cannot *not* give—a definition of their relationship. *How* she asks—the tone and inflection of her voice, her facial expression, and the context of her question—could indicate comfortable friendliness, competitiveness, or some other attitude. B, on the other hand, can accept, reject, or redefine A's message but cannot under any circumstances, even by silence, not respond to it. A's definition may, for instance, be a catty, condescending one; B, on the other hand, may react to it with aplomb or defensiveness. It should be noted that this part of the interaction has nothing to do with the genuineness of pearls or with pearls at all, but with the two parties' respective definitions of the nature of their relationship, although they may continue to talk about pearls.

Whether or not communication closure is reached on the content level will produce agreement or disagreement between the communicants. Laing, Phillipson and Lee (1966) have pointed to these levels in a slightly different framework and have proposed a theory of interpersonal perception which is certainly relevant to this basic property of human communication. They postulate that communication on the relationship level will result in understanding or misunderstanding between the communicants. It is possible for two communicants to disagree about an objective issue but to understand each other as human beings; to agree but fail to understand each other as human beings; or to agree and to understand each other.

A particularly frequent and clinically very important type of communication occurs when the two levels are confused in the sense that the communicants attempt to resolve a relationship problem on the content level—for instance, when they argue about a specific issue in order to establish who is the better person. Asch's experiments (1956) on independence and submission to group pressures provide an excellent example for this sort of communication, and so, of course, do all double-bind situations (Bateson, G., Jackson, D. D., Haley, J. & Weakland, J., 1956).

Another of the basic issues of communication, regardless of the context in which it occurs or of the type of communications involved, has to do with the fact that we must always look at communication as an ongoing process. There are a number of fallacies that I think we all have committed and continue to commit. For instance, if A and B are interacting, that is, exchanging behaviors, these behaviors can be seen as a stream of ordinary communication events, and this stream may be represented as a_1, b_1, a_2, b_2, and so on. That is, an act or piece of behavior by one person is followed by a piece of behavior by the other person, and a continuing stream of events develops therefrom.

There are various ways in which this stream of behavior events can be delineated, both by the interactants themselves and also, of course, by the observers of such an interaction. A common way, one that is nearly impossible to avoid in our language, is to see sequences of individual actions as if they took place on two separate levels. On one level we have a_1, a_2, a_3, a_4, and underneath we have b_1, b_2, b_3, and b_4, and there is a kind of zigzagging that goes on between these two corresponding pieces of behavior. If one of the participants, say A, is the subject of study—for example, if he is a psychiatric patient or an experimental subject—then only the items a_1, a_2, a_3, and a_4 are examined. Laing and his co-workers (1966) have focused sharply on these unproductive errors and, as Laing says: "The failure to see the behavior of one person as a function of the behavior of the other has led to some extraordinary perceptual and conceptual aberrations that are still with us. For instance, in a sequence of moves in a social interaction between person A and person B, a_1, b_1, a_2, b_2, and so on, the sequence a_1, a_2, a_3 is extrapolated."

Laing goes on to show that some generality can then be made about these pieces of behavior so that eventually one finishes up with the sum of "a" that is called the behavior of person A. But very often in these studies the behavior of person B—the experimenter, the observer, or the other interactant—is left out. Since, obviously, one cannot get very far with this kind of analysis, the behavior of person B is frequently introduced in these studies and eventually some kind of correlation between sum a and sum b is established. My contention is that if this procedure is followed, one very important aspect of communication or of interaction—the stochastic nature of ongoing sequences—is lost. Which is to say, as I mentioned earlier, that whatever occurs at one given point inevitably influences the future course of events.

It is of great importance to notice that people will usually, in their own interactions, see only the behavior of the other person. In therapy, for instance, we have noticed over and over again that a person will say, "I am only reacting to the thing that the other person does." There is an old joke that grew up along with the stimulus, response and reinforcement studies. It is the joke about the rat who boasts to another rat, "I have trained my experimenter so that every time I press a button he gives me a piece of cheese." What the rat does we all do in our own lives: We see ourselves only as reacting to a sequence of events and thus punctuate or evaluate it differently than does the other person. What the experimenter considers to be the rat's response, the rat considers its stimulus to the experimenter; what the experimenter then does and calls a reinforcement, the rat sees as a response, and so forth.

What we are proposing, following Bateson (1963), is, in essence, to extend this conception of events to encompass both the experimenter's and the rat's position, and to see clearly that every piece of event, every piece of behavior, is, of course, a stimulus, a reinforcement and a response at the same time.

Far from being spurious, this punctuation of the sequence of events is a highly significant corollary to the premise of an essentially unpunctuated stream. As philosophers of science have pointed out (*e.g.* Popper, 1962), man is born with a propensity to look for irregularities in the constant stream of events surrounding and involving him. The question whether these regularities exist in actual fact or are merely introduced by the observer is of no particular concern. I don't think patterning can be avoided. There is no reason why the day should be divided into 24 hours but this arbitrary division is a very useful one. The same principle is at work in human communication. Man tends to pattern the stream of communicational events into an order which, to him, is familiar and predictable. This ordering, however, presupposes selection, and the criteria applied to this process of selection are anything but simple and obvious. In particular, these criteria need not be shared by or be obvious to the other communicants. Discrepancies in the punctuation of jointly experienced events are, in fact, at the root of many conflicts in most areas of human communication, and the ever-present blindness for the other's punctuation, coupled with the naive conviction that reality is the way *I* see (punctuate) events, often leads to mutual charges of badness or madness.

I hold that this fact is of primary importance to any kind of research one wants to do about interactions between people for the simple reason that I do not think we can get away completely from each person's punctuation of the sequence of events or, for that matter, from our own as researchers. Thus, for instance, nation A may arm to protect itself against a real or imaginary threat from nation B. Nation B considers this a threat and increases its armaments, justifying this step as a purely defensive measure made necessary by nation A's threatening attitude. Nation A now has further "proof" of nation B's aggressive designs, a mechanism extensively studied by Richardson (1956).

Similarly, the paranoid patient suspects the motives of others. This prompts the others to prove to him the honesty and sincerity of their intentions, which not only confirms but increases his suspicions, because, he argues, if they were not out to hurt him they would not be trying so hard to make him believe that they mean well.

The depressed patient withdraws; his withdrawal worries those close to him; they try to help him by increasing their attention; on perceiving their concern and anxiety, he feels doubly guilty for causing them emotional pain and becomes more depressed; on seeing this, they try harder and at the same time feel more desperate about being unable to help him; this in turn compounds his depression to the point of considering suicide for being so "bad" to those who love him.

These examples of vicious circles can be multiplied almost indefinitely. The point is that, when the model of overlapping stimulus-response-reinforcement triads is adopted, no one participant's behavior can be said to "cause" the other's, although the participants themselves, of course, only think in these terms. In most ongoing relationships, it becomes obvious that the behavior of each participant is predicated on that of the other. The exact nature of these relationship links and the more abstract rules that govern them emerge as a new, virtually unexplored, area of human behavior.

One final and very general point derives from the foregoing considerations. In the communication perspective, the question of whether there is such a thing as an objective reality is of relatively little importance compared to the significance of different *views* of reality due to different punctuations. However, awareness of how one punctuates is extremely difficult owing to another basic property of communication. Like all other complex conceptual systems which attempt to make assertions about themselves (for instance, language, logic, mathematics), communication typically encounters the paradoxes of self-reflexivity when trying to apply itself to itself. What this amounts to is that the patterns of communication existing between oneself and others cannot be fully understood, for it is simply impossible to be involved *in* a relationship and at the same time stand *outside* it as a detached, uninvolved observer (which would be necessary in order to encompass and to be aware of the relationship in its entirety). This is essentially similar to the impossibility of obtaining full visual awareness of one's own body, since the eyes, as the perceiving organs, are themselves part of the body to be perceived. As Russell, Gödel, and Tarski have shown once and for all, no system complex enough to include arithmetic can achieve its own fully consistent formalization within its own framework and its own language.

Whether or not human communication and, therefore, human interaction is a comparable system and, therefore, beset by the same problem of ultimate undecidability, is not yet clear at all. There is much that speaks in support of this assumption, mainly the above-mentioned problem of subjective awareness or the fact that to communicate (or even to think) about communication, is itself communication, just as research on communication or on interaction is itself communication. In this sense, both one's subjective experience of communicative processes with others, as well as the study of communication as such, has to employ concepts whose range includes themselves and thus lead into Russellian paradoxes of self-reflexiveness, into an infinite regress of assertions about assertions, and into the problem of undecidability in Gödel's sense (Nagel & Newman, 1958). Bronowski (1966, p. 5), in a lucid study of this vexing problem, has shown precisely that, on the one hand, "any description in our present formalisms must be incomplete, not because of the obduracy of nature but because of the limitation of language as we use it"; on the other hand, he states that it is obvious that the mind somehow solves these problems in a highly typical way for which mathematics or logic offer no analogies.

It seems to us that in the field of human communication, the main evidence for the correctness of this assumption is supplied by the phenomenon of growth and change in relationships which are the equivalent of Baron Munchhausen's feat of pulling himself from the quagmire by his own pigtail. The paradox of change has occupied the human mind since the days of the pre-Socratics and it will not be solved here. But it remains a question of the greatest importance, especially in the light of communicational patterns and the question of their changeability, which, after all, is the main factor in psychotherapy, in conflict resolution on a personal as well as on an interpersonal scale, and ultimately in man's awareness of reality.

REFERENCES

Asch, S. E. Studies of independence and submission to group pressures. *Psychological Monographs,* 1956, *70,* No. 416.

Bateson, G. Exchange of information about patterns of human behavior. In W. S. Fields & W. Abbott (Eds.), *Information storage and neural control.* Springfield, Ill: Thomas, 1963.

Bateson, G., Jackson, D. D., Haley, J., & Weakland, J. Toward a theory of schizophrenia. *Behavioral Science,* 1956, *1,* 251-264.

Bronowski, J. The logic of the mind. *American Scientist,* 1966, *54,* 1-14.

Haley, J. An interactional description of schizophrenia. *Psychiatry,* 1959, *22,* 321-332.

Jackson, D. D., & Haley, J. Transference revisited. *Journal of Nervous and Mental Diseases,* 1963, *137,* 363-371.

Laing, R. D., Phillipson, H., & Lee, A. R. *Interpersonal perception.* New York: Springer Publishing Company, 1966.

Nagel, E., & Newman, J. R. *Gödel's proof.* New York: New York University Press, 1958.

Pittenger, R. E., Hockett, C. F., & Danehy, J. J. *The first five minutes.* Ithaca (N.Y.): Paul Martineau, 1960.

Popper, K. *Conjectures and refutations.* New York: Basic Books, 1962.

Richardson, L. F. Mathematics of war and foreign politics. In J. R. Newman (Ed.), *The world of mathematics.* New York: Simon & Schuster, 1956. Vol. II, 1240-1253.

Rosenthal, R. *Experimenter effects in behavioral research.* New York: Appleton-Century-Crofts, 1966.

Scheflen, A. Stream and structure of communicational behavior, context analysis of a psychotherapy session. *Behavioral Studies Monograph,* 1965, No. 1., Eastern Pennsylvania Psychiatric Institute, Philadelphia, Pennsylvania.

Whorf, B. L. Science and linguistics. In J. B. Carroll (Ed.), *Language, thought, and reality.* New York: John Wiley & Sons, 1956, 207-19.

DISCUSSION

Chairman Ferreira: I shall call now upon the members of the panel to make some preliminary comments about Dr. Watzlawick's presentation, following which you will all be welcome to mingle your own thoughts with those of the panel. I would like to ask Dr. Henry Lennard to begin.

Dr. Henry L. Lennard: This paper is difficult for me to talk about, particularly since Paul is going to discuss my paper later on in the meeting. (Laughter)

I think Dr. Watzlawick has given us a very good summary of some of the important ideas of the Palo Alto group. I particularly like his emphasis upon interaction contexts *per se* rather than upon particular contexts such as family context. Perhaps what we are talking about are patterns of interaction generally rather than about interaction patterns in the family alone. The family has many features in common with other systems and we need to know more about the kinds of differences and similarities between the family and other systems. We can do this only if we have some theory and tools which encompass interaction in the family as well as in other contexts. For instance, interaction in whatever context faces dilemmas such as: the allocation of participation in the system; division of labor among system members; the continuation and maintenance of the system; the organization of action over time, etc.

Let me say something regarding an issue which has now come up a number of times—the impact of the observer or the therapist upon the context to be studied. It has been pointed out that by doing therapy or by observation, the context is changed. Rather than say that this constitutes a liability, I think we should learn much more about this process. What kinds of context do we change? Does an observer change the family more or less than he would an experimental group, a conference group, or a simulated family group? What theory would we use to predict the effect of the observer on interactional variability, and how would we study his effect?

Dr. Salvador Minuchin: Working with disorganized, lower socioeconomic families as we do, we have noticed that they use language differently than middle class families. They put much more emphasis on the relationship messages than on the content messages. I think we feel less impelled in family therapy than in other therapies to pay attention to the content. Since their culture and our culture are so different, we are not interested very much in their content, nor are they interested in our content. This makes it easier to focus attention on other aspects of the context in which the family is functioning.

In relation to that, I want to talk a little bit about the change in the punctuation to which Dr. Watzlawick referred. In terms of our therapeutic approach, we feel that the therapist, in order to introduce change, is introducing a change in the punctuation that the family uses. We have been experimenting with these changes in a variety of ways, using the therapeutic interview to study the "punctuation" of the people. We do that by separating people into different subgroups. We do it by demanding that people change the patterns in which they talk, by introducing the therapist as a modifier, by having the therapist come from beyond the magic mirror or through the magic mirror. We also do it by not really accepting the context in which the family talks and, therefore, being able to put a point at a certain place in the vicious circle.

I liked what Dr. Watzlawick was saying about punctuation. I have always felt that the family therapist was like a play director. Dr. Bowen talks of the therapist as a consultant or supervisor. But this is the first time I have had the pleasure of seeing myself as a grammarian. I think that what happens when we change the punctuation is that we introduce an increase in the ease with which people experience certain areas that usually are outside their area of awareness.

Chairman Ferreira: I would now like to introduce to you the next member of the panel, but I think perhaps a word of explanation is required. You have heard Dr. Paul Watzlawick, you have heard Dr. Henry Lennard and Dr. Salvador Minuchin, and you have heard me. Now I must explain that should you have difficulty in understanding the next speaker, it may be for the simple reason that he does not have a foreign accent (laughter)—Dr. Titchener.

Dr. James L. Titchener: I would like to ask if two very preliminary observations I have made on some video-taped marital therapy might be relevant to this paper. I have been studying a marital therapy interaction system from the viewpoint of observing the flow of kinesic and lexical communication around this three-part interaction system. Here are two very preliminary observations:

After I had made a breakthrough into being able to see the kinesic communication in this system, I became very concerned about how much I was feeding back into the system. I was the researcher, not the therapist, in this system. I was amazed at how much my body movements, gestures, facial expressions, and so on, were regulating, moderating, and modulating the interaction of the spouses. Then, after I had observed *that* for a little while and got used to it, I began to see that I couldn't help influencing the interaction, that I was part of the system, and that the feedback was a necessary element of the system.

A second phenomenon that I have observed is a subjective one. After looking at a videotape of this type of treatment, one in which I have been the therapist, I found that I had a rather exquisite memory for what happened in that session, much better than for any other therapeutic work I have done. The reason is that when I watch this interaction system again, I can recall all of the thought processes within myself at the time, all the things I was considering and observing during that session.

I had just one question about one of Dr. Watzlawick's examples. I think the examples are charming, but they may lead to a too-ready acceptance of his thesis. It is true that we may feed into a paranoid system by our socially regulated responses to it, but I have seen paranoid patients intimidated and they have not behaved any differently. They are no less paranoid. I have seen people threaten to beat them up "If you don't stop doing that," and they are no less paranoid.

Chairman Ferreira: Let me now open the meeting to everyone.

Dr. Rubinstein: I was very impressed, Paul, with the sequence as you described it in your paper—that a_1 produces b_1 and a_2 produces b_2, etc. It occured to me that only at the end of the sequence, where sigma a and sigma b are conceptualized, are we actually dealing with the behavior of the system. Maybe where we get hung up is that once we have created the notion of system we step back again and once more want to reinstate the individuality of the participating units.

Let me give an example of what I mean. Once we are able to see the individual organism as a total system, made up of heart plus lungs plus liver, etc., we can conceptualize this system as a behavioral individual. But we are all too apt to reverse our sequence and go back to the separate identity of the lung, the heart, etc. Is this where we have a methodological difficulty?

Dr. Watzlawick: Yes, this is what I was trying to say. I think that after having paid lip service to the idea of ongoing interaction as a process, very often one finds that this process is made into a "typical" quality of a, a quality such as interrupted sentences, the use of metaphor or literality, ego strength, anxiety, whatever. One comes up with some kind of a sum relating to a, and in doing this one has destroyed the important character- istic of the ongoing process. One has made a cut straight across the whole thing, out of which comes some kind of lifeless abstraction, and one then calls this *the* behavior of the subject.

Dr. Levinger: May I ask for some examples of how you, yourself, have been able to uncover the stochastic nature of these processes? How would you operationalize some of your suggestions?

Dr. Watzlawick: That's a good question. All I am trying to say is this: I am questioning that time-honored and established research methods are adequate for the complexity of the system that we are studying. I am trying to say that this system may not only be more complex; it may be essentially different. The point was raised this morning by Dr. Ravich that the two-person group is essentially different from a three-person group. This is very much in line with what I am thinking.

We are running into differences of structure, into essentially different kinds of phenomena as we look at interaction, and it sometimes seems to me that we are trying to do research as we would if we still believed that malaria were caused by bad air—mal-aria—and we go about sampling air and we do this with a butterfly net, to boot. This is my feeling about the adequacy of most of our research methods. Beyond that, unfortunately, I have no answer to your question.

Dr. Ivan Boszormenyi-Nagy: Two thoughts come to my mind. One is implicit in what you are saying, that every experiment or every obser- vational situation, including the therapeutic one, creates a separate universe which is to some extent discontinuous with what could be seen as the authentic family life or relationship.

The next thought I have is that when we talk about comparing so- called normal or healthy families with pathological (for lack of another word) families of any kind, can we really compare these two types on the same level? Isn't it like asking someone with limited musical ability to make distinctions between one and another of Bach's fugues? Do "normal family interactions" contain any element which is comparable to the interactional system which results in driving a person sick or crazy? A sick family is so much more a family, so much more specialized in its relationships, than the so-called normal family, whose members are involved in the world differently. Anything the sick family can produce at home or under observation is on a basically different level of continuity.

Dr. Fred L. Strodtbeck: If I may just comment on that, I think the gap between the interaction of sick families and the interaction of lower class families is narrower than the interaction differences between lower class and upper class families. I am basing this comparison on their verbal skills and methods of dealing with one another, the speed with which they can survey a large number of cognitive differences and bring about reconciliations, the amount of humor, and so forth, that they display. The thought that there may be stepwise discontinuities between families seems to me a return to the unmaterialized hopes of five or six years ago that there might be enough concrete differences in the interaction of different types of family to allow us to describe families systematically.

Dr. Watzlawick: I don't want to go on record as having said that differences exist between types of families. I was talking about research methods which are derived mainly from work with individuals and are carried over to research with families. If I pointed to a discontinuity a few minutes ago, I should have made it clear that the discontinuity I meant was this: that proven research methods and methodologies for the individual may not be adequate to deal with the complexity of interaction.

Dr. Strodtbeck: Why don't you comment on hypotheses and inquiries that deal with phase emphases of groups or relative allocation of speaking time or relationship between speaking time and power? Why do you fixate on those things which are so individual instead of opening your range of consideration to this other literature?

Dr. Lennard: I'd like to say, too, that what you have in the family field is not so much methods which have come in from individual studies but methods which have come in from the study of other social systems.

Dr. Watzlawick: I would go further than this and include studies that come from a vast number of disciplines, such as biology, physiology, economics, general systems theory, etc. It is my belief that these systems have certain basic properties in common.

Dr. Ravich: In line with the question that you just asked, Dr. Strodtbeck, and Dr. Lennard's response, it seems appropriate to again refer back to a point I made this morning about the difference between a system of two and a system of three. For example, the difficulty of creating a game that involves three people as opposed to a game involving two people, two parties, or two sides, is vast, it is enormous. If we could just make that step, or begin to make such a step, we would have accomplished a great deal. We are not going to do it here and maybe it will never be in the power of any of us to do it. A war involving three parties, for example, is a totally different thing from a war involving two parties, and this is a basic problem. I am trying to conceptualize a game with three people and I don't yet know how to do it.

Dr. Titchener: If you can have a war between three people, why can't you have a game?

Dr. Ravich: Can you have a war between three?

Dr. Titchener: You suggested it.

Dr. Ravich: I don't know.

Dr. Titchener: I was going to suggest a war game.

Dr. Ravich: I would suggest, for example, without meaning to get into politics at all, that at the moment one of the great problems in the world is: Are we having a war in Vietnam with two parties, two other parties, or with one other party? The whole problem hangs literally on that one question, and it can't be solved.

Dr. Strodtbeck: If I may comment, not on the international question but on the two- versus three-person group, I would think, offhand, of some important differentiations there. When you are thinking of a three-person group in contrast to a two-person group, I think the essential ranking processes within the three-person group are continuous. The one thing that shows in interaction process scores is that for two-person groups, in contrast with three-person groups, you have more actions between persons that have the character of asking for the opinion of the other person. This is because the potentiality of the interaction breaking down due to the other person withdrawing is so much greater. If you have two alters to talk to, you can move from one to the other as the tension builds up and not be so solicitous of the other person. Because of this, two-person interactions that reveal differences generally take about 12 to 15 percent more acts than three-person interactions. We don't have sufficient experience with four- and five-person groups, but from the evidence that has been published by Hare, Bales, and Borgatta*, we see slightly more acts of disagreement whenever there are exactly even numbers on each side so that coalitions can be equally counterbalanced.

So, while I am sympathetic both to Simmel and to yourself for emphasizing this difference, I think it could be overemphasized for the purpose of this discussion.

Dr. Ravich: I would like to point out that Von Neumann and Morganstern,** who approached this topic on a most abstract mathemat-

---

*Hare, A.P., Borgatta, E.F., and Bales, R.F. *Small groups: Studies in social interaction.* New York: Knopf, 1955.

**Von Neumann, J. and Morganstern, O. *Theory of games and economic behavior.* 3rd Ed. Princeton Univ. Press, 1953.

ical level, seeking to develop a theory of games to be applied to economic behavior, never actually achieved their purpose. That is, they really developed two theories of games, a theory of two-person games and a theory of three- or more-person games, because as soon as they moved from two to three or more, it tended to break down again into two parties. For example, a bridge game really can be viewed as a game of two parties rather than four parties.

Chairman Ferreira: I would like to put more lumber into the fire by indicating what has been my experience with the two- versus three-person groups. Using a technique similar to and yet quite distant from Dr. Strodtbeck's technique (a technique which, by analogy, I could call *un*revealed differences) I have experienced exactly the same feeling that Dr. Ravich is trying to describe: that a two-person group is a radically different "animal" from a three-person group or a four-person group. As a matter of fact, every time I administered that test to a couple—I have given it to a number of husband and wife teams—I have had the feeling that the only thing they were really excited about was *who* was going to make the decisions. After that agreement had been reached, usually nonverbally, the rest was just a series of "Yes," "I agree," "I go along," "O.K.," "Fine," etc. I never got the kind of natural feeling that I invariably get from using the same technique with a three-person or a four-person group.

Dr. Levinger: I would like to comment here. I believe that the difference between two- and three-person groups is very large. However, as I read Dr. Strodtbeck, the question is partly: "Is it a difference of *kind* or *degree?*" If we are to progress in terms of moving away from discrete typologies and toward variables and continuous formulations, we would want to focus on the *degree* of difference and the *dimensions* along which these kinds of relationships differ. Even though I, personally, also have a preference for studying dyads rather than triads or larger groups, in order to uncover some of the basic processes, I think eventually these pieces are going to have to be put back together. Unless we can conceive of ways of bridging across these units, we are not going to be in that position. This is important for us all to keep in mind.

Dr. Bell: Back to the more philosophic level, I like very much Dr. Watzlawick's emphasis on the stream of behavior, but I would like to ask him a question: Where can one introduce concepts of different levels? Just as in quantum mechanics it is a rather handy idea that everything is basically energy and has different manifestations and functions in stepwise discontinuities, is the analogy in behavioral terms what we have always called personality, group, and culture? Where and how does one introduce those kinds of concepts?

I am one who believes, unlike Dr. Watzlawick, that there is such a thing as memory, that there is such a thing as patterning of behavior characteristics of individuals which carries over time. I am not sure how one fits these kinds of concepts into Dr. Watzlawick's suggestions about the paranoid and the depressed patients. This seems to me to be a kind of reductionism which is quite as dangerous as reducing group phenomena to individual characteristics, or reducing individual characteristics completely to a group process. I don't think that everything is just a mere response.

Dr. Watzlawick: I was unaware that I had given the impression that I don't believe in memory, in the conservation of adaptations once found and, therefore, used again in new situations. I do very much believe, like you, that we have memories, that we carry over from our past certain patterns of behavior and certain expectations. I would try to answer your question, perhaps in a very insufficient way, by saying that what happens in a relationship is precisely that such factors are brought into the relationship by the two communicants and then overlap, interdigitate or are superimposed, thereby creating a new phenomenon that cannot be reduced completely to either of the two. One cannot say, "Here is a crazy person, here is a sane person, and out of this somehow comes something"; but, rather, we are faced with a phenomenon that I like to compare to the moiré pattern in optics when lattices overlap and certain new configurations thereby occur. Also, the model of the moire pattern is very useful because it shows that a slight change in the relationship of the two lattices produces a completely different pattern from the one you had before. So I am talking, really, about what the biologists refer to as the emergent quality and this is the kind of pnenomenon we are faced with as we look at people interacting.

Mr. Weakland: Although there are a number of things I would like to respond to, I will restrict my remarks to what seems to me to be a main point that Dr. Watzlawick was making, which perhaps got somewhat lost in the discussion because we keep coming back to the idea of things being more or less complex.

I think Paul was trying to say that things are complex in different ways, and also that complexity is not just a function of what you are looking at, it is a function of *how* you look at it, so that if you look at something in the right way it is relatively simple. If you take something simple and look at it in an inappropriate way, it becomes complex in a devil of a hurry. Complexity should not be an absolute. The point is whether your methods fit the subject.

Dr. Nathene Loveland: In connection with the discussion of differences between two and three person groups, the size of the group seems to have more of a differential effect on the interaction of the participants in some cultures than in others and in dealing with some tasks (e.g., those that are more highly structured) than with others.

Dr. Friedman: I would like to get back to Dr. Titchener's point about seeing himself in the film, because if you are a therapist in a family or a participant observer, then you can't see the whole picture from the outside; and if you are outside looking in, you can't really know what is going on inside. While you can't completely resolve this question, it is also not that hopeless. As a soft pragmatist, I wanted to say that we can have it both ways. We can have the participant observer giving his self-report and we can have other observers watching the experimenter and therapist through the one-way mirror, or on film, and reporting on his behavior. Then, after the fact, we can put the pieces together and at least we have a beginning solution to the problem.

(Meeting Adjourned Briefly)

Selection of Problems to Be Investigated in Family Interaction Research

LYMAN C. WYNNE

Chairman Ferreira: Our program now calls for Dr. Lyman Wynne to speak on "Selection of Problems to Be Investigated in Family Interaction Research." Dr. Wynne is so well known to all of us that it would be insulting to introduce him to you. Dr. Wynne!

Dr. Lyman C. Wynne: I don't know about being insulted, but I was perplexed I must say by the assignment that I have this afternoon. I spoke on several occasions to Dr. Framo about what concerns he had in mind that called for a discussion of "selection of problems to be investigated in family interaction research." My initial reaction to Dr. Framo's request was to wonder why the selection of problems should be a topic. After all, isn't this a matter of personal preference or taste? With the diversity of problems and the diversity of investigators, isn't there room for all, so that until it is apparent that we are exhausting the field with an abundance of definitive answers, isn't there plenty of room for whatever problem an individual investigator or group would like to pursue? Why shouldn't we go ahead where our whims, our abilities, or our facilities may take us?

This, in fact, is what has been done in the field of family research, and by and large I see no compelling reason for being more selective than our interests suggest. However, on further reflection, it does seem to me that there are some reasons for believing that the time is coming to give consideration to priorities in the selection of problems for family interaction research. Especially is this true when research leads to cumulative confusion rather than cumulative knowledge. It seems to me that Jay

86

Haley's comments this morning help make us more aware of the areas of cumulative confusion, or at least where we should have cumulative skepticism.

Are there certain problems, then, that do deserve higher priorities than others because they need to be clarified and specified before we will be able to understand other problems that will follow? In other words, is knowledge of one sort necessary to pave the way for understanding findings of another variety? More specifically, what major variables may alter family interaction sufficiently so that these need to be noted and controlled in order for us to be able to interpret data about family interaction with reasonable confidence?

Such variables are especially numerous and important in family research because families constitute an area or focus for bringing together data from four major conceptual frames of reference that are relevant to behavior. These are: 1) cultural systems, 2) social structure, 3) personality systems, and 4) biological systems. Comprehensive family studies require observations and controls in all four of these areas, a fact that presents both opportunities and pitfalls for research. Controls and comparisons are both less necessary and easier to provide in other fields of study where the interweaving between factors from different conceptual systems is not so central and obvious. I suggest that priorities need to be given in family interaction research to the selection of those problems which can help clarify which major classes of data affect family interaction and, in turn, are influenced by family interaction.

The question of what problem to select has been well acknowledged in other fields, such as physics. Niels Bohr (1948), in his Law of Complementarity, emphasized how, if one looks at any part of a total range of phenomena, one necessarily has to neglect some other aspects of variability in other parts of the total field. You can't look at everything at once, and as you move from a focus on one part to a focus on another, you are going to have to neglect what you previously were more concerned about. So, it is inevitable that we are going to overlook certain aspects of the subtleties of personality functioning while we are looking at the functioning within the family, and vice versa.

Nevertheless, certain neglected problems deserve consideration and will be emphasized here. First, family interaction research has tended to ignore biologic variables, with the partial exception that sex of family members has been given some attention (e.g., Fleck, Lidz, & Cornelison, 1963). More work is needed to explore the effects on family interaction of brain damage and medical illness in one or more family members, as well as the effects of drugs which alter brain functioning and that may have substantial impact upon interaction. With the widespread use of psychoactive drugs, especially with hospitalized patients, this factor certainly needs to be considered when the interaction of these patients with their families is compared with other families in which no one is receiving drugs.*

The problem of genetic contributions to interaction patterns is still more complex, but a start has been made in the work of Stabenau and Pollin (1968), who have used the Revealed Differences Technique for studying interaction in families with genetically identical twins who are discordant for schizophrenia.

The psychology of individual differences, including response dispositions (e.g., Silverman, 1967), is a burgeoning research field that has much to offer to family interaction studies. We are doomed to confusion and disappointment if we expect family interaction to be understandable purely in terms of family system and situational variables without controlling for, and delineating, stylistic, predisposing personality characteristics of individual family members. These individual differences are, in turn, intertwined with genetic and innate factors that have been altogether too quickly dismissed by family researchers.

Third, at the level of social structure, families are, of course, significant units which we have now become accustomed to call "systems." Since this seems to be a day of skepticism, I would like to take issue with the unquestioning, widespread use of the concept of the family as a system. Almost everybody doing conjoint family therapy and systematic family research employs this concept, implicitly or explicitly, but there has been remarkably little scrutiny of the specific conditions under which families do and do not act as systems. In what sense are families systems? What are the system characteristics of families, both as units of social structure and as patterns of values, norms, and rules? And what are the links between the subsystem of the *nuclear* family to other aspects of social structure—the extended family, social networks within the community, the community as a whole, the family-therapy system of family plus therapists, and so on?

Some of us, including myself, originally became involved in conjoint family therapy because we noticed that in certain families one could see changes in the rest of the family when one family member was changing;

---

*Soon after this conference was held, Lennard, Epstein and Katzung (1967) published a relevant study in which they showed that, in three-person groups in which one person had been given either 50 mgm of chlorpromazine or a placebo, there was not only a decrease of initiation of activity by the "drugged" individual but also, most interestingly, a consistent decrease of communications addressed *to* him by the others. This was not the result of awareness of behavior changes, but was an effect on group interaction operating below the level of reportability by the participants.

for example, the patient in individual treatment is unnoticed by the family until he starts to change and then the rest of the family moves in to disrupt the change, disrupt the therapy or, if the presenting patient persists in his change, other family members may develop symptoms in turn. This has been an hypothesis and an observation that is one of the kinds of problems based upon the "family-as-a-system" concept that I think deserves more direct experimental and research study. It seems to me that this hypothesis is subject to question when we start to look at the cases in which these sequences do *not* occur. In recent years I have been impressed with instances of change in an individual when one might expect reverberations in the rest of the family but the reverberations don't seem to be particularly apparent; the tendency to which a family is equilibrium-seeking and therefore (by definition) tends to act like a system should be much more of an open question for research than it has been so far. The problem arises because families, like all other living systems, are *open linked* systems. Closed systems cannot long endure in the living world; particularly in behavior, links or connections between the open systems are an important object of study in their own right. Thus, in family research, we need to look at the links between related nuclear families, between families and social networks, and so on.

Also, we need to recognize that "families," like "persons" or "individuals," are convenient fictions, heuristic *devices,* not entities "out there," but a way of *sampling* phenomena which are *partially* organized as systems but which can be reorganized for other purposes into other partial systems, such as "personalities," "cultures," "social networks," etc. The concept of the family as a system has been a useful stimulus to theory-building, therapy, and research, but the time has come to question and explore its limitations as well as its continuing conditions of applicability.

Similarly, the concept of family homeostasis, which again is a system concept, has been a very fruitful *starting point* for many studies, but I think at this point we can safely retreat from a belief in the *generality* of family homeostasis and proceed to specify and test out this formulation.

Actually, as Dr. Ackerman (1966) and others have pointed out—and as I pointed out in one paper (Wynne, Ryckoff, Day & Hirsch, 1958) also—the families that rigidly try to maintain homeostasis through successive developmental phases are highly disturbed and atypical. Enduring success in maintaining family homeostasis perhaps should be regarded as a distinctive feature of *dis*order in families. I suspect that the seductive hypothesis of family homeostasis became so widely accepted because we have selectively brought into treatment and research those families that are most likely to confirm this formulation. Family research and therapy, especially a decade ago, emphasized work with *intact* families, who are, it seems likely, apt to be more typical of equilibrium-seeking kinds of families than families which are more disorganized and broken. Fortunately, there are people now, such as Dr. Salvador Minuchin (1967) and Dr. Alfred Friedman here in Philadelphia, and others, who are working with disorganized families in which the family as a system with boundaries is difficult to reconcile with what one sees. Recently, for example, visiting Dr. Friedman's program and seeing a couple of families that Dr. Oscar Weiner was treating, I observed one "family" consisting of a mother and son; in another, a mother, son, a boyfriend of the son, and the boyfriend's girlfriend constituted the family therapy unit.

Under what circumstances can these be considered homeostatic systems? Do these groups have self-equilibrating characteristics? This is the kind of problem it seems to me we need to bring into empirical interaction research, specifying more fully what we think are the system characteristics of the families with which we work.

I also want to comment about the way in which the interaction between the research context and researchers or therapists may act temporarily as a system. Obviously, there may be considerable variation in the extent to which researchers and therapists are, in effect, either shut out or brought into what seems like a family system. Again, the openness of the family needs to be considered as a variable in its own right rather than as something that we try to ignore or eliminate.

Another set of variables linked to families lies in the sphere of culture, especially the values, norms, and rules governing family interaction. Formulations about the idiosyncratic subculture of a particular family, as well as the broader cultural patterns in which a given family participates, can in part be deduced from repeated observations of family interaction. However, interaction and communication are conceptually distinct from culture or subculture, so care is needed in moving from one set of formulations to the other. In my view, high priority should be given to investigating how values and norms of different families relate to their communication in interaction experiments. In some cases, of course, values are highly linked to social class, education, and ethnic variables. In preoccupation with psychopathology, researchers have tended to leave these cultural variables unspecified and unreported, even when there is reason to believe they may be of overriding relevance to communication patterns. The willingness or resistance of families to participate in a study at all is also related to their value orientations. Research on such issues is a good example of the kind of preliminary investigation needed before many of the present and potential issues on family interaction can be meaningfully interpreted.

I have been discussing a series of conceptual frames of reference which go to make up the transactional field of which families are a part. It is worth noting that the family is both context (to biologic and personality systems) and part of a broader context (social structure and culture). This pivotal conceptual location of family work contributes to its special interest.

So far, I have been talking about the context of the family cross-sectionally in time. However, the developmental sequences *through time* seem to me something that deserve a great deal more study and should not be put off. Here I am thinking of a whole series of sequences in time. In this conference reference has been made to sequences within a given experimental procedure, from one phase of interaction to the next. Also, Dr. Epstein talked about the phases within interviews which are relevant to how one selects material.

Second, there are phases in the overall treatment process and sequences in a series of research procedures which are used over time. Each transaction alters both family and researcher, bringing about changes that feed back into the data and alter them rather substantially, especially as the family starts to get clues and ideas about what the researchers want.

Third, on a still broader sphere, there is the problem of the development of families through time—through the phases of courtship, having the first child, having multiple offspring, the children becoming mobile and increasingly independent, of separating from the parents, making for important changes in both the temporal and cross-sectional contexts of families. Reuben Hill (1960) has emphasized the need for a developmental view of families for quite some years now, but this still has not been the subject of much systematic research. Also, there have been few efforts to study how necessary it is to control for the developmental phase of families which are being compared or to study longitudinally patterns of changes and stability in family interaction through the course of family development. Thus, I have sketched out a few major areas in which research problems need to be selected before we shall have an adequate picture of the diverse contexts in which families move—inward to biology and personality, and outward to social structure and culture, as well as longitudinally through time. It seems clear that factors in each and all of these areas are relevant to family interaction—indeed, are continuously operating and affecting the form and content of family interaction, even when we try to ignore them.

REFERENCES

Ackerman, N. W. *Treating the troubled family.* New York: Basic Books, 1966.

Bohr, N. On the notions of causality and complementarity. *Dialectica*, 1948, *2*, 312-318.

Fleck, S., Lidz, T., & Cornelison, A. Comparison of parent-child relationships of male and female schizophrenic patients. *Archives of General Psychiatry*, 1963, *8*, 17-23.

Hill R., & Hansen, D. A. The identification of conceptual frameworks utilized in family study. *Marriage & Family Living*, 1960, *22*, 299-311.

Lennard, H. L., Epstein, L. J., & Katzung, B. G. Psychoactive drug action and group interaction process. *Journal of Nervous and Mental Diseases*, 1967, *145*, 69-78.

Minuchin, S., Montalvo, B. , Guerney, B., Rosman, B., & Schumer, F. *Families of the slums.* New York: Basic Books, 1967.

Silverman, J. Variations in cognitive control and psychophysiological defense in the schizophrenics. *Psychosomatic Medicine*, 1967, *29*, 225-251.

Stabenau, J., & Pollin, W. 1968, Personal communication.

Wynne, L. C., Ryckoff, I. M., Day, J., & Hirsch, S. I. Pseudomutuality in the family relations of schizophrenics. *Psychiatry*, 1958, *21*, 205-220.

DISCUSSION

Chairman Ferreira: I shall proceed now to call upon the members of the panel to make their comments. To be original, I will ask them to do so in alphabetical order. Dr. Ackerman first.

Dr. Nathan W. Ackerman: I might say that I asked to be placed on this part of the program because I always like to hear Lyman Wynne. I have the greatest esteem for him. I like him personally, and I often wonder how it is, whenever he talks, that he just about never offends anyone—which I can't say is true of myself. I think Lyman has an extraordinary sense of fairness, an objectivity, an exquisite sense of tolerance. There isn't a single thing that he has said this afternoon that I want to disagree with. It was a great speech. The only thing I dislike about it at all is that he is deferring to the mood of this group, which is to talk in terms of systems and theory and concepts, and I am going to try, if I can, to change the mood.

At the Family Institute in New York, we started out with a great concern for conformity in a special sense, namely, to be respectable by being preoccupied with systematic research. We have given it up. We are doing only clinical studies now. I could dilate on that but I think you catch my message.

Now, referring for a moment to Jay Haley's paper this morning, I had occasion to read the longer version of his paper and after finishing it my feeling was how happy I am I am not a researcher. It is a terrible burden to call oneself a systematic researcher. I ain't any part of that, either hard or soft. I am a clinician, sometimes hard, sometimes soft, but that's the way it is in family life, you know.

As a clinician, I am loaded with prejudice and my motto is to make the most of it. I think what is important is the open admission that you can't do any of this work on the research side, or on the clinical side, without a bias that challenges you to be explicit about it, honest about it, communicate it, and take it into account in a judgment of the findings.

If, as Jay indicated this morning, family therapy is just plain no good for research, why have this meeting? Where did the researchers come from in the family field? There were family researchers, to be sure, before family therapy became a subject of interest, but certainly the whole field of family research has ballooned out because of the stimulus coming from the clinical side, the tremendous challenge from observations, right or wrong, that various people gathered in doing clinical work with whole families. I will always remember the comment Fritz Redl made in this connection at one of the GAP meetings many years ago, that there is a tendency in the direction of taking the "search" out of "research," and that is a thought-provoking comment, however you want to receive it.

I want to make one quick comment about two or three things from the point of view of the clinician. Taking into account the clinician's particular stance, I must deny that there is any such thing as a two-person group. I don't know of any. I think what looks like a twosome is always something that results from the extrusion of the third party. I think, functionally, there was always a threesome. In the clinical work, it is mother, father and baby, whether baby is already there in the flesh or just a gleam in the woman's eye. If there is a man and woman, there is a baby in the offing somewhere. That is the biological entity, and to my mind the social interactional aspect cannot be separated from the biological underpinning. One can't talk about the biological vectors in any human situation except in social terms, and one cannot understand the social determinants, the molding forces of behavior, except as one takes into account biological differences, sex differences, age differences, generation differences, and whatever else you want to take into account.

After listening to that extraordinarily erudite conversation a while ago, I toss in this naive challenge from the point of view of a clinician. Is there any such thing as a two-person group? If not, what are we talking about and how on earth are we going to get the clinicians and the researchers together? How are we going to mesh our thinking? How are we going to achieve that ideal blend which is the objective of a meeting of this sort?

Chairman Ferreira: Dr. Norman Bell.

Dr. Bell: Lyman Wynne has given us a good lecture on general systems theory, the transactional strategy of looking at the phenomena and constructing conglomerations of variables. I happen to believe in this and I have nothing to disagree with him about. I guess I am like Nathan Ackerman in that I am disappointed that we can't get beyond this level, and I think there may be some questions that could be posed that would help us get beyond it. There are two that I will mention now.

I have heard so often recently, coming from the mouths of others and particularly my own mouth, this notion of the family as a system, that it doesn't make any sense any more. I wish there were another term. I think maybe we could be helped in this if we stopped this baloney and asked: A system of what?

Dr. Wynne: That's my point.

Dr. Bell: A system of people, a system of roles, a system of communication methods, a system of behavioral acts, a system of unconsciouses rubbing up against each other? As you know, one of our extreme friends says that the family is an image which is in the head of every individual, and Ronald Laing goes so far as to say that this is the more real kind of family.

I don't think this business of deciding on the unit is merely a matter of taste. Dr. Wynne challenges the idea that we know what the unit is in his statement relating to homeostasis. This threatens to become another great slogan—homeostasis of what, in what respect, under what conditions? I think we can translate these questions into empirical terms.

To me, one of the more difficult questions that we often assume we know the answer to and need to test is the problem of under what condition you get a shift in the level of action? Under what conditions do you get something triggered off from a group conflict into individual symptoms? What conditions do you need to produce psychological symptoms versus somatic symptoms?

I liked many things that Dr. Wynne said. I liked his emphasis upon longitudinal studies. They must be done, difficult as they are. I liked especially his very basic idea that whatever we are studying, we pay a price. You can't look at everything and you must look at something in detail, but whatever you look at, whatever you bring into focus, distorts the background. These are things which we so commonly and so easily overlook. I join with Lyman in making a plea for bringing them out from under the rug.

Chairman Ferreira: Now we shall ask Dr. Gerald Handel to comment.

Dr. Gerald Handel: I also find myself essentially in agreement with most of what Dr. Wynne said. I agree that longitudinal studies are necessary. I point out in passing that new forms of organization will be required to make such studies possible, involving financing, career commitments, and so on—the whole administrative matter.

I also am somewhat sympathetic to what Dr. Ackerman had to say. This may seem to put me on two sides of the same fence, but I don't think so because the problem is, What is it that we are calling research? The psychoanalyst sometimes uses the term "the flight into reality," and one thing I get, listening to much of the work that has been done, is that there is what I would call a premature flight into coding, a premature concern with how you are to score and create indexes, and so on.

That, it seems to me, is an entirely too limited concept of research, although, obviously, it has some of the appearance of being the wave of the future, or maybe the wave of the present. As the researcher starts interacting more with the computer than with his raw data, it starts to gather momentum, but I think that is unfortunate. Certainly some of the earlier and more interesting or stimulating work has not been of this character. People were interested in understanding how families function, and they turned their minds loose upon the material. They asked questions, they talked to families, and then they tried to make some sense out of what they found. I think these are the initial studies that have gotten this movement under way, if you want to call it a movement.

There seems to be the notion: O.K., we did a little bit of that; that's sort of the early natural history phase of the science, and now let's get on with the real science. I don't think that is so at all. It is not the case in psychiatry. It is not the case in sociology, either. If you look at Philip Hammond's *Sociologists at Work, the Craft of Social Research,* you see ten or twelve very distinguished researchers describing how they went about doing studies which have gained eminence in the field.* Most of what they did didn't hinge upon their coding categories and their indexes or which statistical tests of significance they used. The book shows that what used to be known as the case study, which is now disparaged as a lazy and vague and indefinite way of going at things that doesn't prove anything, has a

---

*New York: Basic Books, 1964.

great deal of value and can be approached in a thoughtful and disciplined way that yields knowledge. I don't think that the more formal methods of research are the only ones that qualify to be called research or that yield knowledge.

Chairman Ferreira: I would like to hear from Dr. Straus.

Dr. Murray A. Straus: I guess I mostly find myself in disagreement with all the speakers so far. If you take as an example the researches cited in Hammond's book, they all have one characteristic in common, which has nowhere appeared in the preceding discussion, and that is an independent variable which varies and a dependent variable which varies. This orientation does not imply premature coding. One can work out one's codes and measurement systems later, but it is fundamental that if you want to find out what affects what, you have to have as a minimum two variables which vary.

All of this talk about longitudinal studies, about systems, is not going to do the job unless we somehow work out a strategy by which we can look at the consequences of something. You can follow families for twenty years and unless you have built in some means of assessing what it is that is going to have what consequences, that twenty years is going to be wasted to a very considerable extent. There will be unintended heuristic byproducts, I would agree.

It seems to me that a lot of research in this area suffers from this shortcoming. It is descriptive. You can be nondescriptive, you can have independent and dependent variables, using informal methods, case studies, through more highly structured methods of self-reports such as interviews, through laboratory experimentation. The method of data-gathering is not the real issue, but essentially whether there is, as I have said, an independent and a dependent variable.

If we then look at what the most frequent kind of dependent variable is in this kind of research, it is some kind of family exhibiting pathology, or a member of the family, whether a schizophrenic or not, and we compare those two groups of families. This, it seems to me, is a step in the right direction but is not really the kind of variable we want to look at. As a couple of people said or implied this morning, it is an atheoretical variable; it is a crude category that we happen to have conveniently available, and also one of some social importance, obviously.

Rather than choose that variable, I suggest that we try to specify what it is in the behavior of families that produces, say, a schizophrenic person, and use that as a variable, present or absent. We should find families in which this type of behavior is present, in which it is absent, and look at its consequences.

Or even better (and this represents my own particular bias and the work I am now engaged in), we should try to manipulate some of these variables experimentally so that we have a surer grip on the question of casual sequence. Just because one studies communication in a laboratory setting, for example, does not make it an experiment, but it is possible to systematically, that is experimentally, vary communication. It is possible to vary expertise, knowledge of family members. Miller's research that was mentioned this morning is an example. It is possible to vary systematically the business of two vs. three. We need not sit here and argue about it. We can have studies in which we get the same observations, choosing one group of sectors of families in which we have just the husband and wife; another in which we have husband and wife and one child; another group in which we have husband and wife and two children; and we can proceed toward resolving this issue empirically.

It seems to me that we are ready to move beyond the phase of systematic study of interaction, whether in a clinic setting, a field setting, or a laboratory, and start adding to it some theoretically based systematic variation in independent variables or dependent variables. I would like to suggest that there is a lot to be gained from doing this by means of experimental techniques such as have been used in social psychology.

Chairman Ferreira: Thank you, Dr. Straus. For the moment, I will confine the discussion to the members of the panel who by now I am sure have rebuttals to what the others have said. Lest I lose my own chance to say something, I will exercise my prerogative as Chairman to speak my mind.

There is a point I want to make in regard to whether or not the family is a system. I look upon the fact that this question even came up as a sure sign that progress has been made in our field. The idea of considering the family as *not* a system could only have occurred after it had been accepted that the family *was* a system. In other words, I believe that we need first to affirm something, to convince ourselves that it is whatever we say it is, before we can start arguing it away. We saw that with schizophrenia, for instance. As you may recall, many years ago it was a very important thing to tell everybody that schizophrenia was an illness, just like chickenpox or measles. It was only after we had convinced almost everybody that schizophrenia was an illness that we were able to start arguing again that it was not an illness—an argument that only became meaningful because we had previously argued the other way around. So, I must congratulate Dr. Wynne and Dr. Bell for bringing this point out and starting the argument against the theory that families are systems.

Dr. Handel: What you have just talked about is one form of scientific thought process. This is one way in which we derive ideas. Somebody says something, makes a strong case for it, and somebody else stands back and looks at it and says, "No, I don't think it is like that."

I don't think that is the only kind of scientific thought process. There is another kind (and this doesn't exhaust the possibilities, either), which is a kind of scanning and searching. One is looking around and responding to things in the environment that impress one, and then one thinks about it and makes comparisons and gathers data, and so on.

Murray Straus was saying that we need to move to a more theoretical kind of variable, that the variable of the family-with-a-schizophrenic-member is atheoretical. I think there is much merit in that way of thinking, but what that does not account for, and what is also in Hammond's book is, Where does one get the hunches and the insights that seem promising and fruitful? What one can do is gather detailed case data of whatever kind and soak oneself in it and see whether that doesn't turn up independent variables every bit as fruitful.

Most textbook treatments of what science is notoriously overlook the whole process of where to get the hypotheses you are going to test and how to decide which ones are worth going after. This is the whole underside of science and I don't think your comment about independent and dependent variables addresses itself to that.

Dr. Straus: No, it wasn't intended to. I was saying, essentially, that however one formulates the problem, we have got to get down to brass tacks in dealing with it—and brass tacks means independent variables that vary and dependent variables that vary.

Dr. Whitaker: Suppose you don't want a tack? Suppose you are looking for a spike?

Dr. Wynne: I would like to both agree and disagree with Dr. Straus. When he talks about specifying variables, dependent and independent, this is something that I had taken for granted as obviously important. However, it seems to me that we have floundered a great deal because we have inappropriately looked at variable A and variable B in isolation. And we have looked at these variables as if there were a necessary connection between them, without taking a multivariate approach, without considering the context of modifying variables that need to be controlled or at least specified. These contextual variables, inevitably present in both contrived and naturalistic family research situations, moderate and often reverse the relationship between pairs of independent and dependent variables. My plea was for a somewhat broader perspective that will allow us to see what is going on that might help account for contradictory findings from different investigators that may be accounted for by different contextual variables. Often, these moderating variables, including such obvious

matters as the instructions and expectations of the researcher, go unreported and even unnoticed.

This holds true even for very simple kinds of things, such as: Who is
present? Who is in the family? What are the family boundaries, either in
fantasy or current interaction? Many reports of family therapy and family
research do not even specify such obvious variables. A story may illustrate
my point. Recently, I was in St. Louis, where the research of Masters and
Johnson on sexual responses takes place. Apparently, they too have been
criticized lately for concentrating on too narrow a set of variables, and
they have set up a new study to look at the communication process in the
sexual part of marital life. Allegedly, they asked one subject the question,
"When you are having sexual intercourse, do you *talk* to your husband?"
The woman was a bit taken aback and said, "Well, gosh, come to think of
it I guess I don't—but I could. There is a phone right by the bed."
(Laughter)

So, we need to specify the context.

Dr. MacGregor: May I offer a hook to hang Dr. Whitaker's problem
on? I think you have been skirting all around the problem because in
choosing variables or in choosing things to study in living systems
variability itself is the measure. I think you get in trouble when you adopt
this idea that living systems are open systems. It is a little easier if you say:
Living systems can be looked at as relatively open or relatively closed.

Dr. Wynne: Right, that's my point.

Dr. MacGregor: And, of course, the more the living system is in a state
of defense, the more it is predictably recurrent. Your sick families have
challenging varieties in behavior but are terribly recurrent in their
repetition of patterns and may be easier to study for that reason.

Dr. Wynne: But it wouldn't be identifiable as a system at all unless it
were partially closed. The point is that an open system tends to maintain
an equilibrium, tends to maintain a steady state, but it does this with
continual interchange with events and persons outside of the system—the
family is in interchange with other persons in the community, and so on, so
that it is not a matter of either/or. It is a matter of how much and under
what conditions the family is closed off or open to interchange with others.

Dr. MacGregor: Variability is still the measure. Two children may talk
to each other and they may find a tremendous number of things that can
be talked about. Put mother in that situation and the number of things
that can be talked about is greatly reduced. These differences are
measureable and they are useful; if you know how one variable varies, you
can control it in order to discover how another one varies.

Dr. Rubinstein: I would like to join you, Dr. Ferreira, in stating that I
am very glad that we are starting to ask ourselves whether the family is a

system. We have taken the idea that it is too much for granted. Traditionally, we have started off by conceiving of father as an abstraction, mother as an abstraction, and son as another abstraction. Then, out of these three abstractions, we created a second order of abstraction that we chose to call "family." Therefore, we were talking about an abstraction of abstractions.

Maybe what is causing our difficulties is that we have to measure the characteristics and variables in the relationships of the particular abstraction that we call "family" rather than simply to ask if the family is a system.

What I certainly have great difficulty with are the terms that have been used throughout the day—"sick family system" or "pathologic family system." I am having difficulty because, to me, a pathologic family system is not the same as a system with a pathologic member. If a family system is pathologic, it is pathologic in its total level of functioning. If it has a pathologic member, it may or may not be pathologic as a system. We cannot take for granted that the two terms are equivalent. The pathologic system at this level may not have a pathologic member or symptomatic carriers of any sort.

Dr. David Reiss: I would like to make a plea for considering such relatively mundane occurrences as embarrassment, serendipity, and accident as useful determinants of research hypotheses and projects. I don't in any way suggest that they replace or supplant the elegant set of conceptual domains that Dr. Wynne presented, but I think that they are relevant to this conference. They need to be kept very much in mind so that our mutual experience, our practical experience, can be useful as a source of stimulation. I think Dr. Epstein treated us to a very open and honest account of some of the embarrassments, accidents, and serendipitous findings of his research efforts on family therapy; for example, his predicament in the time sampling question.

It occurs to me that, independent of one's view of the family as a system, it is obviously necessary for somebody, at some time, to take this question of the unfolding of various time phases in a family therapy session and study it. Some of the kinds of phase concepts that Dr. Strodtbeck has alluded to might be utilized, or an entirely new tack might be taken.

I think that in order to pick up a serendipitous or accidental occurrence in a research program, a person would have to temporarily abandon his interest in either overall theory or in the particular clinical issues of the family, or in the therapy. He would have to follow his nose and see what a serial set of findings on time-related phenomena in family therapy would reveal.

I think it takes a certain amount of courage for a clinically trained person to temporarily abandon his interest in patients in order to find out something that may ultimately be of great use to the very patients that he is working with. I think this would return the "search" to research that Dr. Ackerman talked about, even though it might mean temporarily giving up a lot of one's professional identity and a lot of one's theoretical position.

Dr. Ackerman: I would like to share with you, if I might, a couple of other feelings and thoughts I have about this discussion. We are interested in discovering some useful ideas about the relation of family to behavior, behavior in health as well as in sickness. I am sure it is an axiomatic consideration around this table that in the sickest schizophrenic there are areas of residual health and effective units of adaptation. Similarly, in the family group there are levels of wellness as well as other patterns of behavior that are failing patterns, dysfunctional patterns, nonadaptive patterns. Today we have to think in terms of a certain balance between parts of wellness in people's behavior, whether at the individual level or the family level, and parts that are sick or failing. I don't think we can any longer afford to view pathogenic components of the behavior in isolation, away from the relatively healthy patterns of adaptation.

Coming back to Jay Haley's paper this morning, I felt that it was in many ways a remarkable paper and that he fulfilled his inimitable and responsible function for us all in acting as a gadfly. However, one is forced to draw one of two possible conclusions from that kind of paper. One is that we know virtually nothing to date about the relationship between families and mental disorders; and the other is that the methods that he has surveyed are, in themselves, no good. I feel there is a lack of fit between the methodology and the human problem, and that the latter is the more important question to look at. Are the methodology and the standards of investigation antiquated? Are they inappropriate for this human problem? Must we not now be much more bold and creative in devising new kinds of methodology to test some of our clinical methods?

It seems to me that the human problem comes first and the methodology or the technique of study is entirely secondary. If by traditional standards of systematic research the methods disclose very little, or if they only reveal information about unimportant or peripheral aspects of the phenomena we are looking at, then, by God, change the methodology radically, from the bottom up.

I don't really have a quarrel with systematic research. I just want it to disclose something that is useful for the clinician, and, with some notable exceptions, what I read is simply not useful. Now, why not look at that squarely? Why can't we put our imaginations to work in devising new methods to fit the problem?

Dr. Straus: I think there is a third alternative, which I came to after hearing Jay Haley's paper. One could conclude nothing, one could conclude that the methods are no good, or, as I concluded (and I think this really was the point of his paper), that proper scientific methods have never been properly applied to this issue. Take, for example, the question of the contamination of the ratings with knowledge of the hypothesis and with knowledge of the subjects. Haley, as I understand it, was not saying that we should not use ratings but that we should use them under properly controlled conditions. On the basis of his paper, I come to the conclusion that there is a vast need for objectively done scientific work in the area of family interaction.

Mr. Weakland: We have begun to depart from the topic of Dr. Wynne's paper. It seemed to me that the title of the paper deserved a little more emphasis, because we have been speaking more and more about how we should attack this or that problem whereas the paper was entitled, "The Selection of Problems." As I read it, it was not so much a matter of methods, but a very general matter: What should we be concerned with? In other words, it is not a question of where to attack the problem or how to attack the problem, but where to get the problem.

It seems to me there are two ways to decide what problems to select. They both grow naturally out of our own social context, but they can be discriminated. One way is to give a lot more thought to what we are aiming to find out, and I must say that what Dr. Ackerman has to say on this point seems to me to be relevant. It isn't the only position you can take, but it is a fairly clear position. He has an aim and he wants research related to this aim. I think a lot of the method-focused research that has been discussed would itself benefit from asking, "What do we aim to find out from this method?"

I will close with just one statement in relation to what Dr. Wynne said. He said, "Isn't it a matter of personal preference?" This is something with which I sympathize and something for which there is very good authority. If I may, I would like to quote Freud who said: "Make the small decisions of life consciously, but let your unconscious be your guide on big matters like marriage and career."

There is only one problem with this and maybe Dr. Wynne can help us with it. Unfortunately, it seems to me that sources like NIMH do not look kindly on this approach.

Dr. Strodtbeck: I want to take us from the summits back down to the salt mines. I have a very small question that relates to the ways in which we use the concept "system." Obviously, when we speak of the relative allocation of speaking time by any persisting group and demonstrate the very great stabilities that this has, it is a kind of system effect and can be demonstrated in the successive observations of the same group. However, we occasionally encounter in my laboratory some kinds of observations which we can only understand when we have clusters of groups together. For example, if you ask a wife to rate on Osgood's Semantic Differential how warm her husband is you will find that the correlation between his manifest warmth to her in their interaction and the rating is modest: .25, .32. However, if you correlate her estimation of his warmth with the warmth of his remarks to their son in the family interaction, then the correlation is very much expanded to .65 or .70. When a relationship between A and B is in this sense determined by B's relationship to C, we consider this in our laboratory to be a prototype of a system effect.

Mr. Haley: I would like to make a couple of comments. Before we consider abandoning the idea of the system, I think we should first bring into it a few more people who think in systems terms. "System" is an idea that is thrown about very loosely, but Virginia Satir once estimated that she can talk to a family therapist about a case and it takes her a minute and twenty seconds to see if he has a grasp of what a system is by the way he talks about the case.

I think the problem is that all of us are struggling at a very abstract level with something like a system and at a very concrete level with something like a family, and it is hard to bring these together in any realistic way.

You can say, "Let's start getting new methods," or "Let's start measuring the proper variables," and so on. Well, we have been in this business, some of us, for years, and when we first started experimenting with families we thought it was going to be easy. We thought we could turn to the social psychologists. They had worked out hundreds of small group experiments and we thought we would just apply these methods to families. It has been our experience that they are not applicable. We are dealing with a different order of problem when we are dealing with a group with a history, a future, an ongoing set of relationships, and an ongoing set of repetitive patterns. This process is very different from bringing four strangers together and having them do something.

I think the crucial question for all of us is whether we want to repeat history. There was once a movement called phrenology in which there were a great many people who were sure there was a correlation between the contours of the skull and character and personality. The bumps on the head, they thought, were related to sense of humor and various characteristics of the individual. Now this was a rather large movement, it had an international society, it had national and international journals, it was taught in universities, and all of a sudden it just vanished. One of the reasons I think it vanished was because the phrenologists' measurements were too precise. They could keep it pretty fuzzy on the character and personality side but the contours of the skull could be measured with calipers and therefore their ideas could be refuted. I think if they had kept it fuzzier on the skull end, that movement would still be going.

We are now in a family movement where we assume that there is a correlation between the family and what we used to think of as individual psychopathology. I think part of our obligation, even at great risk, is to formulate our ideas and test them as precisely as possible, even though it might cost us this movement. Even though a lot of us might agree that there is this correlation between families and patients, we can also share a delusion about it. A major function of family research is to test out this idea among others. One of the difficulties is that we have very few observations of families that don't come from family therapy. There has been some observation of families that aren't families in therapy, but very little, and so a lot of the ideas have to come out of this peculiar context of change.

I am not against family therapy as a context for research. What I was saying this morning is that it is not a way of answering questions such as whether an abnormal family is different from a normal one. There are other kinds of questions that can be answered in the therapy context, and it can certainly bring out a lot of ideas we wouldn't otherwise have. But it can also bring out a lot of mythologies that can fool us unless we find rigorous ways of testing them out.

Dr. Levinger: I would like to ask Dr. Ackerman a question about the kinds of problems that he might advise researchers to study. I am really pleased that he said what he said, and I think that the impatience of the practitioners is very important for researchers to consider. Yet one of the researcher's problems is that the clinical language is difficult to translate into research terms. My question to Dr. Ackerman is: What sort of event do you think might have what sort of an effect on another event; and how can we obtain evidence that it does or doesn't? In other words, *what kinds of questions do the clinicians wish to state that are susceptible to research tests?*

Dr. Ackerman: Let me say a word to explain why we at The Family Institute are thankful that we have shelved systematic research and have concentrated instead on careful ongoing clinical investigation of a series of families in treatment. One of the things we are trying to do right now is simply to learn how to describe families with some conviction of accuracy, with some conviction of communicability. I think that is the first responsibility.

Dr. Levinger: How does one know when one has finished "describing"? This is one difficulty.

Dr. MacGregor: Didn't Dr. Strodtbeck just provide Dr. Ackerman with the research evidence for his own statement? Dr. Ackerman says there are no dyads. Dr. Strodtbeck says that when mother talks about father, what she says has to include something about son. So, there aren't two people there, there are three. It seems to me this was very concrete laboratory evidence for what you were saying.

Dr. Levinger: There are semantic questions and there are experimental questions, and it seems to me it is valuable to try to bring these two together systematically.

Dr. Ackerman: May I expand just a little on some of the things that concern us? We are trying to improve what we call our system of family diagnosis. Our assessments are still much too long but they are getting better. At another level, we are trying to come to grips with what is entailed in reconceptualizing mental illness as a family phenomenon across at least three generations. What I am saying is so crude that it is almost self-evident. We are shifting from the idea that mental breakdown is exclusively a manifestation of individual functioning to a concept of a multiplicity of behaviors playing into one another, and a multiplicity of vulnerability patterns among the family members across time. That is, the phenomenon of breakdown now becomes redefined as involving numbers of persons interacting in a special way and reflecting a range of vulnerability patterns within all, or at least some, members of the family group.

We are concerned with the contagion of anxiety across the generations. We are concerned with another problem which has not been mentioned here, which is extremely important. Namely: What are the elements that are lacking in a family that disintegrates? What is the *sine qua non* for the survival of the family group in a social sense and also in a psychic sense? There are certain kinds of elements that must be present or else the family gets smashed, either from without or from within, or both. It falls apart. I am not familiar with any research study of a systematic kind that tries to tackle this question: What are the indispensable elements within the family unit without which that family cannot survive? Clinicians now study these questions in a crude way and turn them over to the researchers, and maybe the researchers can devise a really rigorous kind of study to provide some answers.

Dr. Strodtbeck: Or the question can be asked, What are the inherent wisdoms that drive families apart? I am using Dr. Wynne's phrasing here.

Dr. Ackerman: That is the other side of the same question, I think. At any rate, it is the clinician's job to look for these important problem areas, mark them out, and find a language with which to communicate them. The researchers can then go to work and devise a method that fits that problem.

I am troubled that so much research gets into print that sheds very little light on the clinical problems of the relationship between family and behavior. I would like to see a better fit and more adventurousness in inventing methods that illuminate the really critical questions. Somehow, as I read these studies, I get the impression that the preoccupation with the rigorousness of the method distorts the phenomenon that is under study, perverts it, corrupts it. I get very suspicious of that kind of methodology.

Dr. Bell: Are you more suspicious of the people who are trying to be methodological than you are of the people who are facing problems that don't lend themselves to methodology?

Dr. Ackerman: You mean, am I more suspicious of the researchers than of the clinicians?

Dr. Bell: Yes.

Dr. Ackerman: Well, I am suspicious both ways—suspicious but not cynical. I think there is a difference between skepticism and cynicism. I am being careful for once—it only sounds cynical.

Dr. Bell: This conversation goes back to the issue which Dr. Rubinstein and Dr. Ferreira were discussing. It is a simple point. What I am trying to offer here is a translation in a very truncated form of what Lyman Wynne was saying. In regard to the family as a system, one of the advantages of labeling it that way is that unless we do so, we immediately have to attend to the fact that the family is simultaneously always three different things: It is the context of individual systems, it is the system itself, and it is a subsystem. What Lyman was saying, I think, was that we have made the jump from seeing the family as a context to studying it as a system, but we are very weak indeed on seeing the family as a subsystem of extended kin networks of a larger society, and so on.

Dr. Wynne: In relation to this issue of selecting problems that are meaningful, especially those that are relevant to clinical issues, I would be happy if a study illuminated some aspect of a clinical problem, even though the research might not be too earth-shaking in its own right. It seems to me that we can usefully build up knowledge by small steps, understanding, for example, more about what difference it makes how long a person speaks, or what difference it makes if one sequence of people speaking takes place versus another sequence. Such studies, in themselves, would not illuminate directly clinical problems in the treatment situation, but they may be small, perhaps stumbling, steps en route to understanding more about treatment. I would not want to be so ambitious as to try to devise systematic studies that try to solve important clinical issues all in one fell swoop. I don't feel ready for that and I don't think the field is up to it.

Dr. Handel: I think we may have to face the fact that some of the clinical problems that we feel are urgent may have to be deferred until a later time. I would say there are two main reasons for studying something. One is because it *is* a problem and the other is simply because it is there. A clinician goes after it because it is one of the problems he encounters and he wants to study it and solve it. The formal scientist looks around and when he sees things that are interesting, he wants to understand them.

As I see it, families are of interest because they exist in nature; they are in some form universal. Once we take that step, then the next question of interest is: What is the nature of the bonds that hold families together?

I think that very broad question is one of the most fundamental, encompassing a wide range of work. Proceeding from that question, there are, again, two kinds of things one might go after. One can look for universals; for instance, the incest taboo was considered universal. One can also ask questions like: What kinds of families are there? What different ways are there of being a family? It seems to me that it is necessary to pursue these pathways in a variety of ways in order to form judgments about health and pathology. It may be only at that belated point that the collective judgment of Science may say: O.K., here is something that the clinician can use.

There is another thing that happens, which this kind of meeting discloses, and that is that workers in a field are differentially prepared at any given time to be convinced that something has been demonstrated to their satisfaction. In the papers of the most rigorous scientists among us, there is inevitably at some point in the paper a sentence that says, "I believe that," or "I feel that," suggesting that beyond this point they have to proceed on faith. I think that is one of the realities. There will always be a certain amount of dissatisfaction which will produce a growing edge in the science.

Dr. Bell: Family researchers are not a system as family therapists are.

Dr. Loveland: We have some ingenious techniques for obtaining rich samples of family patterns of interaction but precious few criteria for independent measures of how valid and representative they are. Often, the objectivity and reliability of the measure is in inverse proportion to its clinical usefulness.

Dr. Ravich: I am not nearly as pessimistic as Dr. Ackerman is about the ability to join together the achievements of social scientists with clinicians. In a sense, I have very much the same kind of roots—I am a clinician. As a matter of fact, I am influenced in many ways by Dr. Ackerman, and yet my experience with families caused me to turn to an area of psychology, particularly the work of some social psychologists who have been developing over many years a method for studying two-person interaction. I have been using this, first as a research method, but also as a tool in therapy. Consequently, I don't view family research and therapy as lying so far apart and being so disparate.

Chairman Ferreira: I think Dr. Whitaker has a word to say.

Dr. Whitaker: I have a lot of words to say but I find it very difficult to say them. Like Nate Ackerman, I don't quite know how to bridge the gap between us and the researchers. For instance, I am fascinated by the fact that we have hardly talked about the subsystem of the family which includes the therapists as part of the system. It is as though researchers see the family as a system and don't include us therapists as part of the group that needs to be focused on. I hope we get at this tomorrow. I don't feel we can get at it now, but I feel the kind of tension that Nate has been talking about in myself and I have been sitting here smoking up a storm.

Dr. Bowen: I feel very optimistic. I am in favor of a united family and I think we are getting it.

I am real pleased that Dr. Ackerman would assume the responsibility for getting the researchers and the clinicians together. Jay Haley is much less of a trouble-maker than he was this morning. MacGregor and Strodtbeck put in a little trouble-making but not too much.

I think the only problem now is to get Straus together with the other three discussants and then we will have it solved.

Dr. Strodtbeck: I want to suggest that one of the contributions that those of us from other behavioral sciences have to make is not necessarily restricted to very precise parametric studies. I will use a very brief example. There is in Central Africa a tribe called the Für in which each person has his own plot on which he grows the food that he eats, and except for getting a little millet to one's wife to make beer, and exchanges of cloth, life is kept at a very simple level. The child is reared by the mother until the age of 10 and then for the next five years wanders from village to village and begs and studies sporadically with various teachers.

In a society of that sort, I am sure you would find that the family interaction is, by any standards, very primitive. One of the questions suggested by this example is: Do simpler societies offer less opportunity for problem-solving and therefore limit the problem-solving capacities of its families?

The emphasis that Dr. Straus has placed on having a dependent and an independent variable is intimately related to looking for perspectives in design that are no more complicated than the one I have just given as an example.

Dr. Friedman: I want to thank Murray Bowen for those very healing comments. I always take what he says at face value and I am sure he meant it 100 percent—that we are all getting together happily.

I would like to ask whether, before we adjourn this section, someone on the panel, Lyman Wynne or someone else, would care to comment on Dave Rubinstein's interesting point about family system. He asked whether you could have a pathological individual member in a non-pathological system, and a nonpathological member in a pathological system. This is an intriguing point, and I would like to hear a comment about this.

Dr. Wynne: I think it depends, obviously, upon what *aspect* of pathology you are talking about. Dr. Ackerman pointed out—and it has been pointed out by therapists for many years—that nobody, not even the most regressed hebephrenic, is totally psychotic in all aspects of his functioning. Similarly, with families as social units, I don't think that any family can be appropriately labeled across the board either as totally pathological or not, so again we get into the problem of specifying *what* aspect or dimension of pathology we are talking aobut. Certainly there must be cases where the pathology of the individual is irrelevant to the functioning of the family, and vice versa, in many spheres. There are likely to be some interdigitating effects, however. With certain measures, family functioning can look pretty normal because of the *fit* of two or more individually disturbed people. This, conceptually, makes sense to me and I think it is the kind of problem that would be fascinating to study more comprehensively. This point has both clinical and theoretical significance.

Dr. Handel: May I ask whether, if you have a schizophrenic, it is possible to have a well sibling, or is the sibling really sick, too? This is one version of this question.

Dr. Bell: I can contribute an historical note. From about 1920 on, the idea got around that social disorganization and personal disorganization were closely related to one another, so closely that you could argue it either way. What happened in psychiatry was that they were arguing both ways and it wasn't until 1937 that Herbert Bloomer looked at a bunch of psychiatric studies and uncovered this underlying assumption which had never been tested. He pointed out that it was ridiculous to equate individual disorganization and social disorganization. The question is, rather, an empirical one of functional autonomy, of disorganization balanced by organization at the two levels.

Chairman Ferreira: It devolves upon me to say that we are coming to the end of this part of the meeting. But before I gavel ourselves out of here I would like to say that, until now, I was somewhat apprehensive about the supposed dichotomy between clinicians and experimentalists. I am very pleased to see now that I don't have to make any effort to reconcile both views, since the two camps are perhaps coming together in a much greater harmony than we had anticipated.

I, for one, have always felt that I could very well be a clinician in the morning and a researcher in the afternoon, and again become a clinician the next morning. I've somehow never felt the supposed antagonism or splitting that some have experienced, and I am very gratified to realize that we are becoming both better clinicians and researchers, despite our protestations to the contrary.

I will now turn the meeting over to Dr. Framo before we adjourn.

Dr. Framo: I have been to a lot of conferences and have always wondered how you can determine whether or not a conference was worthwhile. How can you tell if you got something out of it? Sometimes I feel it is like a good therapy session where the impact doesn't filter through until a long time after it's over, and then you remember something you heard that was meaningful. To me, this last half hour was representative of the kind of dialogue between researchers and clinicians that we were trying to achieve. Appropriate questions were asked, I thought, and meaningful issues were being dealt with.

(Friday Afternoon Session Adjourned)

Toward the Differentiation of a Self
in One's Own Family

ANONYMOUS

Dr. Framo: This is the second day of the conference on Systematic Research on Family Interaction. Yesterday, in our attempts to organize the existing knowledge of the field, we made the first tentative steps at trying to communicate with each other and showed the kind of healthy confusion that accompanies the birth of any new field. Most of the confusion, I feel, is a function of the inherent complexities of the subject matter. I, personally, was not unhappy that sparks began to fly. As in every group process—whether conference, therapist, or research group—each of us had to be heard and recognized, and then we could begin to get down to business. All in all, I think it was an excellent beginning.

The discussion yesterday had to be somewhat general and abstract because we were dealing with basic conceptual matters. Today we begin to deal with specifics and will start putting some flesh on the structure and concepts.

May I now present Dr. Paul Watzlawick, who will chair this morning's session.

Chairman Watzlawick: Since we are running a bit late, I would like to turn over the meeting, without further ado, to Dr. ____ and ask him to present his paper, "A Method of Categorizing Some Meaningful Clinical Variables."

Editor's Note: Because the following paper involves personal information about its author's family, the editor and publisher sought legal advice about publication. The

111

conclusion reached was that legal and ethical considerations require that the paper be published anonymously.

The original presentation that the author made at the conference consisted essentially of the last part of this paper entitled, "The Family Experience." The author had originally been requested to discuss the details of his scale of differentiation at this research conference, and when he started speaking the editor was as surprised as everyone else that he departed from his assigned topic and described instead the work he had been doing with his own family. The present paper, based on the extemporaneous talk given at the conference, is considerably longer than the original presentation, and was written long after the conference was over. The author was given this latitude in order to give him the opportunity to expand on the theoretical basis of his presentation. Because of the unusual circumstances that produced it, the paper follows a different format from those in the rest of the book. First, the author explains how and why he decided to present as he did, then the body of the rewritten paper is presented, and finally he presents a version of "The Family Experience" that was originally presented at the conference.

Dr.____: In the months before this Family Research Conference, I had wondered how to do an effective, brief presentation about my family theory and method of family psychotherapy that would be "heard" by more people. My past experience has been that many in my audiences hear the words that go with the theory without really grasping the concepts, and that frequently they perceive the psychotherapy as an intuitive method that goes with my personality rather than as a method determined by theory. In training family therapists I have found that some trainees quickly grasp the theory and go on to duplicate the psychotherapy. Others are slower to grasp the theory, and some never really "know" the theory even after extended periods. I believe a major part of this problem has to do with the theoretical orientation and emotional functioning of the therapists. My theory is best understood if the therapist can listen and observe and function from a position at least partially "outside" the emotional field of the family. Conventional theory and psychotherapy teaches and trains therapists to operate "inside" the emotional field with the patient or the family. In this paper I hope to communicate more clearly my version of what it means to be "inside" or "outside" an emotional system. The Family Research Conference, composed of people important in the family field, was sufficient motivation for me to work at finding a more effective way of presenting my ideas.

In the months preceding the conference, I had been working intensively in a new phase of a long-term effort to differentiate my own "self" from my parental extended family. That effort reached a dramatic breakthrough only a month before the conference. The following week I considered, and then quickly rejected, a presentation about my own family. As the days passed, the factors that favored such a presentation began to outweigh the factors that opposed. The presentation would contain a practical application of the major concepts in my theoretical and therapeutic systems, and, since I know more about my own family than any other family, I decided to use it as an example. I believe and teach that the family therapist usually has the very same problems in his own family that are present in families he sees professionally, and that he has a responsibility to define himself in his own family if he is to function adequately in his professional work. Also, this presentation would be a good example of "family psychotherapy with a single family member." Previous presentations about this subject had only seldom been heard. Another aspect of this enterprise became more appealing as the days passed. For some years I had been aware of the "undifferentiated family ego mass" that exists among the prominent family therapists. The same emotional system exists in the "family" of family therapists that operates in the "sick" families they describe at meetings. In a conference room, talking about relationship patterns in "sick" families, therapists do the same things to each other that members of "sick" families do. They even do the same things to each other while talking about what they do to each other. The final determination of this form of presentation, then, was based on my continuing effort to differentiate my "self" from the "family" of family therapists. I knew, parenthetically, that I would get some of the same reactions from the participants of the conference as I had gotten from my own family members.

In planning the presentation, I had two main goals. The first was to present the clinical material without explanation of theory or the step-by-step planning that went into it. There was reality to support the plan for this goal. The thirty minutes allowed for the presentation would not permit a review of theory. Though not many participants really "knew" my theory or method of family psychotherapy, I could with good conscience assume they had heard or read my previous papers. Also, I was hoping that clinical material without explanation might bring more indirect awareness of theory than another paper on theory. The second goal was the element of surprise that is essential if a differentiating step is to be successful. Rather than trying to explain that here, I will leave it to the reader to remember as he goes along. The plan was not discussed, even with trusted friends. A routine didactic paper about family theory was prepared and the required copies mailed to discussants before the meeting. The stage was set to do either the formal paper or the experience with my own family. I was anxious and sleepless the night before the presentation. Intellect favored the family presentation but feelings demanded that I give up this silly notion and do it the easy way by reading the formal paper. My anxiety would have sufficed to have me abandon the project had I not remembered similar anxiety before each differentiating effort in my own family. Impulses to read the formal paper continued to the very moment of presentation. Even during the presentation I was more anxious than I had anticipated I would be. From past experience, this anxiety was related to the "secret" action move with other family therapists rather than to reporting "secrets" about my own family.

There have been special problems in preparing this report for publication. This final version is being written in 1970, three years after the conference. The emotional forces that operate at any stage of differentiation have operated in this final step toward publication. These forces will be described in detail later in the paper. On one side has been the anxiety of the editor and publisher about publishing personal material, and their understandable defensive posture. The emotional courage necessary for differentiation is nullified by a defensive posture and over-concern about danger. A positive posture that can facilitate further differentiation in me is more important than publication. The anonymous authorship has helped to resolve the issues. Each version of the paper has been a new emotional hurdle for me because I had to respect the realities of publication and at the same time maintain an essential posture for myself. There was a special purpose in presenting the clinical material to the conference without explanation. To publish it as it was presented, to be read by people without knowledge of the special situation, with no awareness of the theory which guided the years of work with my own family, and with a variety of theoretical orientations, would result in the inevitable interpretations and misinterpretations based on each reader's own theoretical bias. The purpose of this written report is to present the theory and the method of psychotherapy based on the theory, and then use the example with my own family to illustrate the clinical application of the theory.

The Theoretical Background

Overall Description

The total theory is made up of six interrelated concepts, only one of which, the "triangle," will be discussed at this point. One of the basic concepts considers the "triangle" (three-person system) the "molecule" of any emotional system, whether it exists in the family or in a larger social system. The term "triangle" was chosen instead of the more familiar term "triad" which has come to have fixed connotations that do not apply to this concept. The triangle is the smallest stable relationship system. A two-person system is an unstable system that forms a triangle under stress. More than three people form themselves into a series of interlocking triangles. The emotional forces within a triangle are in constant motion, from minute to minute and hour to hour, in a series of chain reaction moves as automatic as emotional reflexes. Knowledge about the functioning of triangles makes it possible to modify the triangle by changing the function of one person in the triangle. The therapeutic system is directed at modifying the functioning of the most important triangle in the family system. If the central triangle changes, and it stays in contact with others, the entire system will automatically change. Actually, the entire system can change in relation to change in *any* triangle, but it is easier for the system to ignore a more peripheral or less important triangle. The relationship patterns, based on triangles which function through the years in the total family system, are described by other concepts in the theory. Since the clinical example, described in the latter part of this paper, will not be understandable without knowledge of triangles, a later part of this theoretical section will be devoted further to triangles.

Background Principles

Some of the basic principles that went into the development of this theory and method of family psychotherapy will help in understanding the theory. My primary effort has gone into making psychotherapy as scientific and predictable as possible. Early in psychiatry I was bothered when "intuition" and "clinical judgment" were used to change the course of a plan of psychotherapy or other forms of psychiatric treatment. Gross examples occur at times of crisis when the staff, reacting emotionally, meets to plan a change in treatment that is based more on "feeling" and "clinical hunches" than on scientific knowledge and theoretical principles. It is commonplace for psychotherapists to make changes based more on feeling perceptions and subjectivity than on clinical fact and objectivity.

The theory was developed in the course of family research. The original focus was on the symbiotic relationship between the mother and the schizophrenic patient. The first research hypothesis, based on the previous years of clinical experience, *knew* the origin and development of schizophrenia as a product of the two-person mother-patient relationship. The hypothesis was elaborated in such detail that it anticipated every relationship problem and every clinical situation that could develop. Psychotherapeutic principles and techniques were developed for each clinical situation. The hypothesis also predicted the changes that would occur with the psychotherapy. When research observations were not consistent with the hypothesis, the hypothesis was modified to fit the new facts, the psychotherapy was modified to fit the hypothesis, and new predictions were made about the results of the psychotherapy. When an unexpected clinical crisis arose, it was handled on an interim "clinical judgment" basis, but the hypothesis was considered at fault for not "knowing" about the situation ahead of time, and not having a predetermined therapeutic principle. The therapy was never changed to fit the situation except in emergencies. The goal was to change the hypothesis to account for the unexpected crisis, to change the therapy to fit the hypothesis, and to make new predictions about the therapy. Any failure to change in psychotherapy was as much a reason to reexamine and change the hypothesis as any other unpredicted change. Strict adherence to this principle resulted in a theoretical-therapeutic system that was developed as an integrated unit, with psychotherapy determined by the theory. A major advantage was the systematic utilization of change in psychotherapy as a criterion of hypothesis formation. A major disadvantage was that it required a more consistent and higher grade of psychotherapy than is generally available. However, the discipline of the research improved the skill of the therapists. Similar hypotheses and observations were made on the functioning of staff and therapists to the families.

The research plan was designed to fit as closely as possible to other structured research in science. An example would be the principle used in developing the national space program. The first space probe was based on the best scientific knowledge available at that time. The probe brought new scientific facts to be incorporated into the body of knowledge for making the next space probe. This is an example in which science and technology advance in a teamlike manner.

Our original hypothesis about the mother-patient relationship proved to be amazingly accurate in predicting the details of the relationship within this twosome, but it had completely omitted the observations about the way the twosome related to others. An extended hypothesis was developed to include fathers; new families with fathers were admitted to the research, and a method of family psychotherapy was devised to fit the hypothesis. The relationship patterns observed in families with schizophrenia had been hypothesized to be specific for schizophrenia. Once it was possible to finally "see" the patterns in families with schizophrenia, it was possible to see the same patterns in a less intense form in all levels of people with less emotional impairment. We could see the patterns even in "normal" families, and in the staff, and in ourselves. This development constituted a major change in the research, which was then directed away from schizophrenia to all levels of lesser problems and to people without clinical problems. New vistas were opened up for new hypotheses. Since people with lesser problems change more rapidly in family psychotherapy, new observations and further changes in the hypotheses were accelerated. The theory presented here is thus a presentation of the original research hypothesis, modified and extended hundreds of times, with each modification checked many times in and out of the clinical situation. When a body of theoretical thinking is sufficiently accurate so that it no longer requires significant modification, is accurate in describing and predicting the human phenomenon, and can explain discrepancies as well as consistencies, it is called a "concept." The term theory has not been used loosely. After there are several consistent concepts, the term "theory" is used for the total theoretical system.

The Theoretical Concepts

This family theory is made up of six essential interlocking concepts. All will be described sufficiently so that they can be understood as parts of the total theory. Those that are most important to this presentation will be described in the most detail. The discussion of triangles will be listed last.

Differentiation of Self Scale

This scale is an effort to classify all levels of human functioning, from the lowest possible levels to the highest potential level, on a single dimension. In broad terms it would be similar to an emotional maturity scale, but it deals with factors that are different from "maturity" concepts. The scale eliminates the need for the concept "normal." It has nothing to do with emotional health or illness or pathology. There are people low on the scale who keep their lives in emotional equilibrium without psychological symptoms, and there are some higher on the scale who develop symptoms under severe stress. However, lower scale people are more vulnerable to stress and, for them, recovery from symptoms can be slow or impossible while higher scale people tend to recover rapidly. The scale has no direct correlation with intelligence or socio-economic levels. There are intellectually brilliant people far down the scale and less bright ones far up the scale. A majority of the lower socio-economic group are far down the scale but there are those in the lower social groups who are well up the scale and those from high social groups who are far down the scale.

This is a scale for evaluating the level of "differentiation of self" from the lowest possible level of "undifferentiation," which is at 0 on the scale, to the highest theoretical level of "differentiation," which is at 100 on the scale. The greater the degree of undifferentiation (no self), the greater the emotional fusion into a common self with others (undifferentiated ego mass). Fusion occurs in the context of a personal or shared relationship with others and it reaches its greatest intensity in the emotional interdependency of a marriage. The life style and thinking and emotional patterns of people at one level of the scale are so different from people at other levels that people choose spouses or close personal friends from those with equal levels of differentiation. In the emotional closeness of marriage the two partial "selfs" fuse into a common "self"; the degree of fusion depends on the basic level of differentiation before the marriage. Both partners want the emotional bliss of fusion but it is extemely difficult to maintain this equilibrium. One of the selfs in the common self becomes dominant and the other submissive or adaptive. Said in another way, the dominant one gains a higher level of functional self and appears "stronger," at the expense of the adaptive one who gave up self and who is functionally "weaker." There is a spectrum of mechanisms that spouses use in adapting to the fusion. These mechanisms will be discussed in the concept that deals with the dynamics of the nuclear family system. The lower the level of differentiation or "basic self" in the spouses the more difficult it is to maintain reasonable emotional equilibrium and the more chronic the disability when adaptive mechanisms fail.

The differentiation of self scale is an effort to assess the basic level of self in a person. The basic self is a definite quantity illustrated by such "I" position stances as: "These are my beliefs and convictions. This is what I am, and who I am, and what I will do, or not do." The basic self may be changed from *within* self on the basis of new knowledge and experience. The basic self *is not negotiable in the relationship system* in that it is not changed by coercion or pressure, or to gain approval, or enhance one's stand with others. There is another fluid, shifting level of self, which I call the "pseudo-self," which makes it difficult to assign fixed values to the basic self, and which is best understood with functional concepts. The pseudo-self is made up of a mass of heterogeneous facts, beliefs, and principles acquired through the relationship system in the prevailing emotion. These include facts learned because one is supposed to know them, and beliefs borrowed from others or accepted in order to enhance one's position in relationship to others. *The pseudo-self, acquired under the influence of the relationship system, is negotiable in the relationship system.* The pseudo-self can accept a plausible sounding philosophy under the emotional influence of the moment, or it can just as easily adopt an opposite philosophy to oppose the relationship system. It is the pseudo-self that fuses with others in an intense emotional field. There is so much borrowing and trading of pseudo-self among those in the lower half of the scale that definite scale values can be estimated only from observations that cover months or years, or from a life-time pattern.

People in the lower half of the scale live in a "feeling" controlled world in which feelings and subjectivity are dominant over the objective reasoning process most of the time. They do not distinguish feeling from fact, and major life decisions are based on what "feels" right. Primary life goals are oriented around love, happiness, comfort, and security; these goals come closest to fulfillment when relationships with others are in equilibrium. So much life energy goes into seeking love and approval, or attacking the other for not providing it, that there is little energy left for self-determined, goal-directed activity. They do not distinguish between "truth" and "fact" and the inner feeling state is the most accurate possible expression of truth. A sincere person is regarded as one who freely communicates the feeling process. An important life principle is "giving and receiving" love, attention, and approval. Life can stay in symptom-free adjustment as long as the relationship system is in comfortable equilibrium. Discomfort and anxiety occur with events that disrupt or threaten the relationship equilibrium. Chronic disruption of the relationship system results in dysfunction and a high incidence of human problems, including physical and emotional illness and social dysfunction. People in the upper half of the scale have an increasingly defined level of basic self and less pseudo-self. Each person is more of an autonomous self: there is less emotional fusion in close relationships, less energy is needed to maintain self in the fusions, more energy is available for goal-directed activity, and more satisfaction is derived from directed activity. Moving into the upper half of the scale one finds people who have an increasing capacity to differentiate between feelings and objective reality. For instance, people in the 50 to 75 range of the scale have increasingly defined convictions and opinions on most essential issues but they are still sensitive to opinions of those about them and some decisions are based on feelings in order not to risk the disapproval of important others.

According to this theory, there is some degree of fusion in close relationships, and some degree of an "undifferentiated family ego mass" at every scale level below 100. When the scale was first devised, the 100 level was reserved for the being who was perfect in all levels of emotional, cellular, and physiological functioning. I expected there might be some unusual figures in history, or possibly some living persons who would fit into the mid-90 range. Increasing experience with the scale indicates that all people have areas of good functioning and essential areas in which life functioning is poor. It has not yet been possible to check the scale on extremely high-level people, but my impression is that 75 is a very high-level person and that those above 60 constitute a small percentage of society.

The characteristics of high-scale people convey an important aspect of the concept. They are operationally clear about the difference between feeling and thinking, and it is as routine for them to make decisions on the basis of thinking as it is for low-level people to operate on feelings. The relative separation of feelings and thinking brings life much more under the control of deliberate thoughts, in contrast to low-scale people whose life is a pawn of the ebb and flow of the emotional process. In relationships with others, high-scale people are free to engage in goal-directed activity, or to lose "self" in the intimacy of a close relationship, in contrast to low-scale people who either have to avoid relationships lest they slip automatically into an uncomfortable fusion, or have no choice but continued pursuit of a close relationship for gratification of emotional "needs." The high-scale person is less reactive to praise or criticism and he has a more realistic evaluation of his own self in contrast to the lower-level person whose evaluation is either far above or far below reality.

The scale is most important as a theoretical concept for understanding the total human phenomenon and as a reliable instrument for making an overall evaluation of the course of a life, and accurate predictions about the possible future life directions of a person. It is not possible to do day-to-day or week-to-week evaluations of scale levels because of the wide shifts in the functional level of pseudo-self in low-scale people. A compliment can raise the functioning level of self and criticism can lower it. It is possible to do reasonably accurate general estimations from information that covers months or years. For instance, a detailed history of functional shifts within a family over a period of years can convey a fairly accurate pattern of the family members in relation to each other. The scale makes it possible to define numerous differences between people at various scale levels. The life style of a person at one level is so different from someone only a few points removed on the scale they do not choose each other for personal relationships. There are many life experiences that can raise or lower the *functioning* levels of self, but few that can change the basic level of differentiation acquired while people are still with their parental families. Unless there is some unusual circumstance, the basic level from their parental family is consolidated in a marriage, following which the only shift is a functional shift. The functional shifts can be striking. For example, a wife who had a functional level at marriage equal to her husband's may become de-selfed to the point of chronic alcoholism. She then functions far below her original level while the husband functions equally far above his original level. Many of these functional levels are sufficiently consolidated so that they can appear much like basic levels to the inexperienced.

Nuclear Family Emotional System

This developmental concept deals with the emotional patterns that begin with plans for marriage and then follow through the marriage, the types of relationships with families of origin, the adjustment of the spouses to each other before children, the addition of the first child, their adjustment as a three-person relationship, and then the addition of subsequent children. The level of differentiation of self of the spouses plays a major part in the intensity of the patterns. I originally used the term "undifferentiated family ego mass" to describe the emotional "stuck togetherness" or fusion in the nuclear family. The term is still accurate when applied to the nuclear family, but the term is less apt in referring to the same phenomenon in the extended families, and the term is awkward when applied to the same phenomenon in emotional systems at work, or in social systems. More recently the term "emotional system" has been used to designate the same triangular emotional patterns that operate in all close relationships, with an additional term to designate the location of the system, such as a nuclear family emotional system.

The level of differentiation of self determines the degree of emotional fusion in spouses. The way the spouses handle the fusion governs the areas in which the undifferentiation will be absorbed and the areas in which symptoms will be expressed under stress. There are three areas within the nuclear family in which symptoms are expressed. These areas are 1) marital conflict, 2) dysfunction in a spouse, and 3) projection to one or more children. There is a quantitative amount of undifferentiation, determined by the level of differentiation in the spouses, to be absorbed by one, or by a combination of the three areas. There are marriages in which a major amount goes to one area, with other areas absorbing the "spill" from the primary area. Most families use a combination of the three areas. Marital conflict occurs when neither spouse will "give in" to the other in the fusion, or when the one who has been giving in or adapting refuses to continue. Conflict absorbs large quantities of the undifferentiation.

One of the commonest mechanisms is one in which the two pseudo-selfs fuse into a common self, one giving up pseudo-self to the merger and the other gaining a higher level of functioning self from the merger. This avoids conflict and permits more closeness. The dominant one who gains self is often not aware of the problems of the adaptive one who gives in. The adaptive one is a candidate for dysfunction, which can be physical or emotional illness, or social dysfunction such as drinking or irresponsible behavior. Dysfunction which serves to absorb undifferentiation is difficult to reverse. Dysfunction routinely occurs in one spouse, the other gaining strength in the emotional exchange. Dysfunction in a spouse can absorb large quantities of the undifferentiation, which protects other areas from symptoms.

The third area is the mechanism by which parental undifferentiation is projected to one or more children. I believe this exists in all families to some degree. This mechanism is so important that it is described in the following separate concept. The overall concept being described here is that of a specific amount of immaturity or undifferentiation to be abosrbed within the nuclear family, which is fluid and shifting to some degree, and which increases to a symptomatic level during stress. The borrowing and trading of pseudo-self which goes on with other people at this level of undifferentiation is the point to be emphasized here.

Family Projection Process

This is the process by which parents project part of their immaturity to one or more children. The most frequent pattern is one which operates through the mother with the mechanism which enables the mother to become less anxious by focusing on the child. The life style of parents, fortuitous circumstances such as traumatic events that disrupt the family during the pregnancy or about the time of birth, and special relationships with sons or daughters are among factors that help determine the "selection" of the child for this process. The most common pattern is one in which one child is the recipient of a major portion of the projection, while other children are relatively less involved. The child who is the object of the projection is the one most emotionally attached to the parents, and the one who ends up with a lower level of differentiation of self. A child who grows up relatively outside the family projection process can emerge with a higher basic level of differentiation than the parents.

Multigenerational Transmission Process

This concept describes the pattern that develops over multiple generations as children emerge from the parental family with higher, equal, or lower basic levels of differentiation than the parents. When a child emerges with a lower level of self than the parents and marries a spouse with equal differentiation of self, and this marriage produces a child with a lower level who marries another with an equal level, and this next marriage produces one with a lower level who marries at that level, there is a process moving, generation by generation, to lower and lower levels of undifferentiation. According to this theory, the most severe emotional problems, such as hard-core schizophrenia, are the product of a process that has been working to lower and lower levels of self over multiple generations. Along with those who fall lower on the differentiation of self scale are those who remain at about the same level and those who progress up the scale.

Sibling Position Profiles

The personality profiles of each sibling position, as described by Toman (1960, 1969), have added an important dimension to this theoretical orientation and the therapeutic system. I have found Toman's profiles to be remarkably consistent with my own observations of "normal" siblings. In his initial work, he did not study the "abnormal" sibling who is the recipient of the family projection process. The more intense the projection process, the more like an infantile youngest child this one becomes, no matter which the sibling position of birth. In evaluating a family, a note about the sibling position of each parent and whether or not the profile of each parent was reasonably typical, conveys invaluable information about the way this family will adapt itself to life, to the emotional forces in the family, and to working on its problem in family psychotherapy. For instance a "fusion of selfs" mix made up of an oldest daughter and youngest son automatically conveys a wealth of information about the family, "all things being equal." In addition, this mix behaves differently in conflict, in the dysfunction of one spouse, and in the family projection process. The many details of this concept are of peripheral interest to this presentation.

Triangles

The concept of triangles provides a theoretical framework for understanding the microscopic functioning of all emotional systems. Most important, the step-by-step understanding of triangles provides an immediate working answer that can be used by the therapist, or by any family member, for predictably changing the functioning of an emotional system. The pattern of triangle functioning is the same in all emotional systems. The lower the level of differentiation, the more intense the patterns, and the more important the relationship, the more intense the patterns. The very same patterns are less intense at higher levels of differentiation and in relationships that are more peripheral.

A two-person emotional system is unstable in that it forms itself into a three-person system or triangle under stress. A system larger than three persons becomes a series of interlocking triangles. The following are some of the characteristics of functioning of a single triangle. As tension mounts in a two-person system, it is usual for one to be more uncomfortable than the

other, and for the uncomfortable one to "triangle in" a third person by
telling the second person a story about the triangle one. This relieves the
tension between the first two, and shifts the tension between the second
and third. A triangle in a state of calm consists of a comfortable twosome
and an outsider. The favored position is to be a member of the twosome. If
tension arises in the outsider, his next predictable move is to form a
twosome with one of the original members of the twosome, leaving the
other one as outsider. So the forces within the triangle shift and move from
moment to moment and over longer periods. When the triangle is in a state
of tension, the outside position is the preferred position, in a posture that
says, "You two fight and leave me out of it." Add this extra dimension of
gaining closeness, or escaping tension, and it provides an even more
graphic notion of the shifting forces, each one constantly moving to gain a
little more close comfort or to withdraw from tension, with each move by
one requiring a compensatory move by another. In a state of tension, when
it is not possible for the triangle to conveniently shift the forces within the
triangle, two members of the original twosome will find another convenient
third person (triangle in another person) and now the emotional forces will
run the circuits in this new triangle. The circuits in the former triangle are
then quiet but available for re-use at any time. In periods of very high
tension, a system will triangle in more and more outsiders. A common
example is a family in great stress that uses the triangle system to involve
neighbors, schools, police, clinics, and a spectrum of outside people as
participants in the family problem. The family thus reduces the tension
within the inner family, and it can actually create the situation in which
the family tension is being fought out by outside people.

Over long periods of time, a triangle will come to have long-term
postures and functioning positions to each other. A common pattern is one
in which the mother and child form the close twosome and the father is the
outsider. In this triangle, the minute-to-minute process of emotional forces
shifts around the triangle, but when forces come to rest, it is always with
each in the same position. A triangle characteristically has two positive
sides and one negative side. For instance, one member of the close twosome
has a positive feeling orientation to the outsider while the other member
may feel negative about him. The triangle concept is remarkably more
fluid for understanding a three-person system than the more conventional
Oedipal Complex concepts. For instance, conflict between siblings consists
almost universally of a triangle between mother and two children in which
mother has a positive relationship to each child and the conflict is fought
out between the children. The triangle concept provides many more clues
about what to do to modify the sibling rivalry situation than is provided

by Oedipal theory. In even the most "fixed" triangle, the positive and negative forces shift back and forth constantly. The term "fixed" refers to the most characteristic position. A three-person system is one triangle, a four-person system is four primary triangles, a five-person system is nine primary triangles, etc. This progression multiplies rapidly as systems get larger. In addition there are a variety of secondary triangles when two or more may band together for one corner of a triangle for one emotional issue, while the configuration shifts on another issue.

There are characteristics of the triangle that lend themselves specifically to psychotherapy, or to any other efforts to modify the triangle. The emotional forces within a triangle operate as predictably as an emotional reflex. The reactiveness operates in a chain reaction fashion, one reaction following another in predictable sequence. The therapeutic system is based on being able to observe accurately to see the part that self plays, and to consciously control this programmed emotional reactiveness. The observation and the control are equally difficult. Observation is not possible until one can control one's reactions sufficiently to be able to observe. The process of observation allows for more control, which in turn, in a series of slow steps, allows for better observation. This process of being able to observe is the slow beginning toward moving one small step toward getting one's self "outside" an emotional system. It is only when one can get a little outside that it is possible to begin to observe and to begin to modify an emotional system. When there is finally one who can control his emotional responsiveness and not take sides with either of the other two, and stay constantly in contact with the other two, the emotional intensity within the twosome will decrease and both will move to a higher level of differentiation. Unless the triangled person can remain in emotional contact, the twosome will triangle in someone else.

The Therapeutic System

A very brief review of the therapeutic system is presented to provide an overall view of the place of the forthcoming clinical presentation in the total theoretical and therapeutic systems. The theoretical system conceives of an undifferentiated family ego mass and the therapeutic system is designed to help one or more family members toward a higher level of differentiation. The concepts of triangles provides another theoretical dimension, which says an emotional system is made up of a series of interlocking triangles. The most important therapeutic principle, which is repeatable in an orderly predictable way, says that when the triangular emotional pattern is modified in a single important triangle in the family, and the members of the triangle remain in emotional contact with the rest of the family, other triangles will automatically change in relation to the first.

Family Psychotherapy with Both Parents or Both Spouses

This is the main family configuration for family psychotherapy with any family. The therapeutic method employs the concept of differentiation of self, and of the triangle emotional system that operates in the family. The goal is to work toward modification of the most important triangle in the family, and from experience this has been found to stem from the two parents or the two spouses. I have found that the quickest way to modify the central triangle is to constitute a new triangle with the two primary members of the family and the therapist. When the family triangle includes three or more from the natural family, the emotional system runs its own built-in emotional circuits and it requires much more time for the family to observe or modify the triangle patterns. If the family configuration permits, the family psychotherapy is routinely with both spouses or both parents, whether the initial problem be marital conflict, a dysfunction in a spouse, or a problem in a child. If it is possible to modify the emotional patterns in this central triangle, then all other family members automatically change.

The one basic principle in this method of psychotherapy involves the therapist keeping himself "detriangled" or emotionally outside the emotional field that involves the marital twosome. These two people automatically use mechanisms with the therapist that they use in dealing with any third person. If the therapist can remain outside the emotional field and not respond as others do to the emotional twosome, then patterns between them come to be more quickly modified. I believe this method would work no matter what the subject of discussion, as long as the therapist remained relatively "detriangled," and as long as the twosome dealt with issues that revealed critical triangles.

There are four main things I do in a situation with two spouses or both parents. The first is to keep the emotional system between them sufficiently alive to be meaningful and sufficiently toned down for them to deal with it objectively without undue emotional reactiveness. The therapist is active with constant questions, first to one spouse, and then the other, getting the thoughts of one in reaction to what the other had communicated to the therapist. This prevents emotional exchanges between the spouses and enables each to "hear" the other without the automatic emotional bind that develops in exchanges between them. A second function is to keep self "detriangled" from the emotional process between the two family members. There are many details to this function. The third function is to establish what I have called an "I Position," which is part of the differentiation of a self. The therapist takes action stands in relation to them, which then permits them to begin to do the same to each other. The fourth function is to teach them how emotional systems operate and to encourage them each to work toward the differentiation of self in relation to their families of origin. This step has many important details. It is necessary that the psychotherapy be done in a way that does not involve the therapist in the emotional system between the spouses. With this method, each can differentiate a self from the other as long as the therapist does not get involved in the process and as long as he can keep the process between them active.

Family Psychotherapy with One Spouse in Preparation for Family Psychotherapy with Both Spouses

This method is designed for families in which one spouse is negative and unwilling to be involved in the family psychotherapy. The first part is similar to what will be described in the next section on family psychotherapy with one family member. The goal with this method is to help the motivated spouse to understand the part that self plays in the family system, until the unmotivated spouse is willing to join the therapy as a cooperative effort.

Family Psychotherapy with One Motivated Family Member

This method has been in regular use some eight years. It was designed for unmarried young adults who lived at a distance from parents, or whose parents refused to be a part of the therapy effort. This method is so similar to what will be described with my own family that it will be mentioned only briefly. The initial sessions are spent teaching the characteristics of family systems. Then sessions are devoted to making postulations about the part this single member plays in the total system. Then time is devoted to learning to observe patterns in one's own family, and finally to developing ways to modify one's own emotional reactions in the parental system. This plan involves relatively frequent contact with families of origin to check postulations, to seek new observations that will confirm or refute postulations, and to develop ways to modify reactions. It works best with oldest children who usually feel more responsibility for their families and who are more motivated for such an effort. It requires that the single members be self-supporting, else they never develop the emotional courage for change that might threaten the family attitude about them. An optimum distance from extended families is about 200 to 300 miles, which is close enough for frequent contact and far enough away to be outside the immediate emotional sphere of the family. Appointments are spaced farther apart when distance from family does not permit frequent visits. It is also possible to use work and social relationship systems for learning the properties of emotional systems. The average well-motivated young person will spend about 100 hours spread over a period of four or five years at such an effort. More frequent appointments do not increase the capacity to observe and to control emotional responsiveness. The average result with this method has been far superior to results with conventional psychotherapy.

The Clinical Report

The object of this report is a clinical experience that covered a period of a few months in which I achieved a major breakthrough in differentiating a self from my family of origin. That experience was preceded by a twelve-year effort to understand my family within the framework of family theory. There had been an active effort to modify my self in relation to my family during the last seven or eight years of that period. This slow trial and error effort was intertwined with the stages of my professional work in family research, family theory, and family psychotherapy. Since reaching this evolutionary stage with my own family, I have been able to "coach" motivated family therapists toward significant differentiation in their parental families in as little as two or three years. This goal is achieved by helping them focus on the productive areas and avoiding the time-consuming pitfalls. In an effort to help the reader understand the rationale for this effort, the material will be presented in its evolutionary steps, with each step explained in terms of the theory which has already been presented.

Personal Background Information

There was very little from my conventional psychiatric training that provided a workable understanding of my own family. Most of the useful concepts came from my experience with family research. However, I had some early experiences that may have played a part in the development of my thinking; these will be summarized briefly. Since many ask questions about motivation for working on one's own family, I will begin with some very early trends in my life. During my childhood I possessed two assets that played a part in future choices. One was an unusual ability for solving difficult puzzles and in devising working solutions for insoluble-appearing problems. Another asset was skill in the use of my hands. By the age of twelve I had decided to go into a profession and the choice was equal between law and medicine. After twelve the choice went more toward medicine. At fifteen an incident occurred which resulted in my making a firm decision for medicine. I was an ambulance helper and had to take an unconscious teen-age girl to a university hospital. The girl lay unconscious all afternoon and by early evening she was dead. The vivid memory of the emergency room and the doctors who seemed bewildered, unsure, and fumbling incited me to help medicine find better answers. In medical school, my interest automatically gravitated to areas with the most pressing unsolved problems. First there was neurology, than neurosurgery, and then the challenge of differential diagnosis in medicine. The intellectual challenge of the skilled techniques of surgery did not fascinate me until internship. A series of surgical deaths led to my building a crude artificial heart and being accepted for a fellowship in surgery, and, following this, I was in the military service for five years. The extent of psychiatric dysfunction that I observed in Army personnel and the lack of adequate solutions for these problems led to a decision to undertake psychiatric training. I got involved immediately with schizophrenia, and then explored every known theory and treatment of schizophrenia until my interest settled on the family. Hypotheses about the family led to my devoting myself full-time to psychiatric research on the family a few years later.

I was relatively unaware of psychological or psychoanalytic concepts when I went into psychiatry. Superficial knowledge about these concepts had been compartmentalized as applying to those who were "sick." My close, congenial family had been free of conflict, marital problems, drinking problems, or any diagnosable neurotic or behavior problem for every generation of which I had knowledge. My parental family relationships and my marriage relationship were considered happy, normal, and ideal. My first year or two in psychiatry was a period of near exhilaration as I heard those logical-sounding explanations of human behavior. The exhilaration began to disappear with awareness of logical discrepancies in theory that the experts could not explain. Most psychiatrists did not seem bothered by the contradictions which formed the core of my later research.

In essence, those early years in psychiatry, and my own psychoanalysis, helped me to become aware of a fascinating new world of hidden motivation and conflict. I learned the concepts and became adept at applying them to self, staff, friends, family, and even to prominent people in the news I had never met. Everyone was "pathological," and those who denied it were even more "pathological." Thinking about members of my family took the form of analyzing their psychodynamics and diagnosing them. This stance tended to intensify my previous posture to my family of origin. As an oldest son and physician I had long been the wise expert preaching to the unenlightened, even when it was done under the guise of expressing an opinion or giving advice. The family would listen politely and put it aside as "just psychiatry." During my psychoanalysis there was enough emotional pressure to engage my parents in an angry confrontation about childhood grievances that had come to light in the snug harbor of transference. At the time I considered these confrontations to be emotional emancipation. There may have been some short-term gain from knowing my feelings a little better and learning to "sound off" at my parents, but the long-term result was an intensification of previous patterns. The net result was my conviction that my parents had their problems, and I had mine, that *they would never change,* and nothing more could be done. I felt justified in maintaining a formal distance and keeping relationships superficial. I did not attempt to work on relationships in my family of origin until after the development of my new concepts in family research.

One emotional phenomenon from a system outside the family is of special importance to this family concept. I worked in a large, well-known psychiatric clinic where the emotional system in the "family" of staff and employees was identical to the emotional system in any family. The patterns of all emotional systems are the same whether they be family systems, work systems, or social systems, the only difference being one of intensity. The emotional system where I worked provided valuable observations. I noticed that when I was away on trips I was much clearer and more objective about work relationships, and that the objectivity was lost on returning to work. After it was first noticed, I made more careful observations of the phenomenon. The objectivity could come by the time the plane was an hour away. On return, the objectivity would be lost as I went through the front door returning to work. It was as if the emotional system "closed in" as I entered the building. This is the emotional phenomenon I later came to call the "undifferentiated family ego mass." I wondered what it would take to keep emotional objectivity in the midst of the emotional system. A "differentiated self" is one who can maintain emotional objectivity while in the midst of an emotional system in turmoil, yet at the same time actively relate to key people in the system. I made other observations about the emotional system at work. After a trip, when I returned to the city on Saturday, objectivity would hold until returning to work Monday morning. There was one occasion when the objectivity was lost during a telephone conversation with a staff member before returning to work. On other occasions the objectivity would be lost when greeting a staff member in the parking lot before entering the building. This "fusion" into the emotional system operated most intensely with those most involved in the gossip system at work. Gossip is one of the principal mechanisms for "triangling" another into the emotional field between two people. The details of this phenomenon will be discussed elsewhere in this presentation. In that work system much "triangling" took place at coffee breaks, social gatherings, and bull sessions in which the "understanding" ones would "analyze" and talk about those who were not present. This mechanism conveys, "We understand each other perfectly (the togetherness side of the triangle). We are in agreement about that pathological third person." At social gatherings people would clump in small groups, each talking about someone outside that clump, and each apparently unaware that all the clumps were doing the same "triangling" gossip about them.

I consider involvement in that work emotional system to have been one of the fortunate experiences in my life. It just happened to have been of sufficient intensity to afford observations. After having observed the phenomenon there, it was then easier to see the same phenomenon in all other work systems. It provided a kind of "control" for the very same phenomenon in my family of origin. During the years I worked hardest to "differentiate a self" in my family of origin, I would return occasionally to the old work system for a visit. Some of my best friends are still there. On the average visit, though I had been away for two or three years, it would take no more than thirty minutes to meet someone important to the system, and immediately "fuse" into taking sides in the emotional issues of the system. Finally, after I had mastered the experience with my own family that is reported here, I returned to the old work system for a long visit and was able to relate intimately to those important to the system without a single episode of "fusion."

The Family History

My own family of origin is the clinical example of this presentation. I am the oldest of five children of a cohesive, congenial family that has lived in the same small town for several generations. My parents, now quite elderly, are active in community life and both work in the family business. My personality profile is that of an over-responsible oldest son. I am married to the second of three daughters, who functions more as an oldest. We have four children, ranging from age 14 to 20. My first brother, two years younger than myself, is an outgoing, energetic businessman who established himself in another state immediately after college. He married a college classmate who is a socially active only child. They have one daughter. The third child, my second brother, three years younger than my first brother, is head of the family business and functions as head of the clan at home. He married a second child and oldest daughter while he was in the military service. They have two sons and a daughter. The fourth child in my family of origin, an oldest daughter, is two years younger than the third child. She is the one most emotionally triangled into the family system, the only one who did not go to college, and the one who has made the poorest life adjustment. She married an employee of the family business and they have a daughter and a son. The fifth child is a daughter four years younger than the fourth. After college she worked in another town where she married; she has one daughter. After several years her husband sold his business and they returned to the family hometown where he works in the family business. There have never been any disabling illnesses, accidents, or injuries in any of the five children, in their spouses, or their children.

The step-by-step sequence of events in this family emotional field covers a period of over fifty years. My father was an only child who has functioned as a responsible oldest. His father died when he was an infant. He was reared by his mother until he was twelve, when she remarried and had other children. He was self-supporting from childhood. My mother was a responsible oldest daughter, seven years older than her brother. Her mother died when she was one year old, following which she and her father returned to live with his parents until she was six, when her father remarried. She lived the next 17 years with her father, her stepmother, and a half brother born one year later. My parents first knew each other well when they both worked in town. They were married when he was a station agent for the railroad and she worked with her father in the family business, a department store founded by his father. After marriage, my parents lived in their own home in town for the next five years. I was born a year and a half after the marriage and my first brother was born two years later.

A sequence of events which profoundly influenced the future of the family began shortly after the birth of my brother. My mother's brother was in college several hundred miles away. Her father's health began to fail and my father began spending more and more time in the business, in addition to his regular full-time work. My grandfather had been a responsible oldest son in a large family. His death, when my first brother was two years old, was a nodal point in the family history. My father resigned from his previous job, my mother's brother stayed home from college, and my father and uncle became partners in the family business. My parents moved into my mother's parental home where the household consisted of my parents, then in their late 20's, my brother and myself, my grandmother, then in her 50's, and my uncle, then in his early 20's. The personality profiles of the household will convey something of the family emotional field. My father is an action-oriented oldest son and my mother a responsible "doing" oldest daughter. They are among that percentage of "oldests" who make marriage into a smooth-functioning partnership. My grandfather, as an oldest, had married two adaptive young daughters. My grandmother, his second wife, was quiet and supportive. My uncle, a functional only child by virtue of the seven years between him and my mother, was his mother's only child. He emerged with a profile of a bright youngest son. These particular personality profiles made for a congenial household with a low level of conflict.

About five months after the death of her father, my mother became pregnant with her third child, my second brother. A few months later, my uncle was among the first to be drafted for the war, and my father assumed responsibility for the business. My second brother was conceived within months after my grandfather's death, the reorganization of the business, and the merger into a single household. My second brother was born within the month after my uncle left. It was as if he was born to take over the family business. I and my first brother had been born while my parents had their own home, and we are the only two who moved away and who have no connection with the business. There was no particular pressure on anyone to leave or stay. It just evolved that I and my first brother left. My uncle returned from the war almost two years later, about the time mother became pregnant with her fourth child and oldest daughter. Mother had long wanted a daughter and this child became "special" and over-protected, the one most involved in the family emotional process, and the one who was impaired by it. There is one such child in almost every family. Though the impairment in my first sister did not go beyond overall poor functioning in her life course, the emotional pattern is the same as other families in which the most involved child is severely impaired. With less basic differentiation in my parents and more stress in the family emotional system, this daughter could have later developed severe disabling emotional or physical problems. Why did the emotional patterns involve a daughter instead of a son, and why this child? I believe this pattern is predictable in families and, implicit in Toman's work, are suggestions about whether the involved one is likely to be a son or daughter. In my family, there were reality factors that played into the emotional process. My father was the active responsible one in the family business and my mother assumed responsibility for the family operation at home. There were always chores and need for extra help in the home and business and the children all worked as a matter of course. Clear distinctions between men's work and women's work helped keep my sister in a special category. My older sister has remained emotionally dependent on my parents. School was difficult for her and she was the only one who did not go to college. She has the personality profile of a dependent youngest child, which happens with the one most involved in the family emotional process. The fifth child, another daughter, was born four years after the fourth. She grew up more outside the family emotional system and she has the profile of a responsible oldest daughter.

The period after the last child is born, when the family composition is relatively stable, usually provides the best overview of family functioning. The three boys had about equal levels of adjustment. We spent considerable time with my father in work and recreation while my mother provided more of the reminders about hard work, fair play, helping others, and success. My mother was the active, responsible one in the home. My grandmother helped with fixed chores, and she devoted special attention to my uncle. The major triangle in this combination of home and business involved my father, mother, and uncle. Any member of a relatively fixed triangle perceives his self as "caught." My father was caught between his wife and her brother, my uncle between his sister and her husband, and my mother between her husband and her brother. My father was the one most active in the business and also in civic and community activity. In the business he represented expansion and "progress." My uncle represented caution, and he functioned as the loyal opposition that questioned "progress." In calm periods, a triangle functions as a comfortable twosome and an outsider. My uncle was the outside one, which caused no problems for him since he had the close relationship with his mother who was relatively uninvolved in business issues. In stressful periods, a triangle has two positive sides and a negative side. The negative side in this triangle was between my father and uncle in the business, usually expressed as discontent communicated through my mother. The stress rarely reached a point of overt anger between my father and uncle. The general subject of discontent communicated to my mother was that my uncle was not doing his fair share of the work or that he was obstructing progress, or that my father was getting more than his fair share of business proceeds (he had a larger family to support), or that the business expansions were too costly.

The family triangle illustrates an important difference between family theory and certain conventional psychiatric concepts. There are those who would say that the differences between my father and uncle represented deeply buried hostility controlled by maladaptive suppression, and that healthier adaptation would result from searching out and openly expressing the hostility. Family theory would say that the negative side of the triangle is merely a symptomatic expression of a total family problem and to focus on issues in one relationship is to misidentify the problem, to convey the impression that the problem is in this one relationship, and to make the triangle more fixed and less reversible. There may be transient anxiety relief from direct expression of anger, but to focus on this dimension makes the family maladaptive. The mild symptom expressed only under stress is evidence of a good level of emotional compensation.

The next major shift in the family came as I and my brothers left for college. My grandmother died suddenly a few months before my second brother left for the Army. In the following five years there were several changes. My uncle married and established his own home, my parents and two sisters moved to a house in town, and the old family home was rented. My first brother, who was established away from home, married shortly before entering the Army. During the war my second brother, and then I, were married while in the Army. A few months later my older sister married and joined her husband who was away in war industry. My younger sister was in college during the war. My parents were alone at home. It was difficult to find employees during the war, so my mother devoted full time to helping my father and uncle run the business. There developed a different version of the family triangle, a familiar one in family systems. My uncle and his wife constituted one corner of the triangle; she tended to verbalize her discontent outside the family, and she was seen as the cause of problems in periods of stress.

After the war there was need for young ideas and energy to rebuild the business, which had been merely maintained during the war. My second brother returned with his family to start as an employee with an understanding that he would ultimately have his share of the business. Also, my older sister and her husband returned, and he resumed his employment in the business. A few years later my younger sister and her husband moved back to help in the business. My second brother, as energetic in business and civic activity as our father, was the motivating force in the successful growth of the business. Emotional forces were operating for this brother to become the "head of the clan" and for my younger sister to succeed my mother as the responsible woman in the next generation. Within the family there were a variety of triangles and shifting emotional alignments on lesser issues, but the original triangle pattern continued on major issues. Now the triangle consisted of my father and brother at one corner, my mother and younger sister at another, and my uncle and his wife at the other. During periods of stress the negative issues were expressed between my father and brother on one side and my uncle and his wife on the other. Stress occurred around the issue of expansion of the business and when my brother pressed for his share of the business. Since the family lived in five separate households, there was more of a tendency for family issues to be confided to friends outside the family. With each period of stress there would be discussion about dividing the business, some new recognition of my brother's contribution, and a new period of calm. This sequence continued until the time came when, in a new period of stress, my uncle sold his half to my second brother and retired. The business was reorganized as a corporation, with my brother holding half of the stock and my father and mother each holding one fourth. The family, which had regarded my uncle as the bad guy who stood in the way of progress, tended to see the new arrangement as the final solution. This is another predictable characteristic of emotional systems: When the focus of the symptom is removed from the system, the system acts as if the problem is solved. If the system could think instead of react, it would know that it would be only a matter of time until the symptom surfaced elsewhere. This event in my family occurred after I had learned much about families from research but before I had begun my active effort to use the knowledge in my family of origin. However, I made some postulations about the next area in which symptoms would develop. The next part of the clinical presentation will deal with the course of events for the ten years after the reorganization of the business.

My posture to my family of origin during this period was one of kidding myself that I was "detached" and "objective" and that I was "staying out of the family problem." This stance is the most common misperception that people have when they first begin to become better observers and to be less emotionally reactive in their own families. Actually, I was almost as emotionally involved as ever, and I was using emotional distance and silence to create an illusion of nonresponsiveness. Distance and silence do not fool an emotional system.

Concepts Important in the Differentiation of a Self

New concepts from family research and family psychotherapy provided exciting new ways for understanding my own family that had never been possible with individual concepts. The new ideas were applied to my own family, and other immediate emotional systems, by the time they were fairly well formulated. Observations and experience from my own living situation also made contributions to the family research. Most of the effort went to my own nuclear family (my wife and children), which is a story all in itself. I considered my family of origin as important in understanding my nuclear family, but less important in helping the nuclear family resolve its problems. Very early in clinical work with families, I tried to correlate each pattern in my nuclear family with similar patterns in family of origin. This effort was followed by a short period of precise focus on my nuclear family, with the premise that focus on the family of origin avoided the most important issues in my nuclear family. Gradually I focused more and more on my family of origin, culminating in the present effort being described here. The following is a series of concepts that were important in the effort to differentiate a self in my own family of origin.

Multigenerational Family History

My initial effort in this area was motivated by a research interest. Early in family research I began structured studies to trace the transmission of family characteristics from one generation to another. This was part of the effort to define the "Multigenerational Transmission Process," one of the concepts in the theory. Then I developed a special interest in the transmission of illness patterns from generation to generation. Each facet of the study provided interesting new leads to follow. Thousands of hours went into a microscopic study of a few families, in which I went back as far as 200 or 300 years, and I traced the histories of numerous families back 100 years or more. All families seemed to have the same basic patterns. This work was so time-consuming that I decided it was more sensible to study my own family. My goal was to get factual information in order to understand the emotional forces in each nuclear family, and I went back as many generations as it was possible to go. Until this time I had no special interest in family history or genealogy. In less than ten years, working a few hours a week, I have acquired family tree knowledge about twenty-four families of origin, including detailed knowledge about one that I traced back 300 years, another 250 years, and several that were traced back 150 to 200 years. The effort brought me into contact with genealogists who were surprised that I was as interested in family members who did poorly as those who did well. This is tedious work in the beginning, but a surprising amount of detail can be obtained once the effort is underway.

It is difficult to estimate the direct contribution of family historical information to the understanding of one's family in the present. I believe the indirect contributions are great enough to warrant the effort by anyone who aspires to become a serious student of the family. In only 150 to 200 years an individual is the descendent of 64 to 128 families of origin, each of which has contributed something to one's self. With all the myths and pretense and emotionally biased reports and opinions, it is difficult to ever really know "self" or to know family members in the present or recent past. As one reconstructs facts of a century or two ago, it is easier to get beyond myths and to be factual. To follow a nuclear family of 200 years ago from marriage through the addition of each new child, and then to follow the life course of each child, can provide one with a different view of the human phenomenon than is possible from examining the urgency of the present. It is easier to see the same emotional patterns as they operated then, and one can get a sense of continuity, history, and identity that is not otherwise possible. More knowledge of one's distant families of origin can help one become aware that there are no angels or devils in a family; they were human beings, each with his own strengths and weaknesses, each reacting predictably to the emotional issue of the moment, and each doing the best he could with his life course. My work on multigenerational family history was in progress during most of the period of this report.

Undifferentiated Ego Mass in Family of Origin

I have already mentioned early observations about the emotional phenomenon where I worked, which I later came to call the undifferentiated family ego mass. The same mechanism operated on visits to my family of origin. I made increasing observations about the phenomenon but had no clues about effective action for maintaining objectivity while still in contact with the family. I had long since tried the conventional things for dealing with family emotional situations, such as talking openly to family members about problems, both individually and in groups. The model for this method came from the early experience with family psychotherapy in which open discussion about problems seemed to help. Discussions about family issues seemed to make the family system calmer, but they made the fusions more intense and it was more difficult to get back to objectivity later. When the family was calm it was possible to go several hours or a day before fusing into taking sides on emotional issues. If the family was tense, the fusion could occur on first contact with a key person in the family system. Objectivity would usually return within an hour or two after the visit while enroute home. Then came the theoretical notion of the "undifferentiated family ego mass" and some early principles about "differentiating a self." These principles will be discussed further later. From experience I had learned that the effort to define or differentiate a self is most effective if one is "outside" the emotional system, or before one becomes fused into the system. Since trips home were infrequent, the goal was to maintain objectivity as long as possible and to find ways to extricate myself from the fusion, all during the same visit. One effort was to leave my wife and children at home while I visited among extended family in town. When I became "fused" into the system I would return home and relate intensively to my nuclear family, hoping this would extricate me from the fusion and permit another period of objectivity with the extended family. This plan never worked. In discussions, my wife would communicate some terrible something a sister or my sister-in-law had said or done, indicating that my nuclear family had also "fused into the family system," even though it was relatively isolated from the larger family system. Usually I regained objectivity within an hour or two after the visit had ended. Based on this experience, I tried another technique to extricate myself. I planned two-day visits with the extended family, following which I would "leave" with my wife and children for a two-day subvacation 100 miles or so away; this technique was designed to extricate myself from the "fusion" and to permit another period of objectivity for a second visit. This plan also never worked. It was as if I could not extricate myself until that visit was over and I was an hour or so enroute home. I made one final effort using this technique. This one was based on the experience that it was easier for me to do it alone than with wife and children. When professional trips permitted, I would visit a day or so with my parental family before the meeting in some distant state, and then would make a brief visit after the meeting. This worked somewhat better than the subvacation plan with my wife and children, but I never really regained objectivity until an hour or two after the second visit had ended. During the years that I tried these various techniques, I was also working at "defining a self" by letter and telephone calls with my family of origin, while I also worked at "defining a self" in other emotional systems, such as the effort with the "family" of family therapists. A partial success in a more peripheral emotional system would contribute something to the effort with my family of origin, but significant success had to wait until I obtained a better mastery of the concept of triangles.

My own experience with fusion into the undifferentiated ego mass of my family of origin is remarkably consistent with what I have observed in a broad spectrum of reasonably well-integrated families with whom I have worked in my teaching and practice. I have never seen a family in which the "emotional fusion" phenomenon is not present. Theoretically, emotional fusion is universal in all except the completely differentiated person, who has not yet been born. Usually, most people are not aware of the phenomenon. There are those who can become aware if they can learn to observe more and react less to their families. There are others so intensely "fused" they probably can never know the world of emotional objectivity with their parents. Few people can be objective about their parents, see and think about them as people, without either downgrading or upgrading them. Some people are "comfortably" fused and others so "uncomfortably" fused they use hate or a covert negative attitude (either is evidence of fusion) to avoid contact with parents. There are those of "positive fusion" who remain so attached they never leave home. There are also those who kid themselves into believing they have "worked out" the relationship with parents and who make brief formal visits home without personal communication; they use as evidence of maturity that they do not see their parents. In my work with families, the effort is to help people become aware of the phenomenon and then to make brief frequent trips home to observe and work at differentiation. Frequent short visits are many times more effective than infrequent long visits.

The Differentiation of a Self

Each small step toward the "differentiation" of a self is opposed by emotional forces for "togetherness," which keeps the emotional system in check. The togetherness forces define the family members as alike in terms of important beliefs, philosophies, life principles, and feelings. The forces constantly emphasize the togetherness by using "We" to define what "We think or feel," or the forces define the self of another such as, "My wife thinks that . . . ," or the forces use the indefinite "It" to define common values, as in, "It is wrong" or "It is the thing to do." The togetherness amalgam is bound together by assigning positive value on thinking about the other before self, living for the other, sacrifice for others, love and devotion and compassion for others, and feeling responsible for the comfort and well being of others. If the other is unhappy or uncomfortable, the togetherness force feels guilty and asks, "What have I done to cause this?" and it blames the other for lack of happiness or failure in self.

The differentiating force places emphasis on "I" in defining the foregoing characteristics. The "I position" defines principle and action in terms of, "This is what I think, or believe" and, "This is what I will do or will not do," without impinging one's own values or beliefs on others. It is the "responsible I" which assumes responsibility for one's own happiness and comfort, and it avoids thinking that tends to blame and hold others responsible for one's own unhappiness or failures. The "responsible I" avoids the "irresponsible I" which makes demands on others with, "I want, or I deserve, or this is my right, or my privilege." A reasonably differentiated person is capable of genuine concern for others without expecting something in return, but the togetherness forces treat differentiation as selfish and hostile.

A family system in emotional equilibrium is symptom free at any level of differentiation. The system is disturbed when any family member moves toward regression. The system will then operate to restore that former symptom-free level of equilibrium, if that is possible. The family system is also disturbed when any family member moves toward a slightly higher level of differentiation, and it will move as automatically to restore the family system to its former equilibrium. Thus, any small step toward differentiation is accompanied by a small emotional upheaval in the family system. This pattern is so predictable that absence of an emotional reaction is good evidence that the differentiating effort was not successful. There are three predictable steps in the family reaction to differentiation. They are: 1) "You are wrong," or some version of that, 2) "Change back," which can be communicated in many different ways, and 3) "If you do not, these are the consequences." If the differentiating one can stay on course without defending self or counterattacking, the emotional reaction is usually brief and the other then expresses appreciation. The clearest examples of the steps in differentiation occur in family psychotherapy with husband and wife. The following is a typical example: One couple in family therapy spent several months on issues about the togetherness in the marriage. They discussed meeting the needs of each other, attaining a warm, loving relationship, the ways each disappointed the other, and the making of joint decisions. They discovered new differences in opinion as the process continued. Then the husband spent a few weeks thinking about himself, his career, and where he stood on some central issues between him and his wife. His focus on himself stirred an emotional reaction in the wife. Her anxiety episode lasted about a week as she begged him to return to the togetherness, and then went into a tearful, angry, emotional attack in which she accused him of being selfish, self-centered, incapable of loving anyone, and an inadequate husband. She was sure the only answer was divorce. He maintained his calm and was able to stay close to her. The following day the relationship was calm. At the next therapy session she said to her husband, "I liked what you were doing but it made me mad. I wanted to control what I was saying but it had to come out. All the time I was watching you, hoping you would not give in. I am so glad you did not let that change you." They were on a new and less intense level of togetherness which was followed by the wife starting on a self-determined course, with the husband then reacting emotionally to her efforts at differentiation.

In this example, the husband's effort represented a small step toward a better level of differentiation. Had he yielded to her demand, or attacked, he would have slipped back to her level. When he held his position, her emotional reaction represented a pull-up to his level. This theoretical orientation considers this sequence a basic increase in bilateral differentiation which can never return to the former level. On the new level they both have different attitudes about togetherness and individuality. They say things like, "We are much more separate but we are closer. The old love is gone. I miss it sometimes but the new love is calmer and better. I know it sounds crazy but that's how it is."

The course of differentiation is not as smooth and orderly when one person attempts it alone in his family of origin. One reason has to do with the diversity of issues about which each can take an "I position." Differentiation cannot take place in a vacuum. It has to take place in relation to others, around issues important to both people. A marriage contains an endless supply of issues important to both spouses if they can disentangle self from the emotional system in order to define the issues. Differentiation also has to be in the context of a meaningful relationship in which the other has to respect the belief and the action stand that affirms it. One who affirms a "self" around issues that can be ignored is quickly labeled a fool. It is more difficult to find meaningful issues in a family of origin when one has little or no contact with its members.

The long-term efforts to define my own self in my family of origin have had significant effects, but the year-to-year results have been disappointing. All too often the family would ignore the effort. However, my attempts did result in principles applied successfully in professional practice that were later used with my family of origin in the clinical example to be discussed later. A family system in quiet emotional equilibrium is less amenable to the discussion of emotional issues, or change, than a family system in tension or stress. My most meaningful visits have been during an illness or hospitalization of a significant family member. In coaching others with their families, I encourage visits when the system is emotionally fluid or during family upsets such as deaths, serious illness, reunions, weddings, or other stressful or significant family events.

The Parental We-ness

Until I had experience in family research, I subscribed to the principle that parents should "present a united front to their children." This belief is so common that it has come to be regarded as a basic psychological principle. Certainly I heard this often enough in my own professional training and it is commonly presented as a sound principle in the literature on child rearing. The reasoning states that the united front is necessary to "prevent the child from playing off one parent against the other." Before family research I believed that parents tended to become divided in their approach to children and it was necessary to remind them to discuss differences about the children in private and to present a united front in dealing with the child. With family research I developed the conviction that this dictum is one of the most unsound psychological principles.

All families with whom I have had experience have arrived at the principle of the united parental front on their own. Most sophisticated families tend to present this dictum as a modern principle of child rearing and less sophisticated families present it as a culture-bound principle about children obeying their parents. There is evidence that parents automatically invoke this principle because it makes the parents more comfortable and not because it is good for the child. There are numerous variations of this principle in the triangle between parents and child, but the most frequent pattern is the one in which mother becomes unsure of herself in relation to the child and seeks the father's approval and support. Observation of families in family psychotherapy indicates that parents tend to develop more individual relationships with the child as the family improves.

This phenomenon can be considered from several different levels. On a clinical level, the "parental we-ness" presents the child with a parental amalgam which is neither masculine nor feminine and it deprives the child of knowing men by having an individual relationship with his father, and knowing women from the relationship with his mother. From the standpoint of triangles, the "parental we-ness" presents the child with a locked-in "two against one" situation which provides no emotional flexibility unless he can somehow manage to force a rift in the other side of the triangle. From a theoretical standpoint, the poorly defined selfs of the parents fuse into a common self and it is this that becomes the "parental we-ness." Early in family psychotherapy I began working toward developing an individual relationship between each parent and the child. Nothing but good things have come from this principle. Once the effort goes toward developing an individual relationship between each parent and the child, it is possible to see the intensity of the parental effort to re-establish the "parental we-ness." There are some situations in which the parents fuse into a common self so automatically that it is difficult to establish individual relationships. When it is possible to separate the parental we-ness early, the change in the child is usually rapid and dramatic. Even a very young child is capable of managing a relationship to either parent.

Very soon after working out the principle of each parent having an individual relationship with each child, I began to apply it in my nuclear family. The full implications of this principle, however, were not realized until I knew about the "person-to-person" relationship principle and had more awareness about triangles. The results of these efforts in my family of origin will be presented in another section.

The Person-to-Person Relationship and Related Principles

The person-to-person relationship will be discussed in conjunction with other principles from which it was derived. Early in family research I observed the striking calm and the rapid change in families when one family member could begin to "differentiate a self" in chaotic, disturbed families. This phenomenon would occur after the anxious family had been submerged in symptoms and paralyzed by the inability to arrive at a joint decision for action. Eventually one member, unable to speak for the whole family, would begin to define where he stood on a issue and what he intended to do and not do. Almost immediately the entire family would become calmer. Then another family member would begin a version of the same process. Those families were too impaired for any member to maintain this operating position over long periods of time, but the observations provided ideas for theory and clinical experimentation in less impaired families. In the midst of these observations on families, I noted chaotic upsets within the research staff; staff members complained about each other and efforts to resolve differences in group discussions were unsuccessful. Using a principle developed from the research, I, the director, set out to define my role, and stated my long-term plans and intentions as clearly as possible. The "togetherness" group meetings were terminated. In the course of this rather exacting self-imposed assignment, I realized the degree to which I had infantilized the staff members by instructing them and even functioning for them, while I had been irresponsible in failing to do other things that came within my own area. Almost immediately the staff tension subsided and then another and another of the staff members began to define their responsibilities. Thereafter there were few staff upsets that could not be settled within hours instead of days. This same principle has been used frequently since then in all kinds of clinical, work, and family situations.

The principle of defining a self was later used in a modified form within my entire extended family network. The various nuclear families in the extended family system tend to group themselves into emotional clumps and the communication is often from "clump to clump" rather than from individual to individual. It was common for letters to be addressed to "Mr. and Mrs.____ and Family," or to "Mr. and Mrs.___," and often each nuclear family had one letter writer who would write for the entire family. I had used carbon copy letters to disseminate family information to multiple family members. This method was used during the period I was working on the multigenerational family history and I had more occasion to write than usual. The new plan was to define myself as a person as much as possible and to communicate individually to a wide spectrum of extended family members; I tried to establish as many individual relationships within the family as possible. Every possible opportunity was used to write personal letters to every niece and nephew. The less differentiated family segments still tended to reply with letters to my entire family, but more and more some began to write personal letters addressed to my office, and since they were addressed to me personally, my family never saw them. The return on this endeavor is like a long-term dividend; it has modified my image within the entire family.

Another project was the development of a "person-to-person" relationship with each of my parents and also with as many people as possible in the extended family. A "person-to-person" relationship is conceived as an ideal in which two people can communicate freely about the full range of personal issues between them. Most people cannot tolerate more than a few minutes on a personal level. When either party becomes anxious, he begins talking about a third person (triangles in another person), or the communication becomes impersonal and they talk about things. My immediate goal was to work toward a person-to-person relationship with each parent. Although I made some effort to develop this type of relationship with extended family members by writing letters to individuals, my effort with my parents was more intensive. In such an effort, one encounters every rejection, alliance, and resistance that are present in emotional systems everywhere. In disciplining the self to do this, one develops versatility and emotional courage in all relationships, one learns more about people than in most endeavors, and the family profits too. In some family situations the positive results are sweeping, both for the family and the one who initiated the effort. These experiences were used in clinical practice, which in turn made contributions to the effort with my own family. Most of the patterns in my family are present in all families to some degree. In practice, for instance, a nuclear family out of meaningful emotional contact with families of origin is more vulnerable to intense symptoms, and the problems tend to be more chronic than in families that maintain contact with parental families. The nuclear family is usually reluctant to face the emotional forces that led to isolation, but if they can know that successful establishment of meaningful emotional contact (an infrequent duty visit is not meaningful contact) usually decreases tension in the nuclear family, they are more motivated to make the effort. Progress is several times faster in the nuclear family that is in contact with families of origin than in the nuclear family that is isolated.

Person-to-Person Relationships in the Parental Triangle

In clinical work with other families, I discovered that the pattern in my own family is the most common one in all families. My mother was the most active parent on most issues that had to do with her children. She made it her business to know what went on everywhere with the children. My father played a more peripheral role except on certain issues that came within his sphere of activity. He had to do with money issues, though it was within the rules of the system to speak to my mother before speaking to my father. He always made himself part of the action when anxiety issues developed between my mother and the children, and he made effective comments and actions to allay my mother's anxiety. From early childhood I participated in special activities with my father that did not include my mother. Much was oriented around work chores, but there were also frequent hunting and fishing trips, and in my teen years I took frequent business trips by car with him. We had long conversations about issues of special interest, but a smaller amount of time was spent on personal issues. He had boundless knowledge about nature and observations about wildlife, too little of which has been remembered in my years of urban living. Mother was the letter writer. My father's letters were usually brief and to the point, usually centered around money matters while I was in college. After I left college his letters to me were less frequent. My mother usually wrote for the family and signed her name, and my letters to my parents were addressed to "Mr. and Mrs."

It was a theoretical idea, rather than personal experience, that directed my effort over many years to differentiate myself from my family of origin, and to use the person-to-person relationship for a central part of the effort. At that time I knew a little about "triangles" but I did not have many techniques for using the knowledge to extricate myself from the emotional system. It took much more than the person-to-person relationship to get free of the emotional binds of the triangle, but that will be described later. My first effort with my parents consisted of writing individual letters to each of them. This method did not change the basic pattern. My mother still wrote for both even though her letters became a bit more personal. Then I made an effort utilizing telephone calls. When I telephoned, the usual sequence was one in which my father would answer and within seconds he would call my mother who would do most of the talking from an extension. My goal was to engage him in conversation longer, but this never worked. I rehearsed dialogue designed to talk straight to him but very soon he would either refer the issue to her for comment, or she would cut in and talk for him. If I asked him to silence her so we could talk, she would start a dialogue about that. I have never been effective in using the telephone for this effort. There was always the problem of others on extensions and I could not develop effective feedback.

Time with each parent alone is essential for establishing an individual relationship, but mere private talk with a single parent can accomplish little. One has to be aware that one was "programmed" into the system long ago and it is automatic for both parties to fall back on familiar patterns. An optimum condition for such a relationship is to find a subject of interest to both that does not involve the rest of the family. Each person has his own built-in resistance to working at such a relationship. I have sent people on special missions to parental families and have then had them report that it was impossible to get parents separated, or that there was not an "ideal time" for talking, or that they had postponed the effort until the last few hours, when the effort turned out to be inept. The experience with my parents paralleled that of many. With my father, it was hard to find personal subjects and difficult to keep a conversation alive. When I did introduce a personal subject, he would invoke the parental we-ness and respond with, "Mother thinks. . ." With my mother it was easy to keep conversation alive, but she would invoke triangles by talking about other people and it was just as difficult to keep the discussion on a person-to-person level. My overall aim was to keep the conversation alive with my father, and to eliminate the triangles with my mother. With my father, I tried to prepare long lists of subjects ahead of time, but this was not the answer. To many issues he would respond with minimal comment, the list would be exhausted, and again there would be the uncomfortable silence.

There were some special occasions when I made more progress on the person-to-person relationships than all other times together. Two of these occurred at times of sickness. The first occasion occurred when my father was in the hospital after a moderately severe heart attack. This occasion provided the opportunity to talk about his fears of death, his philosophy of life, and the life goals and aspirations he may not have expressed otherwise. Another occasion occurred when my mother had major elective surgery. There were days with her in the hospital and evenings with my father at home alone. It was there also that I discovered the value of past history as a subject for personal communication. Most people are eager to talk about their own early life experiences to those interested in listening. I was working on the multigenerational family history at that time and I was eager for all that could be remembered. The next opportunity came a year or two later with my mother. In my work on past generations I had discovered a whole segment of her side of the family that she did not know existed. It covered a period from 1720 to 1850 when this segment had moved west. The family name was well-recorded in the area and there were cemeteries where they were buried, churches where they worshipped, lands they had owned, houses they had built, and other items of personal and family interest. I arranged a week-long automobile trip with her to visit all these places. That was a solid week of intense person-to-person contact with very little talking about others. This trip with my mother will be mentioned in the personal experience to be reported later.

In addition to the effort to develop a person-to-person relationship with my parents, I had also continued the effort to "detriangle" myself from the parental triangle. Since the "detriangling" was much more prominent in later family events, the description of that process will be only briefly described. The process of "differentiating a self " from a parental family involves two major steps. The first step is to develop the person-to-person relationships. This step helps to bring relationships more alive, it helps one to recognize old patterns that may have faded from view, and most of all, it results in livelier family response to the effort to "detriangle" or change the old patterns. A parental family can ignore such detriangling moves if relationships are distant. In this report, I have put more emphasis on the person-to-person relationship in relation to triangles than I do in my current work in "coaching" others with their families. There are two reasons for this emphasis. The first is the importance of the person-to-person relationship as a part of the total scheme. The second is that the person-to-person relationship method was in use before the detriangling process was well understood.

Up to this point in my family effort, I had incorrectly assumed that I could differentiate a self from my family of origin by differentiating a self from my parents. I believed that if I accomplished this step well I would not have to bother with all the other triangles in which my parents were imbedded. The notion about interlocking triangles had been in use almost ten years but I had not integrated this aspect of the theory into the work with my own family. As I developed increasing facility with triangles, and as the expected result had not been achieved, it became clear that some kind of a different effort was in order.

The original observation about the undifferentiated ego mass of my family of origin was always an overall guide. My overall goal, it will be recalled, was to be able to have an entire visit with the family without becoming fused into the emotional system. Though the result from all my various efforts with the family had been satisfying, especially the effort at developing person-to-person relationships, I still had not significantly increased the length of time before I would become "fused" into the family system when I visited, nor had I found a way to extricate myself before the visit had ended. The remainder of this report represents a new era in the family effort.

The Family History—Continued

After the reorganization of the family business, there was no obvious disharmony in the primary triangle of my father, mother, and second brother. My original postulation was that the negative side of the triangle would have to occur between my brother and mother, but this prediction was based entirely on theory and knowledge about triangles and not on experience from the past nor anything observed in the family. The relationship between my father, mother, and second brother had always been such a congenial one that it would be hard to conceive of friction between them. Even though I had become enough of a specialist to be a part-time consultant in organizational problems in business, and even with my relatively close contact with the family and my prediction about the next area of disharmony, it was not possible to get definite evidence to confirm my postulation nor to suggest an alternative one. There were superficial discontents expressed here and there between the children and their spouses, or between cousins, but there was no definite pattern and these problems seemed to belong more to everyday minor issues than to basic issues in the central family triangle. I even looked for a common pattern that emerged from my multigenerational studies; it had been predicted that conflict between siblings would be perpetuated by the descendents of these siblings far into future generations. It took some time for a definite pattern to emerge in my family. There are several factors which affect the emergence of the pattern, including the basic adaptability of the family (conflict does not occur between people if the adaptability is good), the absence of stress of sufficient degree to cause symptoms to surface, and the number of subtriangles to absorb minor levels of disharmony.

This pattern in my family is identical to many that exist in businesses and staffs of institutions in which the basic problem which exists on the highest administrative level is triangled and retriangled again and again until the conflict surfaces between two employees low in the administrative hierarchy. The three areas in which "undifferentiation" are absorbed in a nuclear family are marital conflict, sickness or dysfunction in a spouse, and projection to one or more children. The total amount of undifferentiation, determined by the basic level of differentiation in the family, is distributed primarily to one area, or any combination of the three areas. In my parental family the level of conflict is very low, the primary mechanism is projection to a child (lower life adjustment of oldest sister), and the other mechanism is physical illness, usually brief medical or surgical illnesses. These areas provide clues about symptoms when family stress mounted.

Aside from the little subsystems of anxiety and concern in each nuclear family, the prevailing stress in my total family was connected with the business. Early in this period, my second brother developed a brief symptom slightly suggestive of a malignancy. Since the "go power" for the family rested with him, anxiety went very high for a week until the possibility of malignancy was ruled out. Thereafter, the stress was related more to health issues in my parents and disposition of the business in case of their deaths. My parents were getting quite old and each serious-appearing illness in either sent out some kind of an alarm, and precipitated some kind of family reaction. The basic reaction in the central family triangle included my father at one corner, my mother, youngest sister, and sister's husband at another, and my second brother and his nuclear family at the other. One of the first changes in the postorganizational period (from my standpoint) was a cool distance between my second brother and me, initiated by him. He and I had always been close, and this I realized in retrospect, continued until the business was reorganized. After that, he was congenial enough in our brief exchanges, but his business and civic activities were demanding. During the period I was working on person-to-person relationships, he was the one important family member with whom it was not possible to develop a relationship. Time planned to see him alone would be converted into a social event. When it became evident that he was avoiding me, I became more persistent in my effort to see him, and he became equally persistent in avoiding me. When I made a summer trip home, he and his wife took a vacation away during the entire period of my visit. Here was a situation where two of the most important figures in the family system could not get together! He was important at home and I was important because of my position as "oldest" and because I had made myself important through my various efforts. As the distance between my second brother and me increased, the stories about him increased. I was hearing all about him and he was probably hearing all about me from the family network, but I could not see him. He rarely wrote letters, so that communication was cut off.   One summer   I   made   a concerted effort to meet with my second brother. Expecting that he might again leave during my visit, I waited until the last possible moment, about two days before, to announce my visit. He and his wife left on a trip the following day and returned a few hours before my family was scheduled to leave, just long enough to exchange greetings and superficial comments. The trend of events that are the subject of this presentation began about six weeks later.

An important triangle at work at this time was the one between my mother, my second brother, and me. I had worked very hard on the triangle with my parents and me, assuming that my problem would be solved. Now a new version of the problem had been displaced onto the new triangle. When conflict arose in the business, my mother would communicate by some means, if not directly, that I was on her side, and my brother would react as if this was reality. I began to perceive some of this development on trips. The process would emerge in the form of gossip-type stories which in an emotional system communicate, "We two are together on this issue. We are in agreement about that other third person." One of the better ways to disengage from such a triangling "secret" communication is to go to the third person and report the message in a neutral way. I was out of effective contact with my second brother then and the only move I could make was to tell my mother that I was neutral. She would say that she respected my position and I would assume she was acting neutral about me with others. I would leave town and the family would react as if I was on her side.

Action is required when words fail to detriangle in emotional systems. My mother has always used "secret" communications to facilitate her position in the emotional system. One of my early responses to her communication was to listen, and I thought I could listen without taking sides. In retrospect, this maneuver was one of the key triggers for my early fusions into the emotional system. Listening to such communications without response, pretending that one is not involved, does not fool an emotional system. When I was aware that "no response" was not effective, I began using comments such as, "That's one of the better stories." This method was a little more effective. In retrospect, I undoubtedly was responding while I kidded myself that I was neutral. I had worked much more actively on the triangle with my father, mother, and myself and I had been more effective in detriangling from that. There had been several exchanges about "secrets" that turned the tide in that area. The first one was a letter in which mother communicated some negative story about my father. In the next mail I wrote to my father to say that his wife had just told me this story about him, and I wondered why she told me instead of telling him. He showed the letter to her, and she fussed about not being able to trust me. Several letters such as this, plus similar exchanges when I was with both parents, had been reasonably effective at detriangling me from them. During that period, mother made comments about my reading too much between the lines, and I made comments about her writing too much between the lines.

The triangling pattern in my family of origin, which is the usual one in all emotional systems, was most intense during stress periods. Various family members were grouped on the corners of the primary triangle, except that the grouping would be somewhat different, depending on the emotional issues. The two on the togetherness side of a triangle would talk about the outsider. With various versions of different issues being discussed in four separate households, and with me in reasonably good contact with them all, it was possible to keep a good reading of the family emotional tension. My first brother has hardly been mentioned in this report. His life-long position in the family has been one of moderate involvement and acting uninvolved, with statements that he would be willing to help anytime if he was needed but that he did not want to "just talk."

The Family Experience

Prologue

The important sequence of events began when my second brother's wife's brother died suddenly of a heart attack. He, like my second brother, was a vigorous business man who was "head of the clan" for his family in another state. His death left my brother's wife as the next most responsible member of her family of origin. The death of such an important family member can "shake" a family system for months. This was the "shock wave" phenomenon I had investigated in some early research, in which a death can be followed by a series of apparently unrelated human problems throughout the family system. This present situation had the characteristics of one in which there could be such a reaction. I reasoned that, sequentially, this death would "shake" my second brother's wife, that my second brother would help her assume responsibility in her family, that he would become involved in her deep anxiety, that my family would react to his anxiety, and the anxiety could amplify minor problems into major ones at vulnerable points in my family. My first thought was to observe carefully and possibly to lend some help if such did occur. About two weeks later there was an indirect report from friends that my older sister was in an anxious, upset state. She is so attuned to emotional forces in the family that a symptom in her is often an early indication of tension in the family system. There were indications that she was probably responding to the pressure in the larger family system rather than to her own nuclear family. The event was noted. About two weeks after that, there was an episode of overt disagreement in the central family triangle of sufficient intensity that it became an "alive" issue for discussion throughout the family. My second brother was pressing my parents for a small block of stock which would give him control of the family business. My father, in the togetherness side of the triangle with my second brother, was agreeable, but my mother was opposed. I had expected the "anxiety wave" issues that autumn to be expressed more as illness, and I was wondering how to deal with that kind of anxiety should the need arise. It is easier to deal with overt conflict than with internalized symptoms, and overt conflict is relatively rare in our family. My thoughts began spinning about ways I could utilize this conflictual episode to interrupt this anxiety wave for the family, and also to utilize it as a way to further my "differentiation of self." In such an anxiety wave period, the person with the most vulnerable heart can have a heart attack, a chronic illness can flare up, a teen-aged child can wreck a car or break a bone, or any of numerous other symptoms could develop in any member of the family. The overt conflict presented new ideas and challenges, but I did not have a clearly defined plan. I was scheduled for a trip home in about two months, so I had time to think the problem through and to devise a working plan. This is the wonderful thing about triangles. One can construct an amazingly accurate hypothesis from which it is possible to plan a predictable result if the differentiating one can contain his own emotional functioning enough to carry through.

About three weeks after the conflictual issue, my second brother was immobilized for several weeks with symptoms of a herniated vertebral disc.

The Plan

People treat families with great caution, lest the equilibrium be upset. There are situations that automatically disturb families, just as storms disturb a lake, but if one is trying purposely to disturb the surface of a lake, one finds how difficult it is. The carefully worked out specific plans for my visit to the family were some eight weeks in preparation. In my years of family research and therapy, I had diagrammed and successfully blueprinted my way through triangle webs for many other families and I wanted especially to make this effort work for my own family. The overall goal was to focus on the triangle involving my mother, second brother, and myself, and, preferably, also to include my father. With this configuration there would be the original triangle on which I had done most work, my parents and myself, plus the new triangle in which the conflict developed. My second brother and mother were central figures.

For some years my brother had been avoiding me. The issue of making contact with a family member who retreats and who refuses to relate to issues, had long been a special interest of mine. An immediate goal for this project, then, was to create a situation in which my brother would seek contact with me. It was the development of conflict between my mother and second brother that first motivated this plan; it is far easier to deal with conflict than other mechanisms in such an effort. My aim was to have a conflictual issue around which to work. The recent conflict over the business would still be sufficiently alive during the visit, but to focus on that would make that issue into a *reality* issue rather than a manifestation of an emotional system. In addition, I would be more vulnerable to being triangled with that issue. So, I devised the plan to stir up the family emotional system, using old issues from the past around which to work. Said in another way, the goal was to stir up a "tempest in a teapot" from issues of the past that would highlight the emotional patterns among the principal family members. One other item in the planning was a primary focus. In the past I had done fairly well in detriangling myself from one triangle, only to have the tension slip into another triangle; this pattern had been my undoing. In preparation for all the potential peripheral triangles that could align themselves with issues and prove difficult, I worked out a plan that permitted no "allies" in my effort. In other words, it was an effort to keep the entire family in one big emotional clump, and to detriangle any ally who tried to come over to my side for this project. I had used this rationale before on smaller emotional systems in my practice and I knew the principle was workable. A final part of the plan was to involve my first brother. He is an important part of the family and I wanted to find a way to include him too. Very early in my planning I called to tell him about the "awful conflict" in the family; that his help was needed; that I was going to be home on a specific date; and I urged that he return home to be part of this family effort. I was sure he would follow his usual pattern of treating the stock transfer as the reality issue, but I was prepared to deal with his introducing the topic of lawyers and determining which side was right.

My greatest effort went into preparing a long letter to my second brother. First I made a list of old emotional issues that focused on my relationship to him and his to me, the family system's relationship to him and to me, and relationships within his nuclear family. It was my purpose to have an issue for all key family members, especially issues that would touch each relationship cleanly. The letter was written and rewritten in order to eliminate hostile or derogatory comments. If the differentiating one becomes hostile or angry he is vulnerable to losing objectivity and either defending or counterattacking when the issues are hurled back at him. I played and replayed these issues so many times that I could be rather objective about each one. The more I did this, the more it was impossible for me to be angry with anyone. In fact, I had only heightened respect for my second brother who had functioned so well as "head of the clan" at home. I developed a special technique that avoided criticizing him. This technique was to relate "stories" I had heard about him, to tell him that everyone knew these stories but him, state that the family kept warning everyone not to tell him lest he get upset, and to ask why he had not bothered to know what people were saying about him. This sequence is present in every family system—the system talks about the absent one and the system has definite rules about keeping the gossiping "secret." In my letter, my posture to the "stories" was to say they had been going on for years, that some were interesting but most were boring, that the stories seemed to be embellished more during upset periods, that I had long since given up trying to separate fact from fiction in such stories, that I was tired of being admonished about what to tell him and what to avoid telling him and that this letter represented my right to communicate what I wanted to say directly to him without regard for what the system thought was good for him to hear. This technique, designed to present material in terms of "stories," proved so effective I have since employed it routinely in my practice. One always has an adequate supply of appropriate stories to be used for particular situations.

I started the letter by saying that I had wanted to talk to him for a long time but, since he had been away during my recent trips, I had to resort to putting my ideas onto paper. I mentioned that people were saying things about him in connection with the business that were similar to the stories they used to tell about our uncle. I said I did not understand how this had happened, but there it was. In order to touch on his nuclear family, I said there was a "story" about him and his wife being worried about a problem their son had, and that I had been warned to never say a word about it because he and his wife were so sensitive about it. In one paragraph I emphasized that I had no interest in who controlled the family business but that I recognized his contribution to the business and to the entire family. Then I wrote a full paragraph of "reversals," which is a psychotherapeutic principle I have long used of making a point by saying the opposite. This technique works predictably if the therapist is "outside" the emotional system and can be sufficiently casual and detached. Here was my brother who was working a 16-hour day for himself, his nuclear family, his parents, the whole extended family system, and all connected with it. He was doing a wonderful job, except that in periods of anxiety he became overly serious and emotionally "uptight." If I were to tell him to slow down and take it easy and not get so overly responsible for everyone, it would merely be what he has been telling himself and trying unsuccessfully to do. Therefore, the "reversals." I wrote him that I was "shifting gears from my previous posture," and would do something I did not ordinarily do—namely, I was going to give him some good sound advice. I implored him to be more responsible. I said that he had the responsibility for his parents and they were not appreciative enough. Maybe he had not worked hard enough to take care of them, or maybe the problem was in not forcing them to appreciate him better. In any case, he should limber up his back and give it the good old college try. I said that he had all the problems to solve in the business, he had to straighten things out with his parents, his wife and children needed more attention, he had additional problems in his wife's family, and there was an immediate problem with his sister's despondency. I ended the letter by saying that I would be home on a specific date, but since I had already said all that was necessary in the letter, it would not be necessary to see him unless he had something to say to me. I signed it, "Your Meddlesome Brother."

By calculation, this letter was mailed exactly two weeks before my trip home. In the same mail I wrote my first brother to tell him the exact date I would be home and I implied that if he cared about his family he would manage to get home on this date to help clear up this terrible situation. In all these letters, I used words such as terrible, awful, pressing, and horrible to describe the family plight. These words were all designed to stir up the "tempest in a teapot" for the purposes of the visit. I also wrote my oldest sister to say I had heard about her distressing upset and I had written her brother to help her out until I got there. I signed that letter, "Your Worried Brother." Then I waited exactly one week to call my parents under the guise of finding out who might meet the plane when I arrived one week later. Actually, I wanted a reading on the results of the letter. My mother said my brother was furious about "that" letter I had written him. I pretended I did not know what letter that could be, saying he had not written me in a long time and that I did not owe him a letter. She said he had several pages I had signed, that he was showing it to people, he was going to have it Xeroxed, and that he would take care of me when I arrived. I said I was distressed to hear that something had upset him but I would be glad to see him when I arrived. With this new information, I wrote several other letters within the next hour. One was to my younger sister, who lives near my parents and who functions as the responsible woman in the second generation. I wrote that I had just talked with our mother and had found that my second brother was upset about something I had said in a letter. I said that I found this hard to understand because all I had done was write some of my thoughts on paper and send them to him. I wrote that it was a mystery to me how thoughts that came out of my head could upset him. If he was upset, I said, I was deeply grieved because that could upset the whole family, and as "Big Mother" she had a responsibility to do whatever was necessary to soothe him with whatever Big Mothers do to calm people. I asked her to please treat my letter as confidential because I did not want to upset mother too, and to please advise me immediately what I could do to make amends to Little Brother. I said that if my thoughts were upsetting my second brother, maybe I could think different or "right" thoughts. I signed that letter, "Your Anxious Brother." In the same mail, within the hour, I wrote an exactly opposite message to my mother. I told her that I had known about that letter all the time but I was afraid to let her know because she might tell Little Brother and it would ruin my plan, which was going nicely thus far. I said that since I knew I could trust her (she had pledged me to thousands of secrets in the past), I would let her in on the strategy. I said that my plan was to get Little Brother really angry at me in order to draw the fire off the family situation at home. I told her that I had used a few little personal issues to warm him up, but that I had some big issues to fire him up if he cooled off during the week. I ended the letter by saying that this was all very confidential and that one "leak" would ruin the entire strategy—when one is planning strategy it is not advisable to invite the "enemy" to the briefing sessions. That letter was signed, "Your Strategic Son." Later I heard about my mother's reaction to this letter, which was to say, "I got the craziest letter. I did not know what to do with it, so I burned it." The day before the trip, I received a letter from my younger sister saying that my second brother had spent over two hours with my parents after he received the letter, that they thought it was horrible, and that he had apparently won them over to his side. She said that maybe this was one time Little Brother would not leave town when Big Brother came home—that he was mad enough to stay. She reported that he was really going to have it out with me when I arrived and that my older sister's husband was going to "back me into a corner to prove the lies I had been telling about his wife." Then she added that I had really stirred up the family and she hoped that my strategy worked. She ended up with, "I am back of you if I can be of help. I am really looking forward to your visit this time. It should be very interesting."

I hope the reader is clear about the purpose of these efforts. The conflicting messages were designed to prevent any one segment of the family from getting on my "side." Messages run back and forth in such a family system as if by telepathy. The only letter that was not shown to a circle of others was the "Strategic Son" letter to my mother. My younger sister was the only one reasonably outside the seriousness of the family emotional system, as was conveyed by her comment about looking forward to the "interesting" visit. A red flag had gone up from her comment about "I am back of you," which I handled by telling her that I was going to tell the family she had invited me home to help her with her Big Mother role. She retreated from taking sides with me by acting as if the issues I had raised were all very serious.

My younger sister and her husband and daughter met my wife and me at the airport. The trip was planned so that I would spend two days with my family, then three days at a medical meeting at which my wife's presence was desirable, and then two days back again with my family. My wife had no direct knowledge of what I was doing. From long experience, I have found that a differentiating effort routinely fails if anyone else knows anything about it. To be effective, each action and move must come from within the person who makes the effort. These decisions and actions often have to be made instantaneously and, for better or worse, the *individual* has the responsibility. To discuss the plan with another person *who is part of the system* invites certain failure. The first my wife knew of what was going on was when my younger sister began to discuss bits and pieces of the family events after our arrival at the airport. My wife did not ask a single question nor make positive or negative comments about my family at any time during the trip. This had never happened before. It was Saturday midnight when we arrived at my parents' home. The only comment my mother made about the family occurred Sunday morning when she said she hoped things could work out without hard feelings. I said I was glad she was still a good mother who worried about her children. There was not a word from any segment of the family on Sunday morning. Early Sunday afternoon we were invited to my younger sister's home for an early afternoon meal; included were both of my parents, my wife and myself, and my sister and her husband and daughter. Just as we finished desert and coffee, my second brother telephoned to say he had been checking around town to find me and he would be there in a few minutes. My brother was now seeking me out instead of me chasing him. The inclusion of him and his wife made this into the perfect group for this long-anticipated and rehearsed meeting. Every important triangle in the family system was represented. I had purposely stayed close to my parents all morning, hoping to facilitate a meeting of most of these people, but good fortune was with me when it worked out this way. My immediate goal was to avoid defending anything, or attacking any issues, to be able to avoid getting angry even with provocation, and to have an instant casual response to any comment.

My second brother exchanged pleasantries, but after a minute or two he took out "the letter" and said he was there to discuss the epistle I had written when I was drunk. I said that was an advantage in living where booze was cheap and that if his supply was low, I could get some good prices for him. The meeting went on for two hours and was all personal. The principals in the center were my brother, his wife, and me. My wife and my father were slightly out of the group. My mother moved around just back of the main group. Most of the conversation was between my brother and me and mother, with a few comments from my brother's wife. My brother had reacted most severely to a "story" about him that was similar to a story that had been told about our uncle. He threatened a libel suit against me. I agreed that it was awful to start such stories and I thought he should find out who started that story and prosecute the person to the full extent of the law. There was more talk about stories, and I expressed surprise he did not know what others said about him. I hoped he would pay more attention to the stories in the future, since he lived there all the time and I only heard them when I visited. His wife had reacted most to the story about their son, to which she said, "I always say nice things about your children." I responded, "I have heard nice stories about all of you, too. There was just not time to remember all of them." Then my brother and his wife began to report negative stories about me, to which I responded with some version of, "That was a fairly amusing one, but there have been some really good ones about me if you had just paid attention and listened better." Mother was pacing back and forth in the back, with comments such as, "I hope I do not die and leave a divided family." At one point toward the end of the meeting, my brother accused me of being in league with mother, and that the whole thing started when she and I took that trip together to see the lands of her ancestors. I said, "You are really intuitive about some things! How did you know about that? You're right. That's when she and I planned the whole thing." Mother responded vigorously with, "That's the biggest lie I ever heard! I will never tell you anything else again." I turned to my brother and said, "Now you see how she tries to wangle out of things when she is caught with the truth." At the end of the meeting, as my brother and his wife were leaving, his wife said, "I never saw such a family in all my life. I think we should do more talking to each other and less talking *about* each other."

The end of that Sunday afternoon was one of the most satisfying periods of my entire life. I had actively participated in the most intense family emotion possible and I had stayed completely out of the "ego mass" of my very own family! I had gone through the entire visit without being "triangled" or without being fused into the family emotional system. About two-thirds through the meeting I knew I had been succcessful for I noted that the family system had lost its emotional punch, and I knew that, if there was not some completely unanticipated event, I would go through the entire meeting without fusing into the system. Even if I had been slightly or moderately triangled, I would have more than achieved my primary mission for the visit, which was to interrupt the anxiety wave in the family. I *knew* that had been accomplished even by the time the family meeting was well underway. I also *knew* that my postulations about interlocking triangles were accurate by the time the family meeting started. To have completed the meeting without becoming triangled was additional evidence that I had attained the technical excellence to make the theoretical system work. It was the total success of the operation that was surprising, exhilarating, and exhausting. I had spent a dozen years pondering the structure and function of this "undifferentiated family ego mass" and I was so accustomed to each new effort being a partial success that I was hardly prepared for total success. It was equivalent to having finally mastered the secret of the system and having gone all the way to the goal line in one try. Since I believe that one's own life adjustment is dependent on working out a "self" in one's own family of origin, it was equivalent to having reached the summit after a hundred unsuccessful tries. To me the most important long-term accomplishment was the proof that an emotional system has a knowable structure and function, and that one can work out the predictable answers to its problems on a drawing board.

I knew there was follow-up work to be done on Monday, the day after the meeting. To make a differentiating process work, one has to continue in relationship with the family system. Said in another way, it is

necessary to keep talking to the system. This is the point where the feeling
system dictates withdrawal and comfortable distance, which will result in
the system "tightening up" again. On Monday, I knew my brother was still
angry and reactive and I would have to seek him out. I didn't want to go
see him, but I knew I had to; responsibility overcame the feelings. For the
first time in years, I found him alone and willing to talk. There was an
exchange of superficial pleasantry and then, after sufficient time to assure
myself that he would not mention the family issue about the business I
asked, "Are you still mad at me?" He responded with a detached, "Hell,
No!" Then I said that on my way to town I had heard some new stories
about him and would he be interested in what others were saying about
him? He responded with, "I do not want to hear any more stories." I
expressed surprise that a man in his position would not want to know what
people said about him, and that to keep him informed I would be willing
to write the stories on a piece of paper and send the paper in the mail. He
said he would return my mail unopened and unclaimed. I said that I found
his attitude hard to understand, but I would respect it, and instead I
would tell him a compliment I heard about him as I crossed the street. I
had heard someone say that his intentions were good most of the time. He
broke into a wide smile, the first of his old "friends winning" smile I had
seen in months. After that I had the first person-to-person talk I had had
with him in years. He talked about his effort with the larger family system,
his own family, and the business. During the course of this discourse he
talked about our oldest sister and how he had been trying to help her, and
how she seemed to defeat every effort. At one point he said, "Sometimes I
think she is retarded." Immediately after this long talk with him, I drove
down to see my older sister, and said, "Hey, Sis, I have been talking to
your brother about your problems and he said you refuse to listen to him.
What in the world have you been doing to him to make him talk like
that?" In previous years my "detriangling" efforts had been awkward and
forced. Now they flowed smoothly and automatically, and I no longer had
to discipline myself to do them. I made several more smooth "detriangling"
efforts with my parents. That same Monday I wrote a special letter to my
first brother, who had not come for the weekend. I chided him about his
delinquency and irresponsibility toward the family and reported that I had
been home all weekend trying to restore peace and harmony to the family,
but that the harder I tried the more I seemed to upset them. I said, "I have
been trying to establish free and open communications to calm them down.
All I did was tell them some of the stories you have been telling me about
them, and this seems to upset them instead of calm them. This weekend has
been a complete failure and I do not know where I failed. Since I have
failed, it is now up to you to get home immediately to deal with this

emergency situation." I later discovered he had been within 65 miles of home that weekend on a business trip, but that the pressure of business had made it impossible for him to get there.

My wife and I were away from home early Tuesday until late Thursday that week. Then we returned home until Saturday noon. For the first time in my life, I had been completely outside the family ego mass all week. There was no major effort on my part those last days, but merely a casual detriangling of each new situation that presented itself. My younger sister and her husband were even more casual and detached than before. They spoke of how "interesting" and "enjoyable" they found the sequence of events. My parents still voiced concern, but they were calmer than they had been in a long time. My brother's wife sought me out, and I had the first serious person-to-person talk with her in many years. Just before my departure, my second brother's younger son came to say goodbye to me, which was unusual for him. He said, "Thank you very much for coming home this week." A week after the trip, my first brother called to talk for an hour. I did much detriangling with him but it was clear that he and his wife were also relatively casual and "outside" the seriousness of the family issues. His wife later wrote me several letters to ask about my "plan and strategy." In the past I had been "undone" by partners and I was not about to get serious with her and risk spoiling my success. I told her I was hurt by her implications of deviousness on my part when I had spent so much time thinking good things about people and doing good things for them. I assured her that my only goal was to restore the basic love and togetherness in the family. Two weeks after the visit I received a long letter from my mother in which she included one concise paragraph about the visit. In it she said, "With all its ups and downs, your last trip home was the greatest ever." Immediately after the visit, I had written to my older sister again, chiding her about my continuing efforts to get various members of her family to "take care of her and her problems." She responded by kidding me for telling everyone else to take care of her while I did nothing to help take care of her. Then she said she was perfectly capable of taking care of herself, that she did not know where she had been for the last 40 years, but she had a new outlook and a new lease on life. The issue between my parents and brother about stock and control of the family business completely faded after that "family experience" weekend.

In the almost three-year interim since the family experience, the family has been on the best overall level of adaptation in many years. There have been anxieties and small crises, but they have been less intense than formerly. I have come to have a new role in the family which I call the role of "the differentiating one." I have had increasing experience with this phenomenon with others and the usual pattern is similar to that in my family. The one who achieves some success at differentiation has a kind of appeal for the entire family. It is as if any member of the family can approach this one and have the advantage of an emotionally detached viewpoint which in turn helps him or her develop a different perspective. It is more a matter of action than words because words often are negative while the action closeness is markedly better. The family sort of comes to expect the differentiating one always to function well in this position. For instance, there have been other periods of mild emotional "uptightness" in the family in which someone would invite me to get involved or return for a visit and would then administer a stern admonition, "But be sure you do not do or say anything to upset the family." This message is a subtle demand for another miracle performance, but differentiation is a self-motivated, self-energized effort and it cannot succeed with outside stimulus.

An interesting event occurred two years after "the experience." In my continuing multigenerational family history effort, I had discovered in a nearby county, a whole segment of my father's family that he had never known about. I arranged two trips to go with him alone to see the land they had owned and the houses where they had lived. Although I thought I had achieved a good person-to-person relationship with him from the former years, the time spent with him on those long drives was so enjoyable there was not time to talk about all the issues that came up automatically. At this time it was possible to talk about the full range of important subjects without avoidance or defensiveness, and we developed a far better relationship than we had ever had. This experience brought a new awareness that I simply did not know what constitutes a really solid person-to-person relationship. The day after those trips, my second brother asked if I had time for a drink before dinner. He and I spent another period going into issues important to both of us. During the talk he thanked me for what I had done for our father, and for all the effort that had gone into finding that segment of Dad's family. He said, "Dad is ten years younger now than he was when you started this effort." My view of the situation was slightly different. I believe that I had done something to change my relationship with my father, which in turn changed his relationship to all he contacted. I do think, however, that the work on his family was the issue around which the relationship changed.

Finally, there is the family perception of a "differentiating step" such as was described here. No two people who were present at that "family experience" or who participated from a distance would have the same view of what happened. A differentiating step has two sides. Only the differentiating one knows the logical, orderly thinking and planning that has to go into such an effort. If anyone else knows about it, then it is doubtful if any differentiation will result from the effort. The other side is the feeling, emotional response, and if this reaction does not occur there is strong doubt that any differentiation will take place. The initial family reaction is negative and takes the form of surprise, anger, and a "you must be crazy" attitude. When one person is doing a differentiating step the others react emotionally, and people do not think while they react. Immediately after the nodal point breakthrough, there will be certain family members who will offer a spontaneous "Thank you." If the differentiating one requests or demands an elaboration on the initial expression of appreciation, the response is automatically the opposite of what was expected. At this point there will be comments in the direction of the "togetherness" laws that govern the feeling side of the operation. The comments are likely to consist of devaluing or denying the importance of the event, or may even express a critical opinion if a complaint response is desired. A differentiating effort that is successful has to be for "self" alone. If it is done for self alone and the effort is successful, the system automatically benefits also. If it is done primarily to help others or with the expectation that others will approve and express appreciation, then the effort was for togetherness and not for differentiation; an emotional system does not appreciate such stressful nefarious maneuvers in the service of togetherness.

Post-Conference Clinical Experience

In the years before the breakthroughs with my own family, I had been using the theory, principles, and techniques involved in the differentiation of self in a method I called Family Psychotherapy With a Single Family Member. This method involved my "coaching" others as they attempted versions of what I have described with my own family. The results were good, but I still considered formal psychotherapy with husband and wife together to be the most effective of all methods. I urged members of the mental health professions to have formal family psychotherapy themselves as the best possible preparation for the practice of family psychotherapy. A good percentage of my private practice has been devoted to doing family psychotherapy with members of the mental health professions and their spouses; I considered this therapy also as training for the practice of family psychotherapy.

After the breakthrough with my own family of origin, I included my new knowledge about differentiation, illustrated with examples from my own family experience, in formal teaching sessions with psychiatric residents and others in training to learn family psychotherapy. On their own initiative, some of the trainees began to try some of the principles and techniques with their own families of origin. I would first hear about their efforts when they ran into the predictable emotional impasses and then asked for consultation about what had happened and for "coaching" to get themselves free. This coaching was done in the same didactic meetings in which the teaching was done. Over the next months, those who had been most successful with their families developed unusual skill and flexibility as family psychotherapists. They were adept at avoiding intense emotional entanglements with families in their practice, and they could work comfortably with upset and distraught families. They ascribed this ability as being related to their work with their own families, and a new perspective on what it meant to get "outside the family emotional system." The issue of family psychotherapy for these trainees and their spouses had not been considered. They were doing unusually well in their clinical work, and since my focus was on their efficiency as therapists, I paid little attention to their emotional functioning with their spouses and children. After a year or two I realized that the trainees who had devoted primary attention to their families of origin had automatically made as much, or even more progress, with their spouses and children as similar trainees who had been in formal family psychotherapy with their spouses for the same period of time. The experience with this new method provides strong indications that psychotherapy as we have known it in the past may one day be considered superfluous.

There are some tentative speculations I could make about the efficiency of defining a self in one's parental family. One speculation is that it is easier to make valid observations of emotional forces in the more removed, but equally important, parental family, than in the nuclear family in which one's needs are more intimately imbedded. It is also easier to take an action stand in the parental family than in the nuclear family. From my experience, any progress made with one's parental family is automatically translated into the nuclear family. Another speculation is that the parental family effort requires that the trainee more quickly accept responsibility for his own life, and requires him to accept the notion that he through his own effort can modify his own family system. A trainee is more on his own resources when he deals with the emotional reaction in his own family than when he sees his therapist with his spouse.

This approach to training family therapists is too new for there to be more than early clinical impressions. The method is certainly not for everyone. It requires hard work and dedication. It is not possible for a trainee to make progress until he can contain his own emotional functioning sufficiently to *know* the difference between being inside or outside of an emotional system. Until the trainee is partially outside the system, a differentiating technique is either hollow meaningless words or a hostile assault on the system, and an emotional system knows the difference and reacts accordingly. With trainees partially outside the system, it has been possible to help them avoid time consuming pitfalls, to focus on productive areas, and to achieve a reasonably good beginning process of differentiation in a fraction of the time that my effort required. At the time of my own breakthrough in differentiation, I considered it one of the most significant events in my personal life to that point. It is now proving to be a significant turning point in my professional life.

The presentation to the Family Research Conference included about fifteen minutes of my family history and a few background principles, followed by about fifteen minutes of the clinical experience. For listeners who did not have a reasonably firm grasp of my theoretical system, the brief presentation was mostly an emotional experience. From my standpoint, the goal for me and my family in this presentation was a reasonable success. It was not the success within the "family" of family therapists that the original experience had been with my own family, but the family therapists are not as important to me as my own family, and I was not motivated to work on them in such detail.* It is my opinion that most of the participants reacted emotionally to the presentation (it had been planned that way), and that most had no background to regard it as other than a bold, imaginative approach conceived and executed by an intuition that somehow knew what to do at the right time. I hope this present presentation has conveyed sufficient additional data for most to know that it was carefully thought through as a conceptual system and that the ability to execute the theoretical assumptions was developed after years of constant practice and modification of techniques to fit the theory. Most of the conference participants reacted as positively to the presentation as my family did. There were those who reacted emotionally to the extent that they considered the presentation to be selfish and hostile and hurtful, but even they were mostly positive in reserving an overall opinion. Were it not so, then differentiation would not be possible.

Since the 1967 conference there have been concerns from some quarters about my making public this personal report about my family. In the belief that my family is pretty much the same as all families, and that

---

*I might mention that there was one person present at the conference who sensed that part of the presentation was aimed at the "family" of family therapists. Carl Whitaker, whom I consider one of the most gifted and versatile of all family therapists, made the initial "triangling" move in the meeting with his comment about wishing that he was my brother (the great togetherness), which I dealt with (detriangled) by saying that he could not be my brother since Nathan Ackerman was already my brother. This resulted in some playful byplay on the same subject. My impression is that the emotional impact of the presentation did "one up" the others so well that few but Whitaker would have had a ready response.

my family is basically grateful for all the dividends that developed from my assumed role as "troublemaker," and in the deep belief that each in his own way, and each with a different reservation, would be basically pleased to have me do a public report about "us all," I had little reservation about this public report. As families move from the compartmentalized, less mature world of secrets and foibles which they assume they are keeping under cover, and into the world of permitting their private lives to be more open and a possible example for others to follow, they grow up a little each day.

REFERENCE

Toman, W. *Family constellation.* New York: Springer, 1960, 2nd ed., 1969.

Editor's Note: *The reader is reminded that the Conference participants heard only the final section of the former paper labelled "The Family Experience." The discussion following the original speech has been retained in its original form, even though it refers to a slightly different version of the presentation, inasmuch as the points made and reactions expressed still fit with the revised version. In particular it is hoped that the comments betray the freshness and surprise of the material and its impact on an audience which had been expecting a very different kind of presentation. The effect of this presentation on the Conference itself, elaborated further in the concluding chapter, was considerable.*

DISCUSSION

Chairman Watzlawick: I believe I am speaking for everyone present in this room when I say that we are most thankful to Dr.____ for a most enlightening and also entertaining lecture—the two adjectives usually don't go together.

Personally, I admire him for his ability to stay out of such emotional systems for twenty-four hours. With me, it is only fifteen minutes. It bears out the old saying that you can't be too careful in the choice of your family. It also reminds me of something that someone said, that if people define a situation as real, then for all intents and purposes it becomes real.

May I now call on the panel to discuss this paper? Dr. Rubinstein, would you care to start off?

Dr. Rubinstein: I would like to start by saying to ____that now I understand why he has delayed writing to me.

I am fascinated because I was triangled throughout your talk, and I found myself writing and writing notes, trying to detriangle myself. I think the concept of the triangle, which has some continuity with what we were talking about yesterday about triads and dyads, is a fascinating one because it brings our clinical experience into the discussion. I have also operated out of the idea that the dyad is an abstract construct and I have wondered many times, in clinical practice, if such a thing as a dyad really exists. For example, in a mother-child schizophrenic relationship, one wonders if there is not always a third party present. It is difficult to conceive that two people can be related so intensely in a symbiotic way without having to differentiate themselves as a unit from a third party. The third party operates as a differentiating factor which solidifies and reassures the existence of the dyad. I agree fully with you, therefore, that probably the building block in human relationships is the triangle, the triad.

In working with couples, I came across some of Norman Paul's ideas about the mourning process, and they influenced my thinking about the techniques we use in clinical practice in marriage therapy. Aside from changing the rules of the game in the relationship between both marital figures, one useful technique has been to open up the emotional system in which each operates in the triangles with their parents, in the presence of the other mate. By opening up these outside emotional systems, some kind of empathic response is created in the other mate. Hopefully, the empathic relationship between both mates is then going to establish a new sort of triangle on a different level. This is why I would like to qualify your term "detriangling." Are we destroying the triangle, are we detriangling, or are we changing the triangles to a different level of functioning?

I wonder to what extent triangling is really necessary to bring empathy into the relationship between both mates. The therapist who becomes part of the triangle has to prepare himself to work through the separation process. How can he get out of the triangle or change his triangular function to a different level? I hope we will have a chance to talk more about this.

Chairman Watzlawick: Thank you very much, David. John Weakland is going to be the next discussant.

Mr. Weakland: Dr.____began by saying two true things. He said he was going to depart from his prepared paper and he was going to provide an experience. I think that listening to ____ is always an experience, but today was even more so.

I'm going to be very brief, because I don't want to take anything away from the direct impact of the experience which he has provided for us. I think enlightenment in this area comes at the level of experience and not just at the level of ideas, so I will take only one or two minutes, reversing his shift, to return to his prepared paper slightly and to make a couple of general points.

Certainly, the paper he gave me to read, and also the outline which I think was sent around generally, spoke at length about the undifferentiated ego mass and triangles. I must say that I didn't really understand what he was talking about until today—but now I think I do, because he has illustrated it so vividly.

In my opinion, the most important thing he said today, that he did not say in the prepared paper, was to emphasize the importance of getting out of the family ego mass but still keeping one's relationship to it. This sort of going in both directions runs through everything he was telling us today. I think this is very significant, not only for relationships within the families we study but for relationships within our own families. Anybody working in the family field inescapably draws on his own family experience, using this experience in one way or another to inform his work. This is not the kind of work, really, that can ever be put so far away from you that your own life is not involved in it.

So I think that both getting some distance from your own family involvement and yet maintaining some connection is very important to us all. This idea relates to a couple of sentences in his prepared paper that I would like to quote here. He said he believes that, "The laws that govern man's emotional function are as orderly as those that govern other natural systems, and our difficulty in understanding the system is not so much in the complexity of the system as in man's denial of the system." He has a very basic point there. I think such denial often relates to our troubles with our own family involvement. He seems to ask more than we are capable of when he says, "Get with it," and at the same time says, "Get some distance from it." If we do both, we will be better off both in our therapeutic work and, I might say, in our conceptual work. For example, we might be able to look at systems and not dismiss their properties as alien, as we do over and over again with concepts like "mental disorder" or "family disorganization." All our work has been showing more and more that even the most "disorganized" families are highly organized and systematic. If we use such terms and concepts as "disorganization," we don't do anything except obscure the very order that we are looking for.

Chairman Watzlawick: Thank you very much, John. May I now ask Dr. Weiner to comment?

Dr. Oscar R. Weiner: I was really fascinated by____'s talk. I copied down his blueprint and I couldn't help thinking about what this meant to me personally. I found myself kind of wandering a little bit and thinking about going right home and trying it in my own family. Perhaps he has given me something that I might find useful with my own family.

I hope that ___ can respond a little later on as to how he really sees himself in this whole family system. The thought that came to my mind, which was kind of verified by what his mother finally told him at the end about what the weekend meant to her, was that perhaps he was being the family healer. I am not quite sure, in terms of the family projection process, what he had seen himself as being before this.

In terms of his discussion of the individual who tries to differentiate himself yet should keep relating to his family, I have found this concept very useful in my own practice. You have spelled out for me what I have already been doing. I have found this procedure very useful in dealing with individual patients who are struggling to differentiate and at the same time continue to show a great deal of resistance to it. I have also begun to send patients back to their families to relate to their families, and I feel that, in a sense, this gets me out of this triangle that exists between the patient, myself, and the patient's family. I arrived at this procedure because I found myself becoming more and more uncomfortable with the burden that I felt patients were placing on me. They were binding me, resisting growth, development, progress, or whatever you want to call it, and I have found that sending them back to their own families somehow placed me in a better position to deal with them. In the long run it is a much more gratifying experience for the patient because we both get detriangled and he has a different relationship with his own family.

Chairman Watzlawick: Dr. Whitaker, would you care to comment?

Dr. Whitaker: Would I care to comment? Boy, what a question! ___, I wish you were my brother!

Dr. ___: Ackerman is.

Dr. Whitaker: When you said you were boring, it was very clear what you meant. You were boring the hell into me. This is the other end of that probe we were talking about yesterday, which is the one I would like to study.

I think one of the other things you said that nobody has had guts enough to say before is that those people who go into family therapy are really master manipulators. All this cotton-pickin' talk we give out about, "We are going to be sincere and we are just playing from ourselves," has the other side of it, that we are also related to the system. It is very intriguing to me to think about the struggle I have had in terms of trying to differentiate myself as a "separate," as though I was trying to make believe that I wasn't relating to this whole. I wonder if there aren't two groups of us: those who try to separate out from the family or leave home and never come back, and those who stay home and never go away, and each of us is trying to solve the impossible problem of this paradoxical situation in which we go back and forth.

One of the other things that is very inspiring to me is that this thinking helps explain to me the significance of my functioning with cotherapists. I don't have to struggle with working with two's, which you do. To me, working with a cotherapist is a joy. I have the feeling that psychotherapy ought to be originally taught by working with spouses. It occurred to me that what happens when I do cotherapy is that I detriangle by a process of the two of us functioning at one point as a unit and at another point as two separates. Thus, we are constantly free to detriangulate from moment to moment.

This business you talk about of getting thrown into a panic at home is the thing I am more and more sensitive to as a focus for what is going on in the therapy. I picked up the idea first from the newspaper report of the American Chess Master playing with the Russian who won, and he said he knew that at the moment when he was confused that he had lost. When this happens to me in the therapeutic situation, I reach over and get hold of my cotherapist. I have always felt in terms of Lyman Wynne's concept of the rubber fence, that the process of family therapy consists of standing astraddle this family fence. The problem is, it isn't always rubber. Sometimes the damned thing is of steel and it keeps getting higher and I keep getting worried about what it is going to cut. If I have a cotherapist, I can go in with both feet and hang onto his hand so that I can jump back over and get out; or I can stay out and let him go in and then pull him out when he gets entangled with it.

Chairman Watzlawick: Thank you very much. Dr.____, do you want to respond to any of these comments?

*Dr.*____*:* If any of you wonder why I wasn't writing to you, I have just spent a few thousand hours on my own family. I have a folder full of material, the only other copies of those letters about which I spoke. I have spent months on this project and I wanted to utilize this family upset to the full.

I agree with many things all of you say. I don't know about that empathy thing. I don't deal too much in empathy.

Who gets out of a triangle? There is one person who is motivated to do this, if you can find this one. In the average family, if I can get the couple to cooperate, then I do it with them, and if I can't, then I work with the motivated one.

On the question of how do I see myself in my own family, well, it changes from year to year. I used to be myself and go my own way, and I used to sort of stay away and not go back. I think that is one of the biggest delusions that anybody has. I believe it is one of the biggest delusions of psychoanalysis that people have worked things out about their families in their analysis and that they don't have to be involved with them any more.

You talk about resistance to this—it is tremendous. I mean, to force myself to do this was one of the hardest forcing jobs I ever did. It makes you understand a little bit more the resistance of the family member to do it. After I had had this session with my brother, I knew that I had to go back to him the next day. I wished I didn't have to, you know, but I knew I had to go, and that I would go.

Those are all the comments I have at this time. Incidentally, I have had more reports about the way the family situation has settled down. For instance, my oldest sister is on a diet and is losing weight. I have never seen my parents act so alive. They are alive and going like anything. The whole family is.

As for my own emotional part in it, if a person working on a triangle can stay less involved than the others, I think that is to be desired. In other words, I was able pretty much to laugh at my brother while he was shaking his finger at me. But I still get emotional. I get emotional talking about it here. I didn't find a way to get around this last one.

Dr. Whitaker: I hope you won't.

Chairman Watzlawick: Thank you very much, Dr. ____. May I invite brief comments from several of the more research- than therapy-minded participants?

Dr. Bell: There was a very interesting book review back in 1916, the heyday of psychoanalysis. Somebody wrote a review that pointed out that no matter what Euclid did, whether he took a square or rectangle, a parallelogram, a circle, the damned thing always came back to triangles. You take two points on a circle and end up with a third point and you have got a triangle. You take a square and you divide that and it comes out a triangle, as was the fashion in the days of the lovely "demonstration" of the universality of the Oedipus Complex. But two triangles don't make a rectangle, and a circle is something more than a set of triangles.

I guess my question for Dr.____ is not really a challenging of the usefulness of conceptualizing these phenomena as triangles, but what strikes me is that there is no triangle that you can triangulate here without taking into account a much broader context. Another possible strategy would be to talk in terms of larger patterns than triangles—a certain cluster analysis or pattern analysis. But these thoughts are from the top of my head. Further down in the more feeling part, I grasp and appreciate this kind of triangular representation, but I always have this problem as a researcher of wanting to organize things a little bit and then try to put them into a classification, preferably into a classification that might allow for some kind of operational statement and testing out.

What came to my mind was the extensive work done by Caplow and others, drawing on the investigations of Georg Simmel on the different processes that occur in sets of relationships. Caplow has done an elegant piece on the theory of coalition in the triad.

The challenge to me here is whether one can identify a number of variables, power, and so on, and show that what is going on here is essentially what has been called the "mores" of triangles. These are not merely personal relationships; they are sets of power relationships that are also affective relationships. Maybe we could sort them out and describe them in a much more orderly way and perhaps even find some way of testing them.

Dr. Minuchin: I am not a researcher but I still want to comment. I also was impressed that, actually, Dr.＿＿was not talking about a triangle, because he was not dealing with geometry. He is so fast on his feet that, simultaneously, at the point at which he was working with one triangle he was using another triangle to superimpose on the first one. So he was working not only with a rectangle that are the seven members of his family, but with fifteen hundred members in the town.

I didn't understand why, in order to give us an image of what he was doing, he used a geometric metaphor. What he was doing, really, was working continuously with all the members of the family, using them, manipulating them actively in the process of helping. He was almost like a sculptor that is working with wax; sometimes the sculptor is caught so that when he is modeling, he is also destroying or creating something anew.

The family that he describes I would call an enmeshed family. He is working with this enmeshed family in the process of separating and detriangulating, but his style is an inclusive style that is the style of the family. In the work that we have been doing, we differentiate two types of family. Evidently all the families of therapists are enmeshed families. This is why we immediately resound to this presentation, but there is also the disengaged family in which the process is not one of detriangulation, of differentiation, of getting out, but a process of reestablishing and creating units.

Dr. Levinger: I will make my comment quickly, and not discuss my delight at hearing the paper. I do want to add that the concept of a triangle can be related very much to the triangular work of a number of prominent social psychologists—for example, Newcomb's ABX, Heider's POX, Osgood's work on understanding communication and attitude change. If A and B are two people and X is any third object—it could be an attitude, object or any abstraction, or it could be the person of the therapist, or a brother or whoever—this X then is some object to which A and B both relate. And the feelings of A and B toward X, and the balancing of these different feelings, constitute a topic on which there is already a large amount of research.

It seems to me that when Dr. Whitaker talks about "detriangulation," he talks about offering alternative X's to A and B. If A and B get hung up on a particular X where their conflict is maybe at an impasse, then alternatives can be provided. This would be one way one could relate these concepts to existing theory in social psychology.

Chairman Watzlawick: Thank you very much. We will now proceed directly to the next point on our program, a film presentation by Dr. Ackerman.

Dr. Ackerman is going to say a few words and then we will directly start with the projection of the film.

Dr. Ackerman: I have never seen _____ as great as he was this morning. I can't tell you how much I enjoyed that exquisite family tome of his. I am going to talk to him privately about that, especially as he pointed me out as his brother. (Laughter)

Description of Film Presentation of a Family Therapy Session

NATHAN W. ACKERMAN

The family I am going to show you briefly on film is a very different kind of family in some respects, and yet I think the conceptual challenge is to discuss what is the same as well as what is different between ____'s family and this one.

The family consists of five people. The father is 54; the mother 44; there are three children. The oldest is Doris, 25, who is married and has two children, four years and three months, and lives in Pittsburgh with her husband. There is a son, Mel, age 21, who is an engineering student at a local university and who left home a few months back. Then there is a little fellow, Larry, age eight, who remains the baby in the household.

This family was referred in a crisis situation by the mother's internist. A woman with a long history of illness, she had had a severe heart attack in June while visiting her married daughter in Pittsburgh, and between June and September she was repeatedly hospitalized. As the little fellow, Larry, says, he can count the days when he was away from Mama. He measured the absence of his mother precisely, even in terms of hours—twenty-one weeks plus a certain number of hours.

The immediate family crisis is something like this. In September, the mother returned home from the hospital and within a matter of days the boy developed an acute school phobia. He had cramps, he felt sick, and he couldn't go to school. The family was concerned, ashamed, frightened, and frustrated at its inability to get him to go. Each evening Larry prepared

174

for school, expressed disappointment with himself, and worried about losing learning time. He was sensitive about outsiders knowing about his predicament. His sleep had also been interrupted. Nevertheless, all the parents' appeals, entreaties, preachings, scoldings, threats, and sometimes severe physical punishments—none of these devices were effective in any way. The boy won over them. He beat down their resistance, and the parents were pitched into despair and huge anger against the boy. The boy's behavior also changed in that he became overactive, overtalkative, extremely bossy, manipulative within the family group, and showed the kind of silly emotion we shall see in the film.

We were at first reluctant to see this family. Although the mother's cardiologist had stated that her present condition, from a physical point of view, was not so serious, her physician indicated that the severity of the attacks might be attributed to emotional factors. Although these attacks had abated since the onset of the current family crisis, we had some question as to the risk involved in the tension experience of a family interview, and as to whether that would upset the apple cart and precipitate another heart attack in the mother.

However, the internist with whom we checked said, "There is nothing to be lost. This family has burst wide open, it is disorganized, it is out of control because the boy monopolizes the entire situation. The mother is continuously tense." As he put it, "She gets as irritable with him as she can afford, but no more, in terms of her heart condition."

This was a working class family. The father worked 12-14 hours a day as a cutter of slipcovers and upholstery, a pieceworker. Mr. and Mrs. O. are European born. Both are short. Mr. O. denies the obvious inadequacy he feels about this, especially in relation to his tall, well-built sons. When the O.'s married, Mrs. O. continued to be responsible for her brother, six years her junior, in whose education she invested herself against her father's wishes. Mrs. O. worked with Mr. O. in their own upholstery store until Larry was eight months old, at which point the business closed and Mrs. O. became ill with osteoarthritis. Mrs. O. continued to help her husband cut slipcovers until her current illness and she also worked part-time on another job. Mel, too, has worked summers or part-time since he was 14, contributing a large part of his school expenses. Mrs. O. has been the dominant parent both in and out of the home. She explained that Mr. O.'s long working hours and his slow but violent temper made this necessary. Mel and Doris requested stronger intervention in family life from Mr. O., especially since their mother's current illness. The family saw itself as close-knit and, until the recent turn of events, as being able to cope with the frequent periods of Mrs. O.'s illness.

These illnesses had been going on for about twelve years, beginning with an ovarian cyst for which the mother had an operation. She thought she was sterile after the operation and the third child, Larry, an unwanted, unplanned-for baby, entered the family under those special circumstances. When Mrs. O. returned to work seven weeks after Larry's birth, and during the periods of her illnesses, Larry was cared for by neighbors, relatives, and Doris, the married daughter. Doris took Larry to her home for two months when she was newly married and Larry was two years old. He was rigorously disciplined and weaned from the bottle. Although already toilet-trained, he regressed and was retrained at three years of age. Until last year, Larry was enuretic. Occasionally he still needs to sleep with his parents. He handles his penis and anus frequently. Teachers have reported that Larry is bright (I.Q. 133).

After Larry's arrival, the mother had a whole series of operations: two attacks of peritonitis, an appendectomy, a gall bladder removal, and a hysterectomy. During the past six months she had also been plagued with episodes of severe abdominal cramps, presumably caused by adhesions from these many instances of surgical intervention. Prior to the entrance of Mrs. O. into the hospital, Larry witnessed several of the most severe intestinal attacks, and showed obvious fear.

You will have a chance to see in this bit of film what the family looks like and the subtle mood changes that occur, not only in Larry but also in other members of the family—a kind of seesaw pattern of mood shift. When the boy is up, the parents are down, they are dying. When the boy shifts and is depressed, the parents come to life, they become more vocal, more vigorous, more relaxed people.

There are many issues that I hope we will have a chance to discuss after you view the film, issues having to do with the patterning of this particular type of family, my role in response to the family, and the restoration of control once this boy got back to school.

There are many background facts I will have to omit, but bear in mind that just prior to this interview, for some days now, the parents had been making this boy feel enormously guilty. While mother was away in Doris' home, Larry was shifted from father to brother to aunt, and still was too much on his own. Mother expressed distress about this, and also about the considerable demands Larry placed on her when she was home, and her own limitations. Upset about Mrs. O.'s need to convalesce away from home, Mel and Mr. O. often blamed Larry; they said that it was his lack of control that forced Mrs. O. to leave the house. They have also been indicating that his bad conduct, his rebellion, his disrespect, and his refusal to go to school could at any moment cause his mother to have another heart attack, and that he could kill her in that way. Also, the father threatened to have a breakdown himself. So there is a furor raging in this family and no one knows what is going to happen next. There is a kind of rivalry as to who ought, really, to be the sickest in the group.

Now let's look at the film, if we may.

THE FILM

Mr. O. was the first to enter the interviewing room, followed by Mel, Mrs. O., and Larry in that order.* Larry sat between his mother and father, with Mel sitting next to his father and Dr. A. next to Mel. This put Mrs. O. and Dr. A. on the opposite ends of the semicircle. Larry's anxiety was much in evidence during the initial stages of the interview. He was hyperactive, giggling and dominating the conversation as the family spokesman. Both Dr. A. and the parents had to intervene and ask the boy to let them get a word in. With the interview only a few minutes old, Larry said that his mother was "going to have a baby." Dr. A. tagged this as wishful thinking and explored with Larry how much he knew about babies. Larry said that he wanted a baby so that he would have somebody to boss in the family.

At this point, Dr. A. excused himself and left the room for a few minutes. The purpose of his leaving was to give the family an opportunity to be recorded on film in their characteristic pattern of interaction before any therapeutic intervention took place. The parents seemed uncomfortable and whispered together about Dr. A.'s absenting himself. Larry got up and moved around the room. The mother told him to sit down. She then asked him to give them a chance to talk to Dr. A. This was done with a tone of irritable pleading. Larry wasn't about to buy this. Mr. O. stared off into space most of the time. At one point Mel coughed and Larry visibly jumped in response. Stirred by Dr. A.'s previous statement, Larry asked his father if he wanted to give his mother another baby. Mr. O. replied that he didn't want another baby, and Mrs. O. said that they were happy with him, Larry. Larry responded that he was lonely since Mel had left the home. He sat looking lonely and sad indeed.

At this point Dr. A. returned and there was some shifting of the family to allow for better filming. Once they were resettled, Larry wanted to know if everybody was happy. There was more talk about Mrs. O. having a baby and the possibility of her being too old. Larry moved closer to his father, fiddled with the microphone, manifested agitation and hyperactivity. Dr. A. noted that Larry was bossing the situation, that he

---

* In lieu of the film, a description of the film by Dr. Ackerman is included.

didn't allow anyone else to talk. He made this known to Larry and hushed him.

Mrs. O. began to talk about Larry's difficulties in attending school. Mr. O. told about the first day that Larry developed cramps in connection with school attendance. Medical examination proved negative but by the second week of school the boy was not attending at all. Dr. A asked Mr. O. whether he had always spoken so softly, or whether he had only begun to do so after his marriage. Mr. O. denied that he was henpecked and said that he was just unhappy, that Larry's school behavior was depressing. Dr. A. suggested that maybe Larry didn't want to make his family happy. Mrs. O. attempted to excuse herself somewhat from the situation by noting that she was in a hospital when it all started. Dr. A. wondered if she was worried about herself and she denied this. Dr. A. suggested that Larry was plenty worried and he asked Larry about this. Larry said that he had missed his mother and thought a lot about her and then he told of how he was unable to go to the hospital to see her since he was too young. Dr. A. helped him to express his fears that his mother might die. Mel spoke up for the first time and like his father he spoke in an exceptionally low voice. He told of how, when he was twelve and Larry was being born, he too had been unable to get into the hospital to see his mother, although he had tried.

This topic led to consideration of Mrs. O.'s history of ill health. She said that she had had a heart attack eight months ago, after visiting her married daughter. The attack occurred at the bus station just as she was attempting to board a bus for the journey back home. With this illness she was hospitalized eight weeks. Larry pointed out that this was eight weeks he couldn't see her, and then he added to this ten weeks and three weeks during earlier hospitalized illnesses, so that *he went without seeing her for a total of 21 weeks.* During her last hospitalization Larry was taken care of by his mother's sister and by a housekeeper. Larry admitted that he had been very worried about his mother.

Mel, it developed, had only learned the nature and extent of his mother's illness several days after she had the heart attack, but he told Larry only that their mother had a little cold. Mel said that he was worried about his mother and Mr. O. said that he also was very concerned. At this point Larry asked his mother how much she was worried about herself and Dr. A. recognized this as a good question. But, he asked, why should she worry since everybody else in the family was worrying for her? Mrs. O. said that she knew that she was going to get well since she still had so much to do. Dr. A. commented that she couldn't afford to die and she agreed, for she had Larry to bring up, she had Mel at college, and she had a husband at home. Dr. A. commented that all her boys needed her, and she added that she had a new grandchild that she wanted to see. Larry mumbled under his breath and Dr. A. wondered if possibly Larry wasn't nervous for fear that his mother was giving wrong answers; she had earlier assured Larry that she was well and had later gotten sick again, thereby contradicting herself. Because of this, he now found it difficult to believe her. Dr. A. asked Larry if he believed that his mother was going to stay well but Larry did not respond to the question. He said he didn't hear because he was "sky dreaming"—i.e., distracted by some noises that were coming from the floor above. He also spoke of seeing a hand of the man operating the camera in the projection room. Dr. A. noted that he was worried about a lot of things. Dr. A. identified himself with noises coming from upstairs. He said that he was the "ghost" and wondered if Larry was afraid of what he was going to do to him. Larry denied this and denied that he had bad dreams. His mother said that he had difficulty falling asleep, and wanted to have a light burning nearby. Dr. A. wondered if this was to keep ghosts like himself away and Larry giggled and said that ghosts did not smoke.

There was a discussion regarding the family's sleeping arrangements, and from Larry's comments we learned that his and Mel's bedrooms were each adjacent to the parental bedroom, the three rooms forming a "V" shape. Larry's description of the arrangement of the apartment as being "V" shaped seems more in line with the family constellation than Mr. O.'s description of the apartment as being "T" shaped. Larry noted that upon Mel's departure from the household he had moved into Mel's room. At this point Mel attempted to make a comment but Larry cut him off. Mel retreated with what seemed like resigned irritation.

Larry insisted that he was not scared at night, but it was established that he stayed up quite late and that this made his mother "as irritable as I can afford to get." She indicated that before the heart attack she wasn't concerned about how irritable she got. At that time Larry was afraid of her because she would whack him and he would obey. However, now he succeeds in aggravating her and making her sick. Larry attempted to distribute the blame by noting that everybody aggravated his mother. When asked specifically if his father did, Larry responded with "I don't know their business." Dr. A. questioned this, pointing out that he had attempted to move Mom and Pop together in the seating arrangements but that Larry had insisted on sitting between them. With much animation, Larry denied knowing anything about what was going on between Mom and Pop.

Dr. A. then turned to Mel and engaged him. Mel stated that they were coming for the purpose of helping Larry, who was nervous and therefore boisterous. Mel admitted that he himself was normally fidgety and had nervous habits. He voiced confidence that the clinic would contribute to Larry's growth and stability. He said he thought that Larry had been handicapped by having to grow up in a household filled with older people. (Mel was twelve years old when Larry was born.) Dr. A. asked Mel how he felt when he heard that a new child was coming. Mel replied that he had heard it fourth-hand, adding, "I was happy because I knew there was enough love for all." He then doubted that Dr. A. believed him and Dr. A. said he didn't. "You make it sound too smooth. There is more friction in evidence than that." Both Mel and Mrs. O., however, continued to insist that the family functioned well except when the mother suffered her recurrent physical breakdowns.

It was revealed that Mrs. O. began her series of illnesses when Mel was eight years of age, four years before Larry was born. At the time of the filming, she was suffering from lesions stemming from one of her earlier operations. Dr. A. pointed out that she had kept her family hopping with her troubled body and he wondered how the family had managed. Mr. O. commented that it would seem that the greatest amount of mental anguish can be withstood when one feels the weakest and he expressed his surprise that he had been able to survive. Having no help from Mrs. O. in the business, he now found himself working 17-20 hours a day. Larry remembered that in order to see his mother he used to have to go to the store where she worked, and Mr. O. commented how hard a work history they had had, but that they had always been happy.

Mr. and Mrs. O. reported that they had met 28 years ago on a blind date arranged by a neighbor with matchmaking propensities. Mrs. O., who was seventeen at the time, at first felt repelled by Mr. O.'s appearance but continued to date him. Mr. O. "fell like a brick." He referred to his wife as "all a girl should be" and commented on how very close they had always been and how much help they had been to each other. He described how devotedly they took care of each other when one or the other was sick and how all of their misunderstandings were worked out on a "50-50 basis." "Then Larry came and we had our cup full." Dr. A. wondered if maybe they didn't get more than a cupful with Larry. Mr. O. noted that all the time that his wife was ill, Larry had been good, right up to last August. "Then like a bolt from the sky this happened. He's killing me. I'm taking it very hard." Mr. O. went on to describe Larry as a bright boy with good academic potential who at times could behave and talk like an adult, even though now he was acting just like a little baby. Dr. A. wondered just when it was that things got turned so upside down. Mrs. O. noted that it was about the time that Mel moved out of the house. Dr. A. asked Larry if Mel was like a second father to him and Larry agreed that he was. Mel also commented on the closeness of the relationship. Mel spoke of the closeness of the family ties and it developed that he and his mother teased each other about her being his sweetheart. Mrs. O. said she teased Mel about getting married, and Dr. A. said that he would guess that if Mel did, she would break his neck. Mrs. O. defended herself by saying that Mel had to finish school and that she had a happily married daughter. Larry, speaking very quietly, in marked contrast to his earlier animation, spoke of how he wanted a baby to join their family because when Mel got married he would have no brother or sister in the house any more. Dr. A. pointed out that Larry was worried and that he spoke as though his mother and father were already gone (dead). With mother getting sick so often and in the hospital, and father working such late hours, and both sister and brother out of the house, Larry had nobody left for him. Mel had, in a sense, taken his father's place with Larry. Larry defended his father by saying that father always wanted everything that was best for his children. He attacked Dr. A. by saying that he wanted to be either a doctor or a baseball player when he grew up, and if a doctor, "not a doctor like you, but a regular doctor." Dr. A. wondered if Larry would like to be his mother's doctor and Larry made some platitudinous statements regarding how much his mother had done to bring him up. Turning to Mel, Larry asked, "Have you anything to say?" Dr. A. wondered if Larry was wanting to share his sweetheart (mother) with Mel. Larry replied that he had three-quarters of her and then corrected this to 50-50. Dr. A. pointed out that this left Pop out—"He's got no piece of Momma at all." Larry responded: "Pop's had the married piece of Momma for 28 years." Dr. A. noted that apparently Larry did know what was going on between Mom and Pop and pointed out that they had had each other for 20 years before Larry was born. Larry said they had even had each other for nine months before Doris was born, but that, since then, they hadn't had much privacy. "They can have privacy in 20 years when I leave," Larry said, and added that, when he grew up, he would be good to his parents and buy them a house in Texas. This statement made everybody feel good.

Dr. A. returned to the oedipal theme by commenting on how Larry managed to stay awake so as to be around when his mother and father were in bed together. Sometimes he walked into their room. Dr. A. wondered if Larry didn't want to chase his father out of his mother's bed so that he could take his father's place there. Larry responded with, "I'm not married." Larry tried to get Mel into the conversation but, failing, he said that he had sometimes asked if he could get into bed with his parents. He hastened to add, "It's good for me not to sleep with them. I'm too restless. My Pop sleeps very quiet." It developed that Mr. O. was willing to get out of his place in bed in order to keep harmony. Sharing his sweetheart with his two sons made him a "nice pop."

Dr. A. then turned his attention to the school phobia, asking Larry why he did not go to school. It was brought out that Larry had no trouble with school in general, nor with his teachers, his peers, or friends. Therefore, he was not afraid of anything in the classroom setting. The cause for the stomachaches and the school attendance problem had to be sought elsewhere. Dr. A. suggested that perhaps Larry stayed home to keep an eye on his mother, that he was afraid that something was going to happen to her, and he would be left all alone in the world. Dr. A. assured Larry that he would be helped with these fears and worries, but that he had to go to school because there was a law requiring school attendance and the Bureau of Attendance was empowered to make children go to school. "You have to go to school, and that's that." Dr. A. then wondered if "the ghost" couldn't watch over his mother for him while Larry was at school. Identifying himself with the ghost again, Dr. A. said that he would keep his mother for Larry until he got back. "You go to school and I'll worry about your momma for you."

Mrs. O. then commented on the possible significance of Larry's friends being skipped a grade when he wasn't. Larry denied that this was important to him. Dr. A. held to the theme of Larry going to school and it was agreed that if it was absolutely necessary, someone could accompany him. Mrs. O. immmediately responded with, "I'll take him." Dr. A. repeated that Larry had to go to school and there was no choice in the matter, and that, if necessary, Mr. O. could take him. Larry was very silent at this point, on the verge of crying. All agreed that Larry had to go to school and would go. Mr. O. said that if Larry did not go to school, he would get sick too, but Dr. A. told him that this only gave Larry more to worry about. Mr. O. admitted that he was worried about himself and quite irritable and tired. His irritability sometimes caused him to punish Larry by hitting him on the bottom. It developed that all members of the family spanked Larry at times to get him to obey. Dr. A. wondered if Mel didn't do this so Larry would give him the recognition of taking his father's place.

Moving toward the end of the interview, Dr. A. told Larry once more, very firmly, that he would go to school and that "we will help all of your family with their problems and nervousness." He pointed out to Larry that Larry was afraid that the end was going to come to his family soon. He supported Larry by assuring him that nobody was ready to die now so that he really could go to school, either alone or with somebody else in the family.

Mrs. O. and Larry went out the door together. Mr. O. left with Mel, who returned to pick up his mother's pocketbook.

Directly after this first confrontation Larry began to attend school regularly. With Larry back in the classroom, the psychotherapy of the whole family got off to a good start.

DISCUSSION BY RESEARCH PANELISTS

Chairman Watzlawick: I would like to get a discussion going by all of us here on the panel. Dr. Ackerman will have an opportunity to elaborate on the film during the discussion.

Dr. Ferreira: I feel that we should all know something about this family that we don't know—at least that I don't know—and without which I think it would be very difficult for us even to attempt to put into perspective what went on in the film.

Dr. Ackerman: Why don't you ask questions?

Dr. Ferreira: The question I would particularly like to have the answer for is this: Did this family know it was being filmed?

Dr. Ackerman: Yes.

Dr. Ferreira: Was this the first session?

Dr. Ackerman: The first session.

Dr. Ferreira: Were they paying? Did they come on their own or were they pushed into coming?

Dr. Ackerman: No, they were referred, as I said, by the mother's physician, who was concerned about the disintegration of all the family functions, from top to bottom: a disruption of the work pattern, the caring pattern, the eating pattern, the sleeping pattern. Everything had gone off kilter. There was complete disruption.

Dr. Ferreira: They were not paying their own way?

Dr. Ackerman: At the Family Mental Health Clinic in The Jewish Family Service, there is a range of fees according to income. The fee may be nothing, or a family that has a limited income might pay a very small fee of a dollar or a dollar and a half.

Dr. Ferreira: The reason I am asking about these issues is that, to some extent, they can influence the family's whole attitude toward what is going on. But I would really like to comment more as a researcher than as a therapist. From a researcher's point of view, I find myself at a loss. I am not sure what kinds of things one could try to study in such a film or sequence of films that would permit us to conceptualize about either therapy or family interaction in its broadest sense.

Dr. Levinger: Let me ask another question. How was it decided where these people would sit? Did you in any way suggest where they might sit?

Dr. Ackerman: The seating arrangement was initially their own choice. By and by, as other events took place during the session, the parents moved closer together and Larry moved on one side or the other of the parents.

Dr. Levinger: Larry had his cap on when he entered and he took it off sometime during the movie. I was focusing on visual cues, because I had trouble with the sound track at the beginning. So I thought I would see whether I could learn anything from the visual cues, and I diagrammed very simply the position of the people in the room at the beginning of the session.

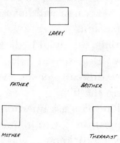

One thing I noticed was that the mother was sitting apart from the rest of the group. Sometime shortly after the movie began Larry started rolling up his sleeves; the older brother already had his sleeves rolled up. I was watching for other visual cues, and I noticed that he put his arms on the chair in a manner very similar to his brother's..

Later I started playing around with Paul Watzlawick's idea of trying to look at sequences in the positioning of the arms and hands. This is the kind of research question that interests me. I didn't arrive at any answers, because I would have to see the movie several more times to begin to understand these repetitive behavioral patterns.

Dr. Ackerman: One can hardly do anything with visual cues in this film because of the interference from the windows and the poor visual conditions under which the film was taken.

Dr. Strodtbeck: At times I looked for evidences of affect by the way the people in the film held their arms, and I watched their feet to see if the movement and emotion was transferred there. I was more interested in doing that whenever I found myself disturbed by Dr. Ackerman's probing associations and the speed with which significant relationships in the family were being opened up. I felt I was in the presence of a man who was behaving like a helpful grandfather to the family. I felt tremendous appreciation for the acuity and sharpness and rapidity with which things moved in this therapy situation.

At first I could not for the life of me understand why Dr. Ackerman offered the cigarette to the mother in such a way that he interrupted the boy's extremely meaningful and poignant speech. He lost nothing because he sat back in his chair and said to the boy, "All right, Son, let's do this over again now." It was a way of putting the lid on this boy's emotionality.

It is my understanding that one of the purposes of this conference is to synthesize clinical findings with the more systematic, scientific literature. One dilemma that exists in the field of social psychology might be characterized as a structural-function interpretation of behavior on the one hand and a symbolic interactional interpretation of behavior on the other. It just so happens that we have a set of theorists in social psychology who explain ordinary behavior under ordinary circumstances, and we have another set of theorists who tend to focus on role distancing, deviant behavior, and behavior under unusual circumstances and in unusual places. We are in great need of a careful theoretical explanation of how a goal-set is interrupted by some monitoring mechanism, such as a role shift as a technique for managing the situation.

To make more specific what I am taking about, a mother and son in a revealed difference discussion may talk along for a long time as if they were intellectual colleagues debating a question. When, in fact, the son does not agree after a time and the mother's monitoring of the external situation causes her to believe that time is being exceeded, she will eventually say to him, "Well, Son, now," and then shift from the debating role to the mother-son role, putting pressure on him to bring about a completion of the situation. In the *Psychological Review* there was an article which took the very simple premise that an organism works on only one task at a time and has a kind of termination rule.* You either do the job, you optimize it, you get bored, or you get discouraged. While this type of computer operation is going on, there is a monitor level—you are going to get hungry, or you get an interruption signal when you bump into anxiety-producing material. When such an interruption comes up, it is the external circumstances to which you are responding. So my conception of Dr. Ackerman's operation is that he puts the family in a situation and actually exceeds their capacity to cognitively monitor what is going on in terms of normal goal achievement. By sending interrupt signals in, by selective use of out-of-role behavior, he brings about the revealing, affective material.

We can take our understanding of what a person like Dr. Ackerman does in the therapy situation and go back to our laboratories and study many phenomena. For instance, we can put people into an experimental situation where they are monitoring, and they know they are going to run

---

*Simon, H. A. Motivational and emotional controls of cognition. *Psychological Review*, 1967, *74*, 29-39.

out of time; then we can watch some of the alternative roles they slip into in the manipulation of others. In this way we may come up with some research that will be less mechanistic and more in tune with clinical matters.

Dr. Tichener: I think that this film can be used as a research document all by itself. You don't have to ask any questions to work with it. But you would have to put a great deal more time on it than the twenty minutes or so that we spent with it.

If I were to study this film I would use a method of context analysis. I would be interested in an exhaustive study of the empathic responsiveness of this whole family system, with particular attention to the communicative units, both lexical and kinesic, occurring in this system. One can accomplish this by getting good transcripts and charting all of the body movements and then looking for the context of those that recur. In this way one can finally build up an idea of the empathic state of this system, possibly with the idea of comparing it with later sessions and with other family systems. A communicative unit is two reciprocal performances. I was able to capture a few such units, although I wouldn't know beforehand whether they were going to be recurring and thus would not be able to compare the context of each of these behaviors.

In the film, there is an interaction between the therapist and the older son; it has to do with mother's illness and possibly some family conflict about it. During this interchange, the little boy pulls back about a foot. The communication unit there might be the exchange between the therapist and the older son reciprocal to the withdrawal of the youngest boy. One would look again for that particular sequence in other contexts.

At a later point, the therapist points at the passive father and, while the therapist is talking with him, there is a great deal of arm activity on the part of the mother. The therapist points and the mother picks up this activity exactly, not in a mirror image but in a parallel manner; she uses the same hand.

There were other behaviors I noticed: Mother touches her face while talking about something in the past, rubbing it in a kind of gesture of resignation, perhaps. Then the older son adjusts his glasses, monitoring or indicating some attitude about whatever touching the face means. Mother pats her legs, and Father points at the little boy and talks about "this one" coming along.

While all this has been going on, there has been some very intense interaction between the therapist and the youngest son, and a lot of hand business by the therapist in eliciting feelings from the boy in reciprocal or complementary responses. While this is going on, Mother wipes her nose and seems to interrupt the interaction between therapist and boy, or at least slow it down.

These are the kinds of behaviors I tend to focus on. Of course, one could collect many more but those are the ones that I was able to pick up from the dim screen in a short period of time. I do think this film could be used as a research document without any need for outside information.

Dr. Ferreira: I am not now at as much of a loss as I was before. Perhaps I even know why I was at a loss. I am really in disagreement with the tone of the comments being made here. I feel that this film is not a research document in the usual sense of the word "research." It is an artful interview and a beautifully done film and I wish I could see it again. I think we are all very much indebted to Dr. Ackerman for bringing us this skillful interview. It is an interesting document, but as I see it it is not a research document.

It is not a research document because to start with we don't know what to observe in it and we don't know what the context is. A while ago, I raised a number of questions which came out of my own discomfort with this kind of data. But as my discomfort went away a bit, I became aware that I could not quite place this type of document in the realm of my experience. First of all, I don't do therapy like that—none of us probably do. That is no bad mark on any one of us or on Dr. Ackerman. The point is that we are all very different in the way we do therapy and for that reason I could not see myself in Dr. Ackerman's role. I found myself in almost constant disagreement with everything he did since I couldn't have done it that way even if I tried. It is not that I thought Dr. Ackerman's approach wrong; it is that I would operate differently myself. Therefore, all the reactions on the part of the family didn't strike responsive chords in me. The family's behavior seemed to be a reflection of Dr. Ackerman's approach.

I don't see how anyone could tell me what to observe there. Of course, there is a great deal we could all see or imagine or fantasize in the film. We are all aware, perhaps, of a research project that took place several years ago involving Gregory Bateson, Frieda Fromm-Reichmann, and others, in which a small fragment of a filmed interview was examined for many hours. They did come up with many interesting observations about just those few minutes of film. And yet that was, to my knowledge, the beginning and the end of that kind of exploration. People interaction is too complex a thing for us to study that way. In that project it took them about one thousand man hours to study five minutes or so of interaction.

So, I feel that if we can use a film like this it must be only in the same way in which we can use our own experience with patients or families in therapy; as a source of inspiration. We may use all of these means solely as ways of getting impressions and of obtaining clues that we can perhaps put together towards the formulation of hypotheses about the system of the family or about our own role as therapists in the presence of the family, etc.

If we are really going to do research, we first need to formulate hypotheses. There is no research without hypotheses. We can go to the top of a mountain to admire the panorama and think it very beautiful or very ugly, depending on the view, but that is not research. Similarly, we can admire the beauty of this filmed interview, or any other interview, but that is not research. If we want to formulate a "before" and an "after," a cause and an effect, as we use those terms, we have to make some sort of prediction and then go afresh into the field to test our hypothesis. We have to see if our hunches, if our impressions, are in any way borne out by the facts. Otherwise, we are going to jump from illusion to illusion.

Dr. Strodtbeck: I don't want to be put in a position of being against hypotheses, but some model of what went on in the therapy session was being developed and you seem not to be paying any attention to that. Can you help me, Dr. Ackerman, in defending my position against what I think is a collective slight here?

Dr. Ackerman: You were wonderful to me so the least I can do right at this very moment is to join you against him. (Laughter)

In the crudest conceivable clinical sense, we have a human situation in which a family falls apart, meaning that it cannot maintain even a semblance of its day-to-day functions. Now, what is the context for this? Here is a child who has been damaged by his family. The child is now punishing the family terribly by wrecking havoc with it. There is a return punishment involved too. He is accused explicitly of wrecking the whole family. He may at any moment cause his mother to drop dead and his father to collapse into some kind of disability.

From the clinical point of view, if we relate the family phenomenon to individual development and individual behavior at any given point in time, we have to concern ourselves with how a family damages a member and how a member can turn around and wreak vengeance in a defined set of like circumstances.

From another point of view, we want to know how many people in this family are disabled emotionally. The boy is the labeled patient. In the first part of the interview he is put out in front. He monopolizes the conversation and is a trouble-maker of the worst kind. He is literally a house-wrecker. The child has a phobic reaction and is depressed. Both parents are depressed. The older brother is barricaded, trying to do what —described so beautifully in the presentation just before mine, to extricate himself and be uninvolved, but he can't succeed. He takes a pose of nonintervention, but he cannot sustain it. He is in it.

Dr. Framo: I would like to ask Dr. Ferreira a short question. Would you agree that, despite the fact that the family therapy situation is contaminated by many factors as far as systematic research is concerned, nonetheless there are probably certain family interactional behaviors and experiences that will only be revealed in that situation and never in the laboratory?

Dr. Ferreira: Probably.

Dr. Framo: And are those behaviors and experiences worthwhile examining?

Dr. Ferreira: Probably, but we will not know about them, either.

Dr. Framo: What do you mean?

Dr. Ferreira: For instance, when Dr. Ackerman described so eloquently how he saw this family, the thought kept creeping into my mind that had you or I been the interviewer instead of Dr. Ackerman, would we have seen the family the same way?

Dr. Framo: I don't mean the therapist. I am talking about an outside research observer watching this whole situation.

Dr. Ferreira: Then, the observer is observing the therapist too, and sees that the family reacts to that therapist in a way different from the way it reacts to another therapist. For instance, I am quite convinced that if I were with that child in the room he would not have behaved that way but would have behaved in a different way.

Dr. Strodtbeck: Let me see if I understand. There is a scientific criterion which says that those matters which enter as scientific data should be replicable by another equally trained investigator. Dr. Ferreira is saying that in a therapy situation, humanistic manifestations of art are involved to a degree, and that the product of such intervention can probably never be brought exactly into the focus of science. My own response is that beyond the concreteness of this particular film demonstration, there is a need for theory which explains the kinds of interventions that a skilled therapist makes in a situation of this sort. Once this theory is articulated, we can design replicable experiments to illuminate it.

Dr. Levinger: That certainly is one way to do a study. There is also a completely different way of studying this film. It occurs to me that one might merely focus on the interpersonal distance of relationships, and make predictions over the course of therapy using distance as a unit and forgetting about what the therapist does. In other words, you could just see what happens to the people who are together in a room. A therapist could deal with another family of four in another longitudinal series, and maybe you could replicate this with a bunch of different families treated by this particular therapist. You could sample several movies, the first interview, the tenth, etc. Predictions could be made about the interchanges, just in terms of distancing or communicating. This is the kind of thing that Dr. Tichener was discussing.

One advantage of movies—videotapes, even more so—is that you can cut out one of the perceptual dimensions. If you want to simplify the problem, if you want the kind of control scientists like to have in the design of experiments, you can take out the auditory dimension completely; or you can take out the visual dimension and just listen to the auditory.

Dr. Framo: The point I was trying to make is not necessarily connected with that. My point is that over a long period of time a family exhibits many behaviors and has a variety of kinds of experiences. I maintain that there are types and ranges of behavior that rarely occur outside the home. You almost never can duplicate typical, unguarded family behaviors in the laboratory because it takes a special kind of situation or issue to bring them out. A family may display regressive behavior only when the issue of jealousy or privacy comes up, for example. Even the family therapy situation is an artificial one in the sense that in such a situation, families behave as they do at home only for brief periods of time when they forget themselves. For example, a parent may curse at his kids all the time at home, and might never do so during a session. Now I agree with Dr. Ferreira that when you use the family therapy situation for systematic research you must take into account the total unit of the family *and* the therapist. Undoubtedly different therapists elicit different behaviors from families, but I think there are certain family behaviors that have such a compelling, regulatory force behind them that they will be revealed regardless of who the therapist is. I still feel that the family therapy situation, over a period of time, is the one situation which can elicit the closest approximation to characteristic family behavior—unless, or course, you could film families in their homes without their knowledge—but ethical considerations prohibit that.

DISCUSSION BY CLINICIAN PANELISTS

Chairman Watzlawick: Thank you very much, gentlemen, and now it is time for the clinicians on the panel to respond.

Dr. Whitaker: I would like to get from the researchers an orientation to what we have just seen as a whole. I am interested in approaching the therapeutic unit of family-and-therapist from a kind of flow orientation over the time of the whole interview—the process, if you will, of the developing transference-countertransference interaction, or whatever you want to call it. Incidentally, I have no problem with the things that Dr.

Ferreira struggles with. I can see myself as operating exactly the way Dr. Ackerman did. I have no problem with the speed; I have no problem with the business of how he goes at it. I think if you are going to be a surgeon you had better not be afraid of blood, and the functioning therapist's role certainly is not palliative.

But I would like to discuss just a few of the artistic bits that I saw Dr. Ackerman do. The first one was a beautiful job of mimicking the family's sweetness. This maneuver made him a part of the family unit in no time flat. Then, they didn't know what to do with it. They had him in and yet he wasn't really in. He was a self, they were clear about that, but at the same time he was constantly involved with them. So they were struggling with the problem of what to do with this endless interactional shift.

I accept the idea that each of us has an artistic style of his own but I don't think that has anything to do with the problem of studying families in research. To me, you study the movement, the process that goes on. For instance, as Dr. Ackerman suddenly flipped from his mimicking involvement with the family to being sarcastic, you had the feeling that the family was suddenly being cut apart. I think it is necessary at times to hurt in order to get at the pathology, in the same way that you can't get at the appendix unless you go through the skin and belly. And then he got sneaky, as a master manipulator, and the rest of the film, to me, could be lumped in this area.

This kind of approach to the whole process is what I would like to see somebody study, and I don't think I have what it takes to do it. I would like to sit down with Tony Ferreira and Jim Titchener and half a dozen of you guys and work on this film in terms of your helping me organize what I think I see in it. But I couldn't do it with a film of one of my own interviews; I would have to do it with a film of Nate's, or he would have to do it with a film of mine.

Dr. Bowen: I have several comments. What we saw in the film, and I would agree with Carl on that, is a package which includes Ackerman and the family. Ackerman is Ackerman, and not everybody can do what he does. It is hard for me to do it. From a research standpoint, I don't think you can think of one film in terms of research. If you know enough about enough kinds of families, then you can begin to draw conclusions, but I think that what we saw today was Ackerman and the family.

Fred Strodtbeck says he foresees a research that is less mechanistic and I say hooray, fine. Heck, when you start thinking about families as constantly moving systems that go in and out all the time, and if you start trying to define all those ins and outs, you sure have yourself a problem. It is hard to do, and that is why I think we have to begin research with some kind of a system viewpoint. I think the pattern of the shifting of the family system is more important than the initiator, whether he be therapist or researcher.

I would like to make one comment in response to Jim Framo's comments. Jim was talking about the extraneous factors or the contaminating factors that affect efforts to study the family. If you know the critical factors, the common denominators, then the contaminants are not there.

Dr. Weiner: It is difficult for me to talk about this particular film sequence in terms of research. What I was tremendously impressed with was how rapidly Dr. Ackerman was able to engage every member of the family with his kind of skillful probing. Each probe cut deeper and deeper, and he did this to make conscious what each member of the family may have been feeling unconsciously. He gave them some things to think about so they could return to them later.

There was one point in the film when Dr. Ackerman gave the mother a cigarette. I felt that this was a high point of this particular film sequence, because up to then Mother seemed to be out of the family group, both in terms of distance and posture. She was sitting back and seemed only slightly involved. I asked Dr. Ackerman how he knew that mother wanted a cigarette. His reply to me was that he saw it in her eyes, that this was something he intuitively picked up. I don't know whether it was really in her eyes or whether he wanted, for some therapeutic aim, to give her something. I don't know how you research something like that, but it became apparent to me that after that, she was in the family and that she, in a sense, was ready to relate to him. I think her own feelings about the family were also revealed when she said, "None of them would have offered this to me." Dr. Ackerman's encounter with mother led to his being involved with all members of the family, and I would say that they were ready to begin to deal with some of their problems.

Dr. Whitaker: To me, the reason why he can go so fast is because the anesthesia for the operation is in his inner self, in his feeling for this family and the individual members in it. They know this and, therefore, the operation is not painful.

Dr. Ackerman: I would like to raise one question that is a little tricky and it bothers me very much. It seems to me that we are coming to a complete impasse in our effort to talk together. I refer to the question: When do we really know anything? It is, I think, crystal clear that Dr. Ferreira has his standards for knowing something, and many others don't agree with him. There are different ways of knowing different things about life. I wish we could unbug ourselves of the question: "What is science and what is not science?" and come back to questions that we considered earlier in this meeting: Wynne's concern with the delineation of the important problem in a definitive study; the question of selection of critical variables—independent and dependent. I echo Carl Whitaker's sentiments in appealing to the more rigorous scientists among you for some special help, not in delineating the problem—I can do that myself—but in relating particular variables that are specific to the content of the human problem, and devising a procedure for examining those variables.

I don't think we are going to get anywhere if people like Ferreira study one set of phenomena and others of us selectively display an interest in a quite different set of phenomena. What is the connection between the kinds of things the researchers want to study and those other kinds of things the clinicians want to study? Are they in different worlds? They shouldn't be. We should be able to define the relation between the things researchers choose to study and what we clinicians regard as important; we need help in examining clinical phenomena in a more precise and reliable way.

I think my friend here, ____ should say a little bit more about his brother.

Dr. ____: If you love him, you don't have to talk.

Dr. Ackerman: You know, we had ____ 's superlative presentation this morning. I was chuckling all the time; it was tongue in cheek. My presentation was of a radically different kind. You could ask yourselves, how does he use himself, and how I do use myself? Is there any common denominator between us at all? I believe that, although on the face of it we seem to function very differently, there are significant common features to our interventions.

We at Family Institute in New York have tried a lot of experiments. We have tried having people on our staff who with no previous knowlege about a given family, observe a film of a family session with the sound turned off. They would study the film over and over again, and try to discern certain units of body interaction. In one family of five, every time this yapping mother hammered at her son, and pointed a threatening, invasive forefinger at him, her 16-year-old boy responded regularly, predictably, with a body gesture as if he were about to puke. It was as if her finger were down his throat and he was at any moment going to retch.

There are a number of sequences of that sort that are quite intriguing to observe, and yet we don't know quite what to make of them, how to use them. We would like some help with that kind of thing. We have about 35 contrasting family types in over 100 hours of film. Sometime back I offered copies to Lyman Wynne to do whatever he wanted with them. He didn't say yes and he didn't say no. I still have the pictures.

Dr. Wynne: I didn't know that you offered them to me.

Dr. Ackerman: Consider that the offer has been made.

Dr. Bowen: May I take just a couple of minutes for something that I think is important? I'd like to relate two experiences. The first concerns the issue of confidentiality. I am running a training program in a medical school, and I was doing demonstration interviews. In this case I was not present until the third interview. In the first interview a wife comes in alone and reports to a social worker she has been having an affair that has been going on for some six months. In the second interview the social worker saw the husband and wife together, and the social worker was hoping that somehow the question of the affair would come up. It didn't, and then there was a staff conference at which it was debated whether it would be a good thing for this affair to be mentioned. I thought, Holy Mackerel! I thought why in heck do these people leave their work for me? So, I started off the third interview, where husband and wife were both present again, by asking the wife why it was she had never told her husband about the affair. She said, "I've been trying to tell him and he won't listen." (Laughter) This is one of those things. Here is a social worker in the business and she had been pussyfooting.

My next example has to do with resistance to family work. I know a young woman who got herself into a school of social work. She wanted to know whether or not she should start talking at the school about the family approach. I said, "Heck, you've got to get a diploma. You had better keep your mouth shut." So she didn't tell anybody at the school that she had any connection at all with me. However, she began treating families, and now the faculty of the school of social work are asking for conferences with her to get her to tell them what she does.

Chairman Watzlawick: The discussion is now open to the group.

Dr. Rubinstein: I would like to introduce a little theoretical speculation if I may. Referring to the film, especially its process aspects, I was impressed with the martyr-like aspect of Mother, like that of a Madonna before the cross. I noticed that every once in a while, especially after you lit Mother's cigarette, the little boy took the same martyr-like position. So then I wondered whether the boy and Mother shifted this martyr role— that is, whether the roles were interchanged in order to maintain the homeostasis of the system.

I then began to wonder about this whole question of homeostasis in relation to our discussion of yesterday about the family as a system. Do we not have to consider that homeostasis can occur at different levels and stem from different sources? I don't think the homeostasis of the family is similar to the homeostasis that occurs at a physical-chemical or mechanical level— for example, the temperature regulator of this room or a physiological homeostasis like the hormonal balance between the thyroid and pituitary systems. Whatever changes occur at these levels of homeostasis, they die off or finish at a certain moment, whereas the human transactional homeo-stasis has a purposive function.

We keep on talking about all the homeostatic arrangements that are in the family but one of the dimensions that we generally forget is where the family is going as an evolutionary system in time and space toward a certain end. Whatever modifications in the homeostatic system are made, they not only keep the system together at a cross section in time but also purposively toward a certain end in time.

Mr. Haley: I would like to address myself to a focus that I think we have in this conference. We have clinicians here who are struggling to change families and do research on that process. We have social scientists who have tried to study families as families, sometimes using family therapy data. Now, there are a few of us around who have had both experiences and Tony Ferreira is one of them. Once you have had both experiences, you think about the problem very differently than if you have had only one of those experiences.

Let me put it this way. We used to think the individual could be studied without taking his relationships into account; he could be autonomous. We then took the big step of saying that he is responding to other people. However, for many years all of us, myself included, began to treat families as if they could be studied as units in themselves, ignoring the context in which they were being studied. We assumed that a family in the home and a family in the testing situation and a family in therapy were all the same family, and the question is whether we are contaminat-ing our results by not differentiating between these contexts. Once you have seen the same family in these three settings, you think about a family very differently.

You have to think in terms of what the family, whatever that is, is responding to in at least two situations: the testing situation which allows an investigator to replicate somebody else's work, and a therapy situation where it is very hard for another person to replicate what that particular therapist is doing. One of the things you have in a testing situation is that the tester or observer is trying to be neutral. The family is responding to a context which somebody is struggling to make neutral. I think the therapy context is a very different one. Among all the things it has, it has at least two levels in it. One is an accusatory level and one is a helpful level. When the members of a family start protesting how much they love each other, I think they must be responding to some indication that they don't. The fact that they are all brought in is some kind of an accusation that there is something wrong with this family. At the same time that they talk about how they all love each other, they may give some non-verbal indication that what they are saying isn't the whole story. There is another level of communication which says: Give us some assistance with the misery we are in. Now that family is responding to a very different kind of multiple-level situation than the family in the testing situation. The context provided by the therapist can vary a great deal too. Carl Whitaker can say he empathizes with the way Nate Ackerman works. I have watched both Nate and Carl work and I don't think the family in the film would be the same with Carl. I don't think the family would respond in the same way.

I don't know what it means anymore when people talk about the family in the clinical setting and family therapy. There are many family therapists who would not bring the whole family together. I don't think Murray Bowen would.

Dr. Bowen: I would see them together at least once.

Mr. Haley: The first time? I think Tony Ferreira would see them individually first and then bring them together. What I mean is, you can see a family very differently in terms of who is dealing with them, how they are dealt with, and how they are dealing with each other on multiple levels of accusation and helpfulness.

Once you have struggled with the problem of how to do family research, you begin to be more and more aware that a family is whatever context it is being studied in. I don't think somebody who has done only clinical work or has done only research can really get the feeling of this.

Dr. Ravich: I think, as Dr. Ackerman suggested, that there may not be a great deal of difference at a deeper level between the process that Dr. ___ described to us this morning, and what Dr. Ackerman was doing in this film. The focus has to be on: What does the third party, the outsider, do? How does he enter the situation and how does he affect it?

I think that this third party role underlies everything that we have been talking about. We say there can be no dyad, that there can only be a triad. The film illustrates this point. In one place Dr. Ackerman asked about the way the parents felt when they first met, and the mother said, "I felt nothing," and the father said, "I fell in love right away." The next point that came up was that the older brother, Mel, was the new lover. He was the one who was not allowed to get married. Then he left, and the little one was designated to be the potential lover. Then Dr. Ackerman came in and took that role away. That, I think, was the dramatic effect of his offering the mother the cigarette. So you see, there is always a triad.

These are all triangular interventions. Research might focus very helpfully on this aspect, not so much on the family but on the impact of the third party if I can use that term to cover the therapist.

Dr. Framo: I want to make a short comment on what Jay Haley said, but before I do I'd like to suggest that someday we have a conference on the *process* of family therapy. At any rate, Jay, in the beginning of family therapy the setting is of course accusatory, but the atmosphere changes as the therapy progresses. After a certain number of sessions, when trust has developed, you get entirely different kinds of family phenomena which I think are unreproducible in the laboratory. There is no substitute for time in the revelation of certain material. The setting does change. It doesn't remain accusatory, although other things can be disturbing to the family as the therapy progresses.

Mr. Haley: I am not saying the setting remains accusatory. Obviously, there are changes in therapy. I am talking about the problem of replication so you can begin to make predictions. The family, after months in therapy, isn't the same as that family without months in therapy. The family becomes a different organism.

Dr. Framo: My point is that if you restrict family interaction research to the laboratory there are certain family phenomena that will never be tapped in that context. When we know enough about family diagnosis and types of families we can compare similar families under different therapeutic regimes and handle the problem of prediction and replication that way.

Dr. Bell: I have watched a lot of these films and I must confess I always feel short-changed. This is not a film of Nathan Ackerman relaxing—he is relaxed but not relaxing. He is a man at work. He has some goals. He is making observations. He is feeding into the system to achieve certain things. Why doesn't someone leave the camera on and let the therapist talk for half an hour about what he was observing while he did the things he did. You, Jay, have done some of this with Virginia Satir's therapy and I found it most enlightening.

While I am a little suspicious about the rationalization that takes place with retrospective data, I would love to hear Dr. Ackerman spend a few minutes saying what was on his mind, what he was observing, and what he was concluding.

Yesterday Jay Haley—and I think this should have been picked up— put a blanket over self-reports as a respectable kind of data. I don't think it is quite as dark under that blanket as Jay may feel. There are a lot of difficulties, but I think we can do something with it; it is the man at work, the sensitive, alive, responding person that I could use as a source of data.

Dr. Ackerman: To respond to your request, what interested me at the outset was the way the family walked in. In the first interview the mother came in last. In the second interview she came in first. This is one small clue to a huge problem which could be expressed in terms of my interest in critical changes of interactional events, changes in sequence that I can detect at the three levels already mentioned: changes in the content of verbal communication, changes in body communication, and shifts of mood.

In this filmed interview I was very much impressed that all three older members of the family sat back and died while they submitted to this boy's destructive monopoly of the entire experience. That was one phase. It also seemed to me that there was a striking similarity between the mask-like faces of father and older son, as contrasted with the affective behavior of the mother and little boy, who also behaved very much alike. This is the way the family was split.

Now it seemed to me that either the three members of the family were allowing this boy to destroy them altogether or they were just piling up an incredible rage and biding their time for an opportunity to kill that little trouble-maker off completely.

I chose to infer that they were biding their time because of their need to defer to the doctor's authority, to be good children with me, and because they did not know what I might do to them if given a chance. They were afraid of me.

At any rate, you have a defensive stance on the part of the three older people. The younger boy is being as destructive as he possibly can be, but underneath he is also deeply frightened. In the midst of this, the mother totally denies the possibility of her own death. Her denial is immediately transparent, and with a little tickling of the defenses it becomes clear that she couples the denial of the death threat with the over-assertion that she is going to live a long time. She says she has a lot to do, working beside her husband and taking care of the children, which in fact she does not do. Then along comes the piece of information, teased out by me, that the whole family had conspired to lie to Larry about why she was in the hospital. They said she had a cold and they tried to maintain that lie, unsuccessfully, of course.

I did two things. One, I challenged the denial. I allied with the boy to stop his omnipotent destructive invasion of the entire interview, and asked him if he was worried about Mother. He turned around and asked her if she really wasn't feeling very well, and so on. When I undercut the mother's denial and reached out for an expression of the boy's underlying panic, the whole mood of the family shifted. The boy became transparently depressed and the mother took control once more.

Most of what I was concerned with was this wavelike phenomenon where, when one part of the family was up, the other part was down; one part trying to come to life and the other part dying. The initial silence of the three older people I regarded as sheer murder. I was waiting for a chance to deal with that openly, explicitly. The opportunity did come, partly in the first interview, partly in the succeeding one the following week.

Once I had punctured the mother's denial and used the boy's

underlying panic to make them more honest with one another about the real threat, I also detected another item that was extremely important to me clinically, namely, that the bond between the mother and father was a very tight one. The father was extremely dependent upon the mother; he felt his very survival was at stake because she was seriously ill, and he bound himself to his woman so tightly that he excluded all the children.

What I did, just to give you an idea of process related to significant events in an interview, was to say to the boy at the end of the first interview, "You know, you have got to go to school and your two parents are going to see to it that you go to school. So will I, but I will take care of your mother. She is sick but she is doing fairly well. I will look after her. You don't have to stay home to watch her day and night, to see to it that she doesn't die."

The boy went to school the next day, in the afternoon because the mother let him sleep late the next morning because he had gone to bed late. You know what that means. That was Tuesday. The next morning they got him to school and there wasn't any difficulty with school after that, but that was only the beginning of the treatment of that family's problems.

(Saturday Morning Session Adjourned)

Techniques for Stimulating Family Interaction in the Laboratory and Methodological Problems of Conducting Experiments with Families

FRED L. STRODTBECK

Chairman Lyman C. Wynne: I would now like to introduce our next speaker, Dr. Fred Strodtbeck, one of the earliest pioneers in interaction research. Dr. Strodtbeck will speak on "Techniques for Stimulating Family Interaction in the Laboratory and Methodological Problems of Conducting Experiments with Families."

Dr. Strodtbeck: I should like to speak today about the search for "true" family interaction. In a sense, the revealed difference technique (Strodtbeck, 1951, 1954, 1958) is similar to the diagnostic operations which occur in family therapy. That is, both involve a process of listening and testing and interpreting. Our technique, however, consists of stimulating in a systematic way a revealed difference in a normal family context, and our objective is to produce a sample of behavior on the part of the family which is revealing and which at the same time is not so excessively revealing that we must accept responsibility for the family by providing further service such as seeing the family in therapy. In setting up a revealed difference study which will gain us entree into families, we ordinarily "search" a large organization like a school or factory with some instrument like a questionnaire. For example, junior high school students can be asked to report on their family structure and the birthplace of their parents and grandparents. We can use this information to identify a given population in which we are interested—say, Italian and Jewish families with fifteen-year-old sons and daughters. We subsequently contact the family and record the interaction in their homes. Our protocols are collected in the home because this is the setting in which normal exchanges of influence and support responses take place between family members. There is, almost surely, a factor of territoriality which monitors human interactions. If a family as a group must move into a new environment, it faces new problems in communicating, moving as a unit, signaling outsiders and the like, thereby requiring a different type of instrumental work. O'Rourke (1963) has reported that fathers (and, more generally, parents) become more task-oriented when the interaction takes place outside the home.

Over the years many variations have been reported on the revealed difference method. Ferreira and Winter (1967) have reported on the philosophy of their technique of stimulating the family interaction. By having the family jointly decide on a color for a hypothetical new car, these investigators get interaction underway *without* revealing the family members' previous individual choices. They thus use an "unrevealed difference method"; they believe that the "lack of revelation" and the "blander" topics produce truer interaction.

It is clear that enthusiasm for one's method is desirable. The investigator probably needs to communicate to the family that he believes that what they are doing is important. I also believe that the family operates best if the members believe that they alone have the resource of common information needed in the reconciliation of their differences.

It is probably necessary to distinguish between approaches which cause differences to be *revealed* (such as ours), those approaches in which differences remain *unrevealed* (such as Ferreira and Winter's), and those approaches which require a group to *discover* differences in the presence of an investigator. In this latter connection, I have felt that Framo (1965, pp. 424, 434-435), in his report on Vidich's (1956) work, might have gone beyond his enthusiasm for the author's candor to look more carefully at the source of Vidich's failure. Framo wrote as follows:

". . .Whereas Strodtbeck presented the couples with *ipso facto* disagreements from the start, Vidich's design was calculated to reveal differences in the course of discussion. A further departure from the Strodtbeck method was that the experimenters stayed with the couples during the discourse, a situation that greatly affected the findings inasmuch as most of his couples directed their statements at the experimenters and the tape recorder rather than toward each other. He pointed out that his couples, in their attempts to come to common agreement about a problem situation, made constant efforts to draw the interviewers into the discussion by requesting an opinion, approval, or agreement. The presence of the tape recorder, interviewers, and the uniqueness of the situation, according to Vidich, introduced artifacts into the situation such that neither the interaction nor the relationship between husband and wife could be understood in terms of their handling of the issues. He said, "A central feature of the interaction was the attempt made by the couple to preserve the private features of their day-to-day modes of conduct from the public . . . Although the spouses attempted to be moderate and to make concessions which they might not make to each other privately, they were still faced with accommodating the existing outlines of their relationship to the interview situation" (p. 237). He went on to say, (p. 238) ". . . the interviewers were 'used' by the informants for private purposes in areas of private meanings. Thus, a third level of meaning is introduced into the responses. In addition to the meaning intended for the tape and the publicly obvious meaning intended for the interviewers was added a loaded meaning intended for the spouse only." Vidich concluded: "It cannot be claimed that the interaction protocol and the meanings represented in it are an accurate representation of the day-to-day interaction of the husband and wife. The protocol merely represents a segment of interaction under circumstances not otherwise duplicated in their lives. The clues to interaction processes and dynamics of social relationships lie beneath the structure of disguises called forth by the situation. Mechanical aids, instructions, interviewers, and the social meanings attached to them define the situation of action for the respondent who, in calculating his situation, responds to its totality. Responses are made at several levels of meaning which range from the publicly admissible to the private. Furthermore, techniques of concealment and standards of admissibility vary from respondent to respondent. An interaction analysis based on standardized categories and made without reference to the totality of this situation would be spurious if any claim were made for generally valid interaction processes, even between husband and wife. To treat the subjects in mechanical terms as only responding to experimental conditions is to distort the data and underestimate the respondent." Vidich has been quoted at length, not only because this writer happens to agree with him, but because it is so refreshing to find an investigator stating publicly the kind of quiet misgivings most research workers have, but keep to themselves, about the flaws in their procedures. Most experimenters in their eagerness to avoid complexity and present neat findings in stereotyped articles, avoid such candor." (Framo, 1965, pp. 424, 434-435).

The Vidich quote is both directly to the point, and at cross purposes with the present presentation. We read Vidich as reporting an instance in which departure from the basic technique is so great that the whole process crumbles. If there is some cohesiveness in a group, we believe that by revealing differences, we mobilize energy to repair the consensus. In the unrevealed approach, individual members are probably more motivated to defend their prior positions by virtue of having reported them to the experimenter; and even if this is not so, the family is given a task which it can respond to as if it were any other job. But in Vidich's approach, the cohesion of the group is mobilized *against* the experimenter. The group is challenged and thereby motivated *not* to reveal their differences. So as an experimenter Vidich is all thumbs, but as a commentator on the fact that the apparatus of the research is a vital factor in the response of the families, he is probably entirely correct.

Whether they are explicit about it or not, it is expressly because investigators do feel that there is a "contribution" growing from the method I have used that they have taken such great pains to invent new methods. Frequently, they are also motivated to cause the family to produce materials which they can quantify easily, and, if possible, in some way which parallels their work with individual psychological tests. That is, along with the question, "Is it true?", they have chosen to ask, "Can it be reliably produced by a different investigator?" and, "Can it be analyzed?"

Before commenting further on the modifications of others, I should like to cite a brief example of a family interaction over revealed differences as it is currently collected in our laboratory. The question which has been given, separately, to father, mother and, in this case, an adolescent daughter, is as follows: "In many states the age for voting is 21. It is argued that, generally speaking, a person younger than 21 does not have enough experience with political affairs to use a vote wisely. Some people, however, feel that the voting age should be lowered to 18. They frequently argue that if a person is old enough to serve in the Armed Forces, or as in the case of a girl, is old enough to marry without her parents' permission, then the person is old enough to vote." In this particular interaction, the daughter is the isolate; she said, "Vote at 21," and the parents answered, "Vote at 18." Since space limitations do not permit inclusion of the full protocol, the following brief summary is given: When the three were all together and the difference revealed, the girl defended her position by saying that in Florida she had heard that children could drive at 13, but she thought this was foolish. The mother countered by indicating how much better prepared she felt children were at 18 now than when she was a girl. When the father supported the mother, there was some brief joking aggression by the daughter against the father in which she stressed that he was an "old man"—almost 45 years old. With this, the daughter conceded that maybe 18 would be all right, and that she was perhaps too much influenced by what she had heard grownups say I want to emphasize that it is necessary to ask the questions separately of each member and then to reveal the differences to the whole group together so that they can arrive at a consensus.

We feel that it is quite important to train the person who goes into the home to avoid getting into entangling relations with members of the family prior to the time he has collected the interaction protocol. Subsequently, he can carry out whatever other conversation with the family he feels is necessary for rapport. The actual management of revealed difference slips, the tape recorder, and the non-involved family members is quite a demanding job. By creating the expectation that after the revealed difference interaction is over something else is going to take place, subjects are persuaded to move along in what they perceive as the first steps in their experimental session.

While it might seem that this quiet directiveness by the experimenter would only work in a culture like our own in which people have been manipulated by teachers, nurses, and the like, it works quite well with groups as different as Hong Kong refugees, Navaho herders, and Mayan peasants. One great advantage of this procedure is that it can be presented in any culture and analyzed in any language. No equipment more elaborate than a portable tape recorder is involved.

Many people, some of them participants in this conference, have utilized variations of the standard revealed difference technique. The procedure has served as a baseline technique in the comparisons made by our coparticipants Drs. Loveland and Wynne (1963) in their description of the Family Rorschach. Like revealed difference, their procedure is relatively standardized, the therapist does not participate, the equipment is widely available, and the protocols constitute a rich hunting ground. While power scores are harder to devise, their stimuli might prove to be more motivating to a schizophrenic subject than the standard procedure. While the Rorschach is uniquely used as a stimulus to promote interaction, the collective interpretations can be evaluated by the same conventions which have been evolved for interpreting the Rorschach. These authors are persuaded that the great variety of individual interpretations of the stimuli, and the built-in pressure for interpretive transactions, causes their method to have particular relevance for clinical research. I believe Drs. Levy and Epstein (1964) would essentially agree, though the teams differ on details of administration and interpretation. The advocates of the Family Rorschach would not argue that the interaction is more typical of everyday interaction than that produced by the standard procedure; they would believe it was "truer" only in the sense that it is more revealing psychologically.

This tendency to opt for a still different fraction of what might be present in everyday interaction is also the line followed by Dr. Arden Flint. He felt that revealed differences over the communication of feeling rather than cognitive, mediated experiences would be more desirable to have, so he set up a stereognostic test whereby the families reached into a darkened enclosure and were encouraged to work out common interpretations of what it was they felt. This primitive sensory level taps phenomena not reached by cognitive approaches. The Bonner and Goodrich team (1963) had couples who were facing different comparison panels match a sample color swatch visible to both of them. This technique meshes inputs from different sensory modalities in addition to producing information pertinent to coping styles. From my brief observation of subjects at work on these tasks, I find them objectionably passive and experimenter-oriented. When a family is ushered into place before a fairly complicated piece of equipment, I believe it is difficult to remove their sense of subordination to both the experimenter and the task. This is a method effect of the type that investigators are usually unaware of.

Beyond "who wins and how" there is the question of the collective thought quality of the family or couple as a whole. Dr. Reiss (1967), who uses problem-solving tasks, and Drs. Roman and Bauman (1960), who have couples taking the Wechsler-Bellevue together, pursue this approach. Farina (1960) used nondichotomous revealed differences in his study. We always ask a series of questions and the answer requested is simply agree or disagree; our procedure actually heightens the differences between the family members. Farina's approach was to use a 5 or 7 point scale so that the differences would be recorded within a somewhat smaller scatter. Titchener et al (1963) had their families reconcile a series of differences instead of the investigators interrupting after each decision. Minuchin and his group (1967) utilized family tasks as well as a variation of the family TAT with his population. Another participant of this conference, Dr. Ravich (1966, 1969), adopted the two-person bargaining game of Deutsch and Krauss (1964) to develop a train test for couples which has interesting clinical implications for marital dynamics.

Frances Cheek (1964) compared a group of normal three-person families with a matched group of three-person families containing a discharged schizophrenic patient. She focused on the discrepancy between questionnaire responses and behavioral samples of family interaction involving a 15-minute discussion of questionnaire responses on which the triad had separately disagreed. Dr. Cheek was one of the first to note the difference in interaction patterns when the three-person family involves a

girl as contrasted with a boy. Mishler and Waxler (1968) have been
working in ways similar to our own, and Hetherington and Brackbill
(1963), working with families of nursery school children, used revealed
difference inquiries in a fascinating study which correlated personality
traits with identity.

Sex differences in families have been a central concern for Margaret
Parkman, who has been working with me at Chicago and is now at
Cornell. She and I are systematically concerned with the patterns of
unconscious masculinity and femininity in boys and in girls. She studies
families with two children and counterbalanced in her design half boys
and half girls, half with older siblings and half with younger, and half male
siblings and half female; with this design the interaction effects as well as
sex and ordinal position variables could be contrasted. In those instances
in which siblings were of the same sex, the allocations of task dominance
between the parents were contested in ways that were not present when the
two siblings were of opposite sexes. When the siblings were of opposite
sexes, mother took more responsibility for the direction of the girl and
father more responsibility for the boy. When we relate this sex difference
finding to a fourth member of the family as a classificatory variable you
begin to approach experimental evidence of family system effects.

About the time that the Head Start programs were getting under
way, we concerned ourselves with looking at the differences in family
interaction which were a function of intelligence. We compared families
with children whose IQ was very high, in excess of 160, with families
whose children had IQ's in the range of 125; both sets of families were
normal and highly privileged. Our major finding, which was not what we
expected when we began this study, was that the very high I.Q. families
exchanged greater support and warmth toward each other than did the
lesser I.Q. families.

The only latitude that we experimenters have for the kind of
versatility that clinicians display is when we create and commit ourselves
to an experimental design. This aspect of a research career is the most
demanding but also the most meaningful. I'd like to trace briefly for you
how I have used the revealed difference technique to learn something
about the contrasts in family organization, power in the family, child
development and so forth between different cultures. After initially
reporting on the technique (1951), I looked for cultures that were
maximally differentiated as to the relative power of the husband and wife,
and compared Texan, Mormon, and Navaho couples. I was able to
demonstrate that the sex role supported in the larger culture tended to be
more powerful in the revealed difference situation. The revealed difference
technique was then applied to the three-person family situation (1954),

and my purpose then was to contrast power relations in the family with those in *ad hoc* groups. Subsequently (1958), I worked with Jewish and Italian families in New Haven, and with these families I was concerned with whether, in addition to achievement values that are transmitted from the culture, there is a kind of relearning that takes place during family interaction. That is, we learned that those boys whose decision-making role was dominated by their fathers felt more subjugated to destiny than did those boys whose relationship with their fathers was more democratic. This finding was further tested by using still another culture grouping, Japanese Americans in Chicago.

My contemporary work is related to the cultural contrasts that I began with; this current work stems from some protocols we collected from refugee Hong Kong Chinese a few years ago, as well as from our hypotheses about authority and unconscious sexual identity in the family. I am presently working in Yucatan in Mayan peasant villages; the revealed difference findings are translated from Spanish into English and we do our standard analysis. We have come up with the interesting finding that the high power accorded the father in decision-making, arising as it does in a traditional society, is not perceived by other family members as an exercise of dominance comparable to the way it is viewed in our own society. The father's indication that Jose should be chaperoned when he goes out with his fiancee seems to be responded to as if he were simply the person transmitting the lore and accumulated wisdom of the village rather than a father making an independent kind of intervention.

These are some of the background concerns that I bring to share at this conference. I'd like to say a few words about procedural matters. Once the protocols are collected, the steps for their analysis are quite routine. We type them out, and then score them, listening to the taped interchanges while viewing the typed protocol. The fact that we use the Bales Interaction Process categories is, I think, quite unimportant, just as I believe that the technique by which the revealed difference is stimulated is relatively unimportant.* The protocols, once they are analyzed by any category system, can then be judged by people of whatever degree of naivete or wisdom you choose. Following a given revealed difference session, you can always ask the participants in a family interaction what their own perceptions are, and the problems of collating, factoring, and of relating these levels of postinteraction experience is, with the advent of the modern computer, quite a straightforward process.

Clinicians might ask whether the revealed difference method is useful

---

*Bales, R. F. *Interaction process analysis.* Cambridge, Mass.: Addison-Wesley, 1950.

enough to justify the difficulty of obtaining such protocols. The gain in insight into a particular family is probably not worth the effort, since you can get the data you need in other ways. But in the search for "true" family interaction, what we are doing when we design this or any other systematic intervention procedure is to find a way of getting standardized data such that they can be collected epidemiologically. I have determined, for example, that a Mayan peasant family produces protocols that have much less cognitive complexity than a middle-class family in the United States. While we are guided primarily by a concern for systematic theory in child development and socialization, we are not oblivious to the concerns of the clinician. I see no reason why at a later time some further simplification of techniques can't be brought about which will come to be more clearly related to phenomena that matter to clinicians.

REFERENCES

Cheek, F. E. The "schizophrenic mother" in word and deed. *Family Process,* 1964, *3,* 155-177.

Deutsch, M., and Krauss, R. M. Studies of interpersonal bargaining. In M. Shubik (Ed.), *Game theory and related approaches to social behavior.* New York: Wiley, 1964.

Farina, A. Patterns of role dominance and conflict in parents of schizophrenic patients. *Journal of Abnormal and Social Psychology,* 1960, *61,* 31-38.

Ferreira, A. J., & Winter, W. D. Decision-making in normal and abnormal two-child families. *Family Process,* 1968, *7,* 17-36.

Framo, J. L. Systematic research on family dynamics. In I. Boszormenyi-Nagy & J. L. Framo (Eds.), *Intensive family therapy.* New York: Hoeber Medical Division, Harper & Row, 1965.

Goodrich, D. W., & Boomer, D. S. Experimental assessment of modes of conflict resolution. *Family Process,* 1963, *2,* 15-24.

Hetherington, E. M., & Brackbill, Y. Etiology and covariation of obstinacy, orderliness, and parsimony in young children. *Child Development,* 1963, *34,* 919-943.

Levy, J. & Epstein, N. An application of the Rorschach test in family investigations *Family Process,* 1964, *3,* 344-376.

Loveland, N. T., Wynne, L. C., & Singer, M. T. The Family Rorschach: A new method for studying family interaction. *Family Process,* 1963, *2,* 187-215.

Minuchin, S., Montalvo, B., Guerney, B. G., Rosman, B. L., & Schumer, F. *Families of the slums.* New York: Basic Books, 1967. Appendix.

Mishler, E. G., & Waxler, N. E. *Interaction in families.* New York: Wiley, 1968.

O'Rourke, J. F. Field and laboratory: The decision-making behavior of family groups in two experimental conditions. *Sociometry,* 1963, *26,* 422-423.

Ravich, R. A., Deutsch, M., & Brown, B. An experimental study of marital discord and decision-making. In I. M. Cohen (Ed.), *Psychiatric Research Reports,* 20, American Psychiatric Association, Washington, D. C. 1966.

Ravich, R. A. The use of an interpersonal game-test in conjoint marital psychotherapy. *American Journal of Psychotherapy,* 1969, *23,* 217-229.

Reiss, D. Individual thinking and family interaction. *Archives of General Psychiatry,* 1967, *16,* 80-93.

Roman, M., & Bauman, G. Interaction testing: A technique for the psychological evaluation of small groups. In M. Harrower, P. Vorhaus, M. Roman, and G. Bauman (Eds.), *Creative variations in the projective techniques.* Springfield, Ill: Thomas, 93-138, 1960.

Strodtbeck, F. L. Husband-wife interaction over revealed differences. *American Sociological Review,* 1951, *16,* 468-473.

Strodtbeck, F. L. The family as a three-person group. *American Sociological Review,* 1954, *19,* 23-29.

Strodtbeck, F. L. Family interaction, values, and achievement. In D. C. McClelland, A. L. Baldwin, U. Bronfenbrenner, & F. L. Strodtbeck (Eds.), *Tulent and society.* New York: Van Nostrand, 1958.

Titchener, J., D'Zmura, T., Golden, M., & Emerson, R. Family transaction and derivation of individuality. *Family Process,* 1963, *2,* 95-119.

Vidich, A. J. Methodological problems in the observation of husband-wife interaction. *Marriage and Family Living,* 1956, *18,* 234-239.

DISCUSSION

Chairman Wynne: Dr. Strodtbeck has referred in passing to a number of techniques which have been used for stimulating family interaction and he has given us some very interesting data on some of the findings in his own work. Fortunately, we have here today various people who have devised family interaction procedures, some of which have been referred to by Dr. Strodtbeck. One of the things that maybe we could do during the course of the discussion now is to consider the kinds of data that these different techniques seem to elicit as well as the kinds of problems one has to deal with in using them.

I would like to throw it open to the panel at this point for further comments, either in terms of discussion between the panel members or in some further illustrative comments. Who would like to start?

Dr. Roman: The data that Dr. Strodtbeck has talked about and all the various techniques for stimulating family interaction touch upon a theoretical point that I think relates very much to this morning's discussion. Perhaps we might discuss a concept which to me encompasses a variety of situations—the family therapy situation, the situation of observing a family in another context, for example, the home, and the situation of observing the family in a laboratory. That concept is power. One of the things that one could say about the presentations of both Dr. Ackerman and Dr._____is that they illustrated the use of the therapist's power to produce a certain kind of redistribution of power in the family. Even a specific manipulation like the offering of the cigarette in Dr. Ackerman's filmed session was a decision-making crisis. When Dr. Ackerman made the decision and, in a sense, went against a subgroup in the family by allying with the mother, it seemed to me he was establishing himself as a power in that situation.

The issue that is of special interest to me is to develop a measure of decision-making or power distribution in families that is useful to clinicians. In the work we have been doing we were interested not only in the dominance patterns within families but whether dominance had anything to do with competence. To what degree was the dominant person the person who was the most competent to be dominant in that situation? Another way of describing it would be: Is leadership in the group process related to competence? If husband dominates more than wife or, as we have found, nonpatients dominate more than patients in the marital interaction, it certainly does matter to clinicians whether that dominance is appropriate or not. Does the person dominate because he is more in touch with the situation or is the dominance based on inappropriate reasons?

There is one brief bit of data that we have recently come up with which I think very much relates to this question. We have found, in testing marital pairs in which one of the spouses was a patient admitted to a day hospital, that the nonpatient spouse dominated significantly more than the patient spouse. For a variety of reasons one can expect this finding. We found that after discharge from the hospital, the nonpatient spouse did *not* dominate more than the patient spouse, even though the responses of the expatient spouse did not change. While the actual correctness of the patient's responses did not change, something else changed. In a sense, we were able to show that the interaction of this marital pair in their decision-making processes changed very significantly, even though the individual in terms of past competence did not change. I think this issue is of very special relevance to clinicians, whether one uses a confrontation technique or whether one simply wants to assess system pathology, if we define system pathology as the degree to which leadership is not associated with competence. We are dealing here, essentially, with the reality testing capacity of the family.

I will stop there because I think many of you people who have been working with similar kinds of techniques have moved in interesting directions.

Dr. Loveland: I would like to talk about a few of the problems, other than the more general ones such as adequacy of independent criteria and controls, which beset us when we try to make research use of the samples of interaction obtained from the various techniques mentioned by Dr. Strodtbeck. One such problem is that the negative aspects of human relations have been spotted, described, and categorized more than the positive. In using the Relation Rorschach Technique for studying families with identical twins, for example, the designated patient and the "well" sibling not infrequently showed similar kinds of limitations. But even when it was possible to identify the sick twin from a greater piling up of pathology scores, only vaguely and subjectively could we identify and describe the strengths that enabled the one twin to cope more adequately than the other. And in the current form of the Relation Rorschach scoring system, subcategories for interactions which limit and preclude task achievement are more numerous and highly differentiated than those for interactions that facilitate task achievement.

Finer differentiations of both positive and negative aspects of interaction may become possible when working with families with very young children. Their interaction patterns seem less crystalized or system-atized and are more easily spotted and described than when the children have reached adolescence or young adult age. There were often striking differences in the way different families recognized and interacted around the natural limitations of preschool children in the Relation Rorschach situation (i.e., their language handicaps, their limited grasp of the concept of consensus assessment, their inability to unite in the inquiry, etc.). For example, adults usually see the black area of Card III as human, whereas very young children see it, if at all, as animals. Some parents immediately grasp how their children see it or, if not, listen or ask until they do, and settle on the child's perception as the agreement. Some then also try to show the child how they, the parents, saw it. Others insist that their child accept the superiority of the human interpretation and then, in the inquiry, write it as the consensus of "the whole group": some write it as the spouse consensus, making the assumption that for a task such as this, the child must be ignored, etc.

Some parents are ingenious in devising ways by which the child could validly record his understanding of what they agreed on—the child is encouraged to draw it in, or to tell them, and they write it in for him, identifying themselves as the child's secretary. Others write in their own ideas of what was agreed upon, one or both parents also writing for the child without having first consulted him. Still others ignore the child completely. And some of these preschool children reinforce or passively go along with the adults, while some rebel against *whatever* system the older members of the group follow. Longitudinal studies of such families may help answer such questions as to why one offspring mirrors while another complements, positively or negatively, the parents' functioning.

To step back to my first statement, I think that, for me, one of the biggest problems in all these techniques is to find ways of handling and analyzing the very rich material that all these techniques give us.

Dr. Reiss: I would like to pick up on some points you are making, Dr. Loveland, about handling the data, once interaction is stimulated. I am hoping, Dr. Strodtbeck, that you will make some further comments because I want to raise a couple of questions.

Most of the studies I am familiar with on revealed differences use a coding method that requires a coder's judgment or several coders' judgments about behavior; the particular items of behavior are then grouped in one or another category, depending on Bales' definitions or the category systems of other investigators.

What I would like to propose—and it is by no means a novel proposal—is a continued development of what might be called an "analog" means of dealing with the data. What do I mean by "analog"? As I use the word, I am thinking of the kinds of kymographic studies that might be done. I remember from my physiology course many years ago that when the heart beat, a pen on a smoked drum jumped, and then one had, not a record of anybody's judgment as to whether or not the heart beat, but a direct and permanent record that was a direct analog of the behavior of interest.

I believe Dr. Ravich's description of the position, speed, and course of the trains in his study constitutes a permanent analog record of the interaction that was stimulated.* I would propose that this is a useful record even if we completely miss the boat in understanding what the behavior is, because at least we have a permanent record of what it was and can understand it perhaps at some future date.

I would like to raise just one more point in connection with the comments of both Dr. Strodtbeck and Dr. Roman, and this is a question relating to how you stimulate interaction, and whether it makes a difference what the stimulus is. I think the bulk of the discussion in this conference so far suggests that maybe it doesn't make too much difference. I would like to submit, on the basis of my personal experience, that it does make a difference as to how you stimulate interaction. I have used problem-solving techniques with whole families that very much require competent cognitive and perceptual functions. Competence as a family characteristic has often been over-looked by family clinicians and researchers. As Dr. Loveland was discussing in terms of her own work, it is easy to overlook some of the competences of family members. This is not to say that either the clinical or the experimental setting is an artifact. It is to say that one of the really human and quite clinical problems is that people, in families, behave competently one moment and incompetently the next. I recall a father, for instance, who behaved very competently in a problem-solving session only to return to family therapy where he was again, as before, humbled and made inadequate by the demands of his chronically psychotic daughter.

I believe that the contrast of behavior as produced by different means of stimulating interaction is a very rich and poignant question, and I would hope to hear the experience of others along this line.

Dr. Loveland: I think we need to study family relations not just in standardized situations but also in a variety of other situations such as structured and unstructured interviews, various types of screening and therapy sessions, and so forth.

Dr. Otto Pollak: Dr. Strodtbeck's contribution to sophisticated research methodology in family interaction is part of the established consensus in the scientific community and we would add nothing to his

---

*Ravich, R. A. The use of an interpersonal game-test in conjoint marital psychotherapy. *American Journal of Psychotherapy*, 1969, *23*, 217-229.

stature nor to our work by repeating our acceptance and reverence for that. The question is what we do with it.

I learned this morning, if I didn't know it before, that one of the functions of family therapy is to challenge denial, and I would like to bring my contribution to you as a challenging of denial. We deny that there is no real cooperation between the clinician and the researcher. I challenge that. I think there is an essential divorce between research and clinical work.

Nonetheless, I wonder whether Dr. Strodtbeck would be good enough to tell us at least his fantasies about applying his methodology to family interaction as it happens in the therapeutic situation.

Dr. Strodtbeck: From the perspective that my own research has given me, one thing that appears to me to be important is to have persons who are in therapy situations observed in each of their manifold relations in the larger community. The notion that for all illnesses the family should be the focus of the relevant therapy is probably disconfirmed.

Some years ago I visited an area of England out along the Thames and found that the family members used highly systematized techniques to avoid each other. The younger people who are working do not stop at the pubs on the way home; instead, they put on their modish clothes and go out. When the old man comes in from the pub the adolescents are at a local dance place in the community which closes just before the pubs close later in the evening. So people can go to sleep at night without really interacting with one another. These cultural styles for reducing the amount of family interaction enable certain transfers of energies outside of the family system. Nowhere in our discussions have I heard a theory that explicitly deals with ways of teasing people out of the family context other than those that are focused on the reevaluation of family experiences. One could examine the group orientations of people in work situations. You could also get coordinated data generated on two or three members of the family seen in different T group situations. This heuristic approach would bring to the surface a level of theory that we have not yet considered—i.e., the relationship between family and extrafamilial experiences.

Going back to Dr. Reiss' comments, the general paradigm of multimethod, multimatrix examination is important. That is, if you feel that you have a particular intervention technique that you would like to have more experience with, link with that particular method some alternate method for which there are norms and see whether or not you get similar findings. Considering the cognitive quality of family problem-solving, for example, one could add the Wechsler-Bellevue test to the repertoire of tests because this test has well-established norms.

With regard to the other aspect of Dr. Reiss' comment, what he calls the "analog" and I would call the "gram-centimeter-second" tradition of research, I can only share with you the knowledge that we have been down that road before. Along these lines, there is, of course, the work of Chapple,* and then Matarazzo and Saslow,** who, with tremendous expenditures of energy, found ways of getting nice parametric measures for the two-person interaction. My own feeling is that all that can be read from the markings of those various techniques can be read virtually as easily by simply counting the number of sentences, and anything that distributes the sentences through time helps you to work with the same materials. So I cannot imagine that in the analysis of interpersonal interaction, we are going to find the thing to hook our kymograph to that will give the measures that will bring about the simplification that is desired. However, there is now a new information revolution in the behavioral sciences associated with computers that may enable us to handle our protocols in a much more efficient way.

Those are my associations to your questions.

Mr. Weakland: All or at least most of the people who have commented from the panel have spoken about the analysis of materials collected as distinct from the materials themselves. I want to address myself to this same question of analysis of materials from a slightly different angle. In the first place, I think there are many of the researchers present here, and certainly elsewhere, who have grave doubts about what you can get out of the Bales' category system. Many of the people here who have done clinical work would not look at revealed difference interaction in anything like the same terms as Dr. Strodtbeck's scoring system describes it. I wonder, for example, how Lyman Wynne's pseudo-mutual families would respond to revealed difference test situations.

Chairman Wynne: Unfortunately, there is not time for Dr. Strodtbeck to respond to your interesting question, John, as we have to move on. Dr. Henry Lennard is going to deliver the final position paper of the conference.

---

*Chapple, E. D. The Interaction Chronograph: Its evaluation and present application. *Personnel,* 1949, *25,* 295-307.

**Matarazzo, T. D., Saslow, G. and Matarazzo, R. G. The Interaction Chronograph as an instrument for objective measurement of interaction patterns during interviews. *Journal of Psychology,* 1956, *41,* 347-367.

Criteria for the Development of an Inclusive Coding System for Categorizing Family Interaction

HENRY L. LENNARD

Chairman Wynne: Dr. Henry Lennard will bring together a number of issues that have been brought up both this afternoon and previously. We will then consider whether the research implementation that has been mentioned in the last discussion has reached a stage of development which offers the possibility of breaking through some of the impasses with which we are all so painfully familiar. Dr. Lennard's topic is: Criteria for the Development of an Inclusive Coding System for Categorizing Family Interaction. Without further ado, Henry Lennard.

Dr. Lennard: If I had given this paper yesterday I would have known what to say, but now it is getting to be more and more difficult. I can see merit in each of the positions that have been advanced, and I would like to join this or that faction. I am reminded of the story of a wife who went to a therapist to complain about her husband. The therapist told her, "You are absolutely right." The husband, in turn, talked to him about his wife's faults, and was told, "You are absolutely right." An observer, witnessing both situations, was puzzled, and asked the therapist, "How can you tell both of them that they are absolutely right?" The therapist pondered this remark for a moment, and then said, "You know, you are absolutely right."

After having listened to what has been said about category systems for the study of family interaction, I feel like that therapist. Many things have been said about their advantages and their limitations, and I agree with many of the comments made. Yet, permit me to make some general

216

remarks about the purposes category systems serve in the study of human behavior—specifically, by the development of category systems and the act of classifying *per se*.

      1. Systems of categorization permit a student of human behavior to summarize diverse observations and to separate out common aspects in complex behavioral data. Thus, actual coding or categorization makes analysis of the "stream of behavior" a more manageable objective.

      2. The reduction of complex "living" data by common sets of categories permits comparisons between systems and between social contexts. Indeed, Bales (1950), who is the creator of perhaps the most widely used set of categories for analysis of social interaction, explains that he was motivated to undertake this task so as to provide students of small groups with measures somewhat analogous to those available to students of large social structures in the form of rates and indices (e.g., suicide, crime, birth, death, and divorce rates). In this way, not only can overall comparisons be made between different kinds of systems, but also with respect to specific dimensions.* In comparing distributions of behavior in different kinds of systems, similarities as well as differences emerge.

      3. Category systems permit an investigator to test hypotheses regarding the presence or absence of specific interactional processes and sequences. As a variety of behavioral data is worked with and scrutinized, new hypotheses are generated.

      4. The act of developing a category system proceeds by stages, involving various conceptual tasks at each stage. The solving of such conceptual problems progressively increases our understanding of the relation between the raw data of human interaction and the theoretical frameworks which have been constructed to account for these data. Categories are often derived from prevailing theories and perspectives. The first step, then, is often to achieve an understanding of the diverse theories that have been advanced by clinicians and investigators, so that categories relevant to such theories can be appropriately constructed.

Once concepts have been translated into categories, the behavioral

---

*It is interesting that despite this initial motivation, few such between-systems comparisons are available in the literature. Such an attempt to make comparisons is reported in: Lennard, H. L. and Bernstein, A. *Patterns in human interaction: An introduction to clinical sociology.* San Francisco: Jossey-Bass, 1969.

data itself has to be closely examined and numerous decisions made as to which verbal acts and which behaviors are subsumed within a particular category. Very often one learns that the categories developed are overlapping and not really clear. Not only do the categories then have to be revised, but the investigator has to set down the set of rules that govern each act of classification, often providing illustrations of which behaviors fall into one or the other of the categories. All of the efforts described here are extremely useful in helping a researcher learn what it is that he and the clinician are really talking about. Like other learning experiences, engaging in the steps inherent in the procedures of defining categories and classification is painful, and not as immediately satisfying as the noble art of theorizing. This may well be one of the reasons why far less people and effort have been invested in such activities than has been suggested. In searching through the clinical and research literature on the family, one will locate very few comprehensive category systems, especially ones which are well-described and replete with definitions and indicators that make a system useful to other students.

I believe, Dr. Wynne, that you and Dr. Singer (1966) have only recently published *your* coding system in detail. Goldfarb and Meyers (1966) have only recently published criteria for *their* category system, after having worked with it for many years. I have so far published only one section of the category system I have been working with (1965). A preliminary category system with clinical utility was published by Riskin (1964). The most widely used system, that of Robert F. Bales, though it has many advantages and is an important research instrument, may only be suitable for particular purposes.

I believe that there are many significant areas in family research that would benefit from the development of research instruments analogous to category systems. I am referring, for example, to studies based on the self-reports of family members of their everyday interactions. Family interaction inventories might well be constructed on the basis of a classification of family interactional behaviors.

Let me now turn to some methodological problems and decisions which an investigator faces when he engages in the development of a category system. Shall he devise a system of categories limited to the system he is studying (e.g., the family), or one that is useful and relevant to a large number of social interaction systems? As I have already mentioned, I am biased in favor of the latter alternative. Such an all-purpose system directed to the study of interaction contexts and relationship systems *per se* provides an understanding of similarities and differences in system functioning and variables that would not be available to an investigator who uses research instruments specifically designed for the study of *one* particular system.

It is interesting to note that most of the sophisticated category systems devised for family study (Wynne-Singer; Goldfarb-Meyers) lend themselves, without great modification, to the study of communication systems other than the family.

Another issue that needs to be resolved deals with how comprehensive a category system should be. Should it be inclusive enough to permit the assessment of multiple hypotheses or be restricted to the operationalizing and investigation of one set of concepts only? Since data collection in family research is a very time-consuming business, I would consider an epidemiological or survey research model to be more practical than the one-variable model favored by psychological investigators.

In long-term epidemiological studies, especially in the area of chronic illness, where there are many competing hypotheses and so little hard knowledge, information may be obtained on a variety of relevant variables in the same study. The collection of a variety of data does not commit the researcher to analyze all of the data collected, but it permits separate analyses for each set of variables, and does not foreclose on the possibility of combining several approaches to the data in a subsequent analysis. This reasoning applies to the use of a multiple coding system in family analysis as well. In the family studies we have undertaken, each verbalization contributed by a family member was classified along ten dimensions. We were subsequently in a position to carry through an analysis of the formal or process features of interaction separately from an analysis of content dimensions. In addition, we could combine elements of both analyses.

Finally, one must consider the issue of unitization. Categorization, classification, or coding requires decisions as to how to slice or anatomize human behavior sequences. Which segment of behavior or communication is to be classified or categorized? Some students of interaction process feel very strongly that most efforts at categorization involve arbitrary units which do violence to the "stream of behavior." While the issue has been discussed in relation to social interaction process *per se*, it is, of course, equally relevant for the development of categories of family behavior. There has been little agreement so far as to what constitutes a "natural" and what constitutes an "arbitrary" unit of behavior. Most investigators tend to work with fairly simple units such as statements or interchanges or sentences. Students of paralinguistic and kinesic behavior have worked with even smaller units; but little systematic attention has been given to the delineation of larger and more comprehensive interaction sequences as units.

A number of other general objections that have been raised with regard to the use of category systems should be briefly discussed. One, that the phenomenon of communication involves multiple channels, and that the category systems constructed so far, are limited to one channel, usually the verbal one. A second objection is that the parameters selected for study, and that are amenable to measurement, are really not the significant ones. By a significant variable the critic usually means the variable he is most interested in.

At this stage of knowledge about the family and of other interaction systems, it does not seem to me that there is a consensus on what the significant variables are. What seems to be called for, first, is some consensus on what methods could be used discovering what the significant parameters and variables are.

A third criticism, which is certainly not unjustified, is that the reliability of category systems is often not adequate; that categories are often insufficiently well-defined; and that the amount of inference involved in using them is not substantially less than in the use of clinical judgments.

I share some of the discomfort expressed in these objections. However, their degree of relevance depends on the purposes to which the category systems are put. For example, there is a considerable body of interest in the study of family interaction which is not centered around the "disturbed" family, but centers around intrafamilial behavior in relation to socioeconomic, ethnic, or cultural differences. Whenever the object is to study gross differences between systems, an inability to assess the subtle nuances of interaction may well be less significant.

In general, however, I believe that only through the continued attention to improving sets of categories and systems of classification can these achieve the degree of usefulness needed in the field.

Disenchantment with the kind of measurement of family processes represented by the more rigorous systems of observation and categorization has led to divergent responses by clinicians and by researchers. On the one hand, there has been a call for "clinical research," for the student of the family to become more adept in clinical description and to become a more sensitive and insightful participant-observer.

On the other hand, a great deal of interest has been generating in developing family experiments in which specific parameters of family interaction can be studied under controlled conditions. The interpretation of the findings of such experiments, it is claimed, would require less degree of inference than categorization of "natural" family interaction. Without in any way wishing to discourage this burgeoning development in family experiments, I would like to suggest that this approach, too, creates problems, and perhaps raises new questions that it may be unable to answer.

One such question relates to the applicability of the "languages" used in family experiments to the medium used in "natural" family interaction. How is family interaction constrained by experimental "languages," such as playing a game, pushing buttons, or passing notes without speaking? Experimentation provides a new medium of interaction, and, to paraphrase McLuhan, I believe that the medium not only contains a message but also constrains messages. I have, for example, had occasion to examine some of the messages passed between family members in a "family experiment," and it appeared to me, on a basis of a preliminary review, that certain kinds of content (messages dealing with affect) are not likely to be contained in such notes.

Similarly, to use the pushing of a button as an indicator of "dominance" in the family requires perhaps no less of an inference than locating a verbal exchange in a category of disagreement.

I would, however, encourage this line of family study to the same extent that I favor studies employing systematic classification of "natural" interaction. An important task would be to compare the different kinds of information yielded about a family from the employment of different methods, such as systematic observation, self-report by family members, and a family experiment.

In conclusion, I would like to offer some criteria, or, if you will, personal preferences for the direction that should be taken in the further development of category systems. One, as I have already said, is that category systems should be applicable to a range of interaction contexts rather than to only one system, such as the family. Categories should be oriented to the similar problems that different interaction contexts present, such as system maintenance, the allocation of action between participants, and information exchange. Two, categories should be sensitive to clinical formulations and have some bearing on the assessment of alternative clinical models. And three, efforts at categorization and unitization should be directed to the description of interaction flow over time; that is, to the developmental and emergent aspects of interaction. For example, categories to describe differentiation in process changes in the tempo and rate of behavior interchanges, and larger sequences involved in both the integration or disintegration of a system.

I think that I have talked enough for now. Maybe I can expand on these comments during the discussion.

REFERENCES

Bales, R. F. *Interaction process analysis: Method for the study of small groups.* Cambridge, Mass.: Addison Wesley, 1950

Goldfarb, W., Levy, D. M., & Meyers, D. L. The verbal encounter between the schizophrenic child and his mother. In Goldman, G. S. & Shapiro, D. (Eds.), *Developments in psychoanalysis at Columbia University:* Proceedings of the twentieth anniversary conference, psychoanalytic clinic for training and research, Columbia University. New York: Hofner, 1966.

Lennard, H., Beaulieu, M. R., & Embrey, N. G. Interaction in families with a schizophrenic child. *Archives of General Psychiatry,* 1965, *12,* 166-183.

Riskin, J. Family interaction scales: a preliminary report. *Archives of General Psychiatry,* 1964, *11,* 484-494.

Singer, M. T. & Wynne, L. C. Principles for scoring communication defects and deviances in parents of schizophrenics: Rorschach and TAT scoring manuals. *Psychiatry,* 1966, *29,* 260-288.

DISCUSSION

Chairman Wynne: Before we go ahead with the panel, I would like to make a few comments and tie together the subject matter of the first paper this afternoon with the second one. The official title for the first paper, as you can see in the program, was "Techniques for Stimulating Family Interaction in the Laboratory," and now we are dealing with the problem of categorizing the material which has been stimulated or elicited. It seems to me that as a further tie-in with the clinical material that came up this morning, the person of the family therapist, and what he does and says, can similarly be regarded as stimuli for family interaction. This, then, raises the question of the extent to which similar methods and criteria for coding categories of family interaction may be applicable after interaction has been stimulated in these diverse ways. Whether the same sets of categories are relevant or not is an empirical issue we should discuss. At any rate, we end up not simply with the interaction *within* the family but also with any transactional process that has been set going between the family and the tester or therapist. Therefore, you have a new superordinate system, if you will, or a transactional process which includes what the instructions or stimuli have been and the whole process that goes on between the therapist or investigator and the family.

One is not simply dealing with the family as a context for individuals but the family as part of a broader context which also includes, most immediately, the test instructions and the tester, or the interviewer, or the therapist. Dr. Loveland has actually applied her technique of the Relation Rorschach to the family therapist meeting with the family together; in other words, she has applied this standardized test technique to a group that constitutes a larger system than the family alone. This is an example of the way in which research techniques can be applied with some inventiveness and imagination to diverse theoretical issues which are relevant to the clinical problem of what effect a particular therapist has on family interaction. I think if this issue of the interaction between therapist and family is left out, clinicians may feel that a lot of interaction research is irrelevant to their concerns, which always include the personality and behavior of the therapist. By transposition of some of these research methods to include the therapist, it may be possible to study the "fit" between therapist and family and also to evaluate therapeutic changes over time, using the same research procedure with therapist and family at regular intervals.

Thus, we need to look at these newer research methods that are being discussed this afternoon, and the newer categories that are proposed. When we consider that new alternatives are becoming available, I think that the potentialities for application of these experimental methods to problems that are vital to clinicians will become more and more apparent.

I would like to go ahead with some remarks by the panel members, starting with Dr. Titchener.

Dr. Titchener: There are many directions one could go with Dr. Lennard's paper, but I just want to pick up on the phase differentiation idea which, as I understand it, means that different things happen during different phases of a process. I like this idea because it gives one a sense that there is some regularity and pattern to a psychotherapeutic process.

I would like to ask if Dr. Lennard has noticed phase differentiation in a single hour of family therapy? Or is it that therapists act differently one week later or two or three weeks later than they did in the beginning? I would tend to think that there is a different kind of behavior by family and therapist late in an hour than there is at the beginning. In fact, maybe the behaviors occur in cycles so that phases repeat themselves.

Dr. Lennard: I don't have any data for phases within a family therapy hour. Scheflen's work, as you know, does deal with phases during the single therapy hour. He presents a very interesting differentiation of the changes that occur.*

Chairman Wynne: Bales' work and Fred Strodtbeck's work would also be involved in this.

Dr. Watzlawick: There is one type of work that Henry Lennard just mentioned that hasn't been referred to during this meeting, which I think is extremely relevant. This work was done here at Eastern Pennsylvania Psychiatric Institute by Scheflen**and his coworkers. He has shown that there is a patterning to therapy sessions; that therapists and family members, or in his case individual patients, are governed by very definite patterns in their interaction. He has, moreover, blown a hole in the more orthodox idea of rigid role concepts; he has shown that interaction patterns persist irrespective of who contributes to them—i.e., if one member fails to perform a part of a pattern, other members in the group will take over for him.

One general question that came to my mind at the beginning of Dr. Lennard's talk was: Do we have to reach agreement at this point of development of our work? My personal answer is that I don't think we have to. I see something very positive in the divergence of ideas. I think it is excellent that we are going in seemingly very different directions, because this, as far as I know, has been the case in most advances of science.

My very firm conviction is that we are going to arrive at our aim, for the simple reason that the computer up here [brain] works with these categories. We all know them without knowing that we know them, and it is "only" a question of discovering them and formulating them eventually.

Dr. MacGregor: I would like to characterize Dr. Lennard's work, subject to later correction. As I see it, he has confused the problem of content analysis or category sets with the problem of statistics. The problem of statistics has to do with summarizing observations, condensing information. As I see what Dr. Lennard does, he asks the other fellow what his theory is and then he condenses the theory into a set of propositions which are very troublesome to him, mostly because the other fellow's theory has holes in it. The question, then, of what is to be the unit becomes a very puzzling question because the units are going to be those appropriate to the question.

---

*Scheflen, A. E. Communication and regulation in psychotherapy. *Psychiatry*, 1963, 26, 126-136.

**Strategy and structure in psychotherapy: Three research studies of the Whitaker-Malone multiple therapy,* English, O. S. (Ed.), Scheflen, A. E., Hampe, W. W. and Auerbach, A. H. *Behavioral Studies Monograph,* Eastern Pennsylvania Psychiatric Institute, Philadelphia, Pennsylvania. 1965

The set of categories is not necessarily an instrument for analysis of data. For instance, I circulated to this group an outline that summarizes a chapter in a book. If you tried to use those categories like rating scales, you would become extremely frustrated and the product would make me look like a monkey. But those catch phrases from chapters of a book are condensed material. This outline of mine is related to some hypotheses about types of families. The question of whether those types are valid or not depends on a content analysis that I have under way. In order to do this content analysis I would rather rely on an outside set of categories, an *a priori* method, that there has been a lot of experience with, not one produced from my data. So I have selected Ralph White's Value Analysis. I will find frequencies in his scheme that I can correlate and then factor and find out if, indeed, there are four types in this propaganda analysis that match my four types of families. Then I will be able to say that indeed this type is different from that type. This type of family has one characteristic propaganda output, whereas that other type of family has another.

Dr. Lennard: Bob, when you say "propaganda output," you have delineated a category. You are summarizing your observations by the notion of propaganda output. In essence, you are using categorization to summarize, which is what I said categories are for.

Dr. MacGregor: Yes. Ralph White would call this question, "What is the value system of type A, type B, type C and type D family?" I am only interested in whether I can get a long list of items suitable for factoring to find out whether type A, type B, type C and type D are somehow different, and if Bales' Interaction Process Analysis would do it, I would take that.

I am not so sure that we are short on bundles of items. If you go out to San Antonio where they have a personality research laboratory, every psychologist running around has a bundle of items. The trouble is that he hasn't found a population he can standardize them on. So for the purpose of making my bundle of items useful, I will have to code quite a number of families to know whether type A uses, say, the term "sex" more frequently than my sample of families do. I will have to normalize; indeed, I will have to find out if my distributions in these categories look normal so that I can find out where the assumptions for normalizing apply.

In his comments today, Melvin Roman mentioned the power dimension and whether dominance is related to competence. You can find out whether dominance is related to competence by looking at influence. If your category includes only an item about time, all you will be able to find out is that monopolizing takes up a lot of time; but if you have a richer set of categories, you may find out that the dominant, competent fellow influences content one way whereas the dominant noncompetent fellow influences content another way.

Dr. Lennard: I don't know whether we understand each other, Bob, because to me, at least, it seems obvious that if you describe two families in a variety of ways, it is going to be difficult in reviewing your pages of notes to infer that "one family is type A and the other family type B" without some way of putting together all the things which you have said about the family. The term "category" simply refers to the procedure of putting together observations which are similar and can be subsumed by the same concept, variable, or dimension. These categories can, in turn, be put together in different ways, so that you may subsume a number of sub-categories under a major category.

Dr. MacGregor: But then you don't get findings. You just get orderly descriptions.

Dr. Lennard: No, no; this is where you begin to do the work and it is at this point you feed in the statistical methods, but not before.

Chairman Wynne: I am not sure if what we have done since yesterday morning is to come full circle or perhaps some other arrangement like a triangle, but, at any rate, the first shall be last and the last shall be first— Jay Haley.

Mr. Haley: I am not sure I like that position. I will make some general comments, partly because I don't know quite how to be specific in discussing what Dr. Lennard said.

I find it hard to agree with him and hard to disagree with him, because I am not clear what his position is. But there is one thing he said that I would disagree with and I think it has some general application to this group.

I don't think we should look for an all-purpose set of categories that apply to mothers and daughters, and fathers and sons, and two strangers, and the psychotherapist and a patient, and a prisoner and a jailer, or any of the varieties of kinds of human relationships there are. I think there has been a tendency to do that and we need to differentiate ourselves from the interdisciplinary ego mass, if I might put it that way.

I have looked over quite a few category systems—I used to collect them as I went around watching researchers—and I think one of the reasons they are not published is that they are pretty dull unless you are particularly interested in the specific focus they are aimed at. But there is another thing about these category systems. Many of them seem to me to be attempts by people to be quite broad and draw ideas from a variety of places and fit these into categories. A useful analogy could be made here to cooking. You can take an Italian chef who makes a wonderful spaghetti sauce and then you can take a French chef who makes a delicious onion soup, and you can have some good roast beef, and then you can have some shish kebab. Now, each of these people has worked very hard to get the right kind of dish. But you can have a super-chef come along and say, "If all of these are very good recipes, when I put them together I will have a wonderful dish." So he puts them in a blender and he can toss in the spaghetti sauce, the shish kebab and the roast beef, and I don't think that out of this comes a marvelous new entity. A bunch of mush comes out.

I think one of our difficulties is that we have gone after categories by pulling ideas from various fields. Many of the ideas came up before families were ever seen as systems. I do not know if Bales ever looked at a family. He made a category system of what a family is supposed to be and people have been trying to use it for a long time. People have tried to use in their category systems something that is relevant to clinical work and character and individual personality. They have dragged in ideas from communication; they have dragged in ideas from role theory; they have tried to use Birdwhistell's kinesics; they have made a big thing about how a male-female differentiation is important. All these things get put into a category system, a couple of contrasting families are put into a situation and stimulated to talk in some way. Then they go after these families with these categories, and I think there is a tendency to come out with quite a bit of mush.

What I would hope is that after ten or fifteen years of this we could begin to move more in the direction of formulating questions more precisely, of formulating an experimental context of some kind which will test these questions, and come to some conclusions, rather than trying to bring in all kinds of ideas which may or may not be useful. We have to learn to discard as well as accept, I think.

Dr. Lennard: I would like to comment on this. I understand very definitely what you are saying, Jay. (Laughter) You sound like a member of a study section who says: "There are too many variables. Limit your variables!"

But as I suggested before, in a new field where you don't know very much, it is advisable to build into what one is doing as many different ideas, as many variables, as possible and then one can determine those which pay off and those which don't.

This is the kind of methodology which is used in epidemiological surveys such as, for example, in relation to heart disease. The researchers ask: Is it diet, is it exercise, is it marital stress, etc.? In a long-term longitudinal study, one doesn't want to test diet only, because it may turn out that diet is not correlated with coronary artery diesase and that the opportunity for the collection of more relevant data has then been lost for some time.

What do you lose by taking seriously what other people have to say in addition to focusing on your own favorite ideas?

Dr. MacGregor: If you try to study everything at once, you are not going to get any payoffs at all because you are always going to say that this thing doesn't pay off because the other thing you are studying interferes. I suggest that you apply measures to a situation that don't alter the situation. They should be measures taken from the natural situation that tell you something, not measures that you deduced from the theory you are trying to understand. When possible I believe one should apply existing, standardized instruments.

Dr. Lennard: Yesterday, Jay said that in the studies which have been done, there is little evidence for differences between the so-called normal and the abnormal or disturbed families. Somebody then said, "Well, we didn't study the right variables."

Dr. Framo: What has actually happened in research is that we have been measuring the things that are easy to measure, agreed-upon observable behavior, and where is it getting us? I would like to ask Henry a question and to mention a dirty word. Can we ever find ways of measuring, inferring, or operationally defining the "dynamic unconscious?" Can we study multiperson motivational systems that interlock? Can the deeper motivational levels be put into relational categories? For example, if I talk to you while smiling, and you get angry, your behavior might be a response to an unconscious hostile motive of mine. Perhaps, operationally, you can determine unconscious motives by the reactions of the person to the behavior. I would like to believe that the psychological sciences can eventually move into this area instead of always repeating again and again precise measurements of relatively trivial behaviors. Our psychological journals are full of these kinds of studies, and few people even read them anymore.

Dr. MacGregor: Don't fuss at the measures for counting insignificant stuff. Fuss at the people who ask the questions. We need better questions such as, Do flexible people influence rigid people? First, you have to get something that measures who is a flexible person and who is a rigid person.

I submit that in Vincent Nowlis' work with the Mood Adjective Check List you have a good description of a flexible end and a rigid end.* Then you know that you are dealing with a flexible or a rigid person and you can make your postulates as to what are the operations by which the flexible person influences a rigid person.

Dr. Titchener: That is not a family interaction, though. Dr. Framo was

---

*Nowlis, V. Research with the mood adjective check-list. In Tomkins, S. S. and Izard, C. E. *Affect, cognition, and personality.* New York: Springer, 1965.

talking about interaction categories and you are talking about individual behavior.

Dr. Lennard: I think we are at a point where the most we can do is to map out a territory, and I, for one, would be in favor of putting in more lobsters and steaks, to use Jay's metaphor. For example, there are psychophysiological variables operating here about which we know very little. Also, I believe that you should focus on a particular issue when you *analyze* your data, not at the time of collection of your data.

Chairman Wynne: Dr. Reiss is the next contributor.

Dr. Reiss: I think we have strayed from the question of coding and the usefulness of a variety of coding systems which Dr. Lennard originally discussed in the position paper, to the virtues and pitfalls of measurement. This is an unfortunate diversion, largely because the problem of coding, as such, and particularly the problems of the codes that Dr. Lennard mentioned, do add something quite specific to the deliberations of this group apart from the general issue of: How much can you measure, what should you measure, what theories should you use?

Coding, as I understand it, is a special kind of measurement, and one of the particular characteristics of the coding operation as a measurement is that it specifies what the context of the judgment should be. Specifically, most codes specify how much of the protocol the coder can read before he makes the coding judgment. A particularly restrictive context is one that was used by Mishler and Waxler where a number of their codes specify that you can only look at an isolated statement and you may not pay any attention, in making your judgment, to anything said by that person before or after that statement was made.*

What this procedure of measurement highlights—and the procedure is certainly very much in the tradition of coding—is the notion of: To what extent can you, by canon or by edict, legislate a specific ignorance in the measurer and come up with something useful? Or, what particular use does canonic ignorance, as you might call it, have in studying families?

I would hope, Dr. Lennard, that you can make some suggestions as to how much restriction ought to be made in creating a useful coding system, and what are some of the pitfalls of such restrictiveness?

Dr. Lennard: You have raised a very important issue. One limitation often imposed by a coding system is that the coder cannot use everything he knows. To be specific, in our research we were interested in discontinuity, that is, in determining whether a statement is a discontinuity in terms

---

*Mishler, E. G. and Waxler, E. G. *Interaction in families: An experimental study of family processes and schizophrenia.* New York: Wiley, 1968.

of the feeling, the topic, theme or mood. To make a determination as to whether a statement represents a discontinuity with everything that has been said before would be a terribly difficult undertaking. One would have to go back to every statement and look at everything to make this determination. A coder could not possibly do this. But I don't think that such knowledge is available to an observer, either. The most sensitive observer, I think, leaves out 95 percent—99 percent—of the phenomena which others looking at the situation may eventually pick up.

Chairman Wynne: Along the same lines, Harry Stack Sullivan was quoted once as saying during a psychotherapeutic hour in which he was at his very best in noticing what was going on, he might have picked up 10 percent of what was really important. He said that he felt very proud of this level of accomplishment. This is also applicable to the research situation, without any question.

I would like to call on Dr. Ferreira who has been wanting to speak.

Dr. Ferreira: I would like to sound a conciliatory note over a controversy which I don't feel has too great a reason to exist. This controversy is due mostly to an ambition, which, though laudable, is nevertheless very premature, namely, to try to bring research methodology as we conceive of it into the whole field of clinical work and therapy. We are perhaps in the same position Democritus and Lucretius would have been in twenty-five hundred years ago, if, upon visualizing the existence of the atom, someone had demanded that they build an atomic bomb, or something of the sort.

I think it is much too early for us researchers to bring our incomplete knowledge into the field of clinical work, and into what the therapist is doing with his families. I see no reason at all, as I have said before, why both facets cannot be followed in a sort of parallel way: on the one hand, with the clinician trying to struggle artistically with his family, hoping for the best and sometimes getting it, and on the other hand, with the experimenter controlling his variables and trying to get some meaningful and solid raw data about what families are, and what interaction is. We would have the right to expect that both facets could meet, hopefully, before infinity.

Dr. Levinger: I was a little distressed today because I had been hoping that we would come closer together in understanding what each other's problems are. To go back to the cooking metaphor, we have been talking about the kinds of tools to be used for cooking the food, or the spices to be used for seasoning it, when perhaps the *real* problem is to decide what it is we want to have for dinner.

The statement of the problem seems to me to be the crucial thing, and we have really spent far too little time on it. I think part of Jay

Haley's distress may have been occasioned by this. For example, this morning, Dr. Ackerman talked about three different areas of investigation for his therapy case: the verbal, the body movement, and the mood. It seems to me that the Bales' method will yield data on only the first of those levels, although it might give indirect evidence about the mood. So it seems to me that *"What is it we want to know?"* is the problem that we must spend more time discussing and thinking through.

Dr. Strodtbeck: In making a classification system, one of the kinds of problems that you always encounter is taking a ribbon of continuous interaction and making some rules about chopping it into units. Once the units are chopped into whatever series of classifications you wish to use, you either have to make the decision: Are you going to use successive multiple dichotomies, with positive or negative dimensions, or are you going to use a cafeteria list of five to fifty-nine different varieties?

If you want reliability, the cafeteria method mitigates against it very rapidly. If you have successive dichotomies, you can get reliability much faster. But by far the most important consideration is getting some contrasting protocols which tend to represent differences that you are concerned with. You can use any category system that you can put together hurriedly without estranging all your personnel, and then see whether or not that category works. Then you can determine how it might be improved by looking back more carefully into the empirical indices that you have, and go out and get additional cases. The theory you espouse interacts with whatever empirical material you have collected to build your category system.

If you have any questions as to whether or not you are getting more information from a new category system, there are statistical operations to see whether or not the new category system is independent from the first, and with computers you don't even have to know how to do a correlation coefficient to use them. It seems to me that progressive, active engagement with your data is *the* solution to the sense of doubt that people are bringing to this matter of categories.

Chairman Wynne: I would like to underline this last point by saying that a thoughtful effort at coding and working out empirical categories for coding can help clarify one's concepts. Actually, I think this is a circular process. It has been emphasized, appropriately, that we have to think about the questions we have in mind to know what kinds of categories are appropriate. On the other hand, in the process of starting with a somewhat vague question and then trying to work out criteria and categories and codes, my experience is that we then start to realize in what ways our questions have been vague and diffuse and unclear; so that we then start to ask better questions. Then we can, from the better questions, work on to better categories, so this is a continuous process. We needn't expect to have the ultimately clear questions at the beginning, nor the definitive categories. It is very much the business of both the therapist and the researcher getting in there and getting their hands dirty with questions and methods and categories that admittedly are never as cleaned up as one might ideally prefer.

At this point, I think we should turn to the summarizers.

Dr. Bowen: I'm bugged. Let me say this word. I am sort of disappointed in you, Lyman. You got the differences going over there between Henry Lennard and Jay Haley and you didn't get any of the differences solved in that panel this afternoon. I was hoping that by the end of this meeting we would get all of our differences solved so that we would be in a position to pass a resolution about solving Vietnam. (Laughter) You didn't even get the differences solved at the head table and we are in a bigger mess than we were when we started.

Chairman Wynne: We just *know* that we are in a bigger mess. It is now time for our summarizers, Drs. Friedman and Handel, to speak. Let's go ahead with the trends that Dr. Alfred Friedman thinks we have developed.

(Editor's Note: *The reader is advised that the following summarizing comments were spontaneous reactions to the conference based on notes made during the conference, and were not studied critiques of the proceedings.*)

Dr. Friedman: First of all, I will not so much discuss trends as try to review for you some of the issues that were raised during this conference.

There will be at least four limitations to this summary. It will certainly miss some important ideas or trends that were expressed. It will not identify those who expressed the ideas, except for the position paper presenters. It will probably place more emphasis on clinical research than social system research, because I am more familiar with the former. And, like the conference, it will list more problems and raise more issues than it will answer.

Dr. Framo, our Chairman, first charged us with our task and stated some of the challenges and hopes of this conference. The conference led off with Mr. Haley's position paper, which was a comprehensive review and critical analysis of the current state of family interaction research. This report took a hard, rigorous line with a skeptical eye toward global theorizing and speculation about family dynamics. It did, however, set a mood of mild enthusiasm which was held back sharply by skepticism.

The studies summarized by Haley which met rigorous experimental tests were very few. These studies were largely restricted to comparisons of so-called normal and abnormal families and covered only narrowly circumscribed elements of process and outcome of interaction. More conflict was found in abnormal families than normal families, and abnormal families required more time to complete an assigned performance task.

The widespread research method of employing clinical judgments and even of using carefully defined rater judgments for coding categories of response was declared by Haley to be all but worthless. There was some difference of opinion among conference participants as to whether these rater judgments could be made sufficiently independent and blind and still be reliable and replicable.

Another topic to which the conference addressed itself, after the presentation of Haley's paper, was whether the typological approach of comparing interaction samples of so-called normal families with so-called abnormal samples of families, was the most useful approach. The question was asked whether families could be more meaningfully typed by some other variable such as the functioning of the whole family system or family role distribution rather than by the pathological symptom picture of one family member. It was pointed out that it might be possible to have a family in which the family system was malfunctioning or unsuccessful while at the same time there was no apparent symptomatic member in the family. The reverse could occur where there was a symptomatic member but the overall family system appeared to be working quite successfully.

With respect to typology and research controls, more systematic observation of so-called normal families was called for to determine whether real differences could be found between them and the problem families. It was also suggested that research studies should include normal samples as well as samples of two or more types of abnormality, such as neurosis or schizophrenia, so that differences could be related to a particular type of pathology which occurred in a family member.

We moved to the second position paper of Dr. Epstein, who pointed to a similar need to study more homogeneous rather than heterogeneous samples and types of families, and to control for such variables as size of family, sex, and ordinal position of children. This research report of Epstein's was one effort that dared to study systematically change and improvement occurring in families as the result of the therapeutic enterprise. It was a hopeful report in that it indicated that many of the problems involved in such a study, such as identifying and quantifying meaningful criteria for improvement, could be wholly or partially solved. One of the hopeful aspects of this research report was a finding of a positive relationship between the quantity of interaction found in a pretreatment assessment of the family and the amount of movement or change independently reported by therapists after an initial phase of six sessions of family therapy. While this short-term result did not hold up for long-term therapy, it could still have considerable value in selecting families for short-term family treatment in situations where there are limited staff resources and a large number of cases.

Dr. Wynne's position paper dealt with the question of how we select the important variables for study regarding family system and family interaction. He first asked: If the family really is a system, in what sense is it a system? If the system is not completely closed but always partially open, we cannot clearly know what its boundaries are. The family has to be seen as part of, and in the context of, its own extended network and the broader community and social system. Is the family a system of rules, or of task assignments, or of roles, or of conscious and unconscious biological and affective relationships of persons, or is it the sum of all of these?

Certain more or less accepted assumptions used by theorists to differentiate well-functioning from pathological families should still be tested by more systematic study. Thus, is rigid homeostasis a sign of family disturbance or is it that we tend to see and treat close, nuclear families and this leads to the impression of homeostasis?

Wynne asked whether the family really resists change and improvement in the scapegoated member, the designated patient. He pointed out that there is need for longitudinal studies of various developmental phases of whole families.

Wynne also proposed that family interaction studies are central to the study of society in general, because the family is the link between at least four types of systems: biology, personality, social role structure and culture. Is it partly for this reason that so many different variables have to be controlled in the systematic study of family interaction?

Dr. ____'s position paper, which came next, was a high point of the conference. ____ used a unique, fascinating analysis of his own personal family and of the forces and maneuvers at work in the family, to demonstrate his principles of family relationship and family system. These principles have to do with: How does a family member free himself from the family undifferentiated ego mass; how does one detriangle oneself from the triangle which one may be involved in with one's parents or with one parent and a sibling? The triad or triangle is the basic building block of the family and this is what has to be dealt with in therapy. One has to get out of the pathological part of the mass while still relating to the family and not rejecting it completely.

According to ____, the therapist works with two family members at a time and uses his own separateness to detriangle the triangle which this

family triad tries to induct him into. Also, it is most difficult to deal with
the family member who is going away from you and is trying not to deal
directly with you on a genuine affective level. You have to get "in" with
that person or with that dyad before you can get out again on a better
level. Good therapists are expert manipulators in maneuvering family
dyads and in moving in and out of their own families.

One difficulty with this type of family research is not only the
complexity of the family system but also our own need to deny some of the
important, intimate family issues which we experience ourselves.

Next, we went to Dr. Ackerman's film presentation and analysis of a
family therapy session. This film demonstrated, first of all, Ackerman's
skillful techniques for getting inside important aspects of the family system
quickly and eliciting key family problems. Secondly, the film demonstrated
how the therapist effectively controls the whole family in the therapeutic
session without getting involved in countertransference with any one
member. He gets inside the family but stays outside at the same time. The
film and the discussion about it that followed also demonstrated the
extreme difficulty in subjecting to controlled research process the kinds of
therapeutic insights, process and intervention which may be quite powerful
and meaningful but elude systematic analysis.

Dr. Strodtbeck's position paper was primarily a review of a variety of
research applications of the revealed difference technique for stimulating
and studying family interaction. Several interesting points were made.
Differences were found in parental interaction depending on whether a
female child or a male child was present in the family interaction process.
When the two siblings were of opposite sex, the mother took more
responsibility for the girl and the father took more responsibility for the
boy, but when the two siblings were of the same sex, there was more
competition between the parents for role responsibilities.

The revealed difference technique provides a method of obtaining
large-scale, standardized epidemiological data from cross-cultural samples.
One surprising aspect of the technique is that the results apparently do not
depend too much on the particular family and cultural setting in which it
is used. On the other hand, it was proposed in the discussion that it makes
a difference what kind of stimulus, problem or situation you use to
stimulate family interaction, whether it be a Rorschach card, revealed
difference questionnaire, and so on.

Since the time is short, I will skip to a kind of impressionistic
overview of the conference. During the afternoon session of the first day, a
split developed and widened between the clinicians and the family
therapists on the one hand, and some of the global family theorists and the
systematic, research-oriented members of the conference on the other hand.

This split also reoccurred, but to a milder degree, during the second day. The globally and genotypically-oriented clinicians and theoreticians were saying that the exact researchers were studying trivial and meaningless problems, and were not contributing much to the basic understanding of the family or to the family therapy process. On the other hand, it appeared that the experimentally and phenotypically-oriented researchers were saying that the clinicians were perpetuating their own biases and myths by descriptive generalizations and global theories of family dynamics, and that there was no real evidence that any of their generalizations were true. It appeared for a while that these two diverging points of view could not meet or integrate in a useful partnership, but after some frustrations were expressed, in which each side indicated that the other was not supplying what was needed, a bridging and healing process began to develop in which the two sides came closer together. They did not reach complete agreement or unanimity, but I felt that they were not in a worse mess than when they began. (Laughter)

Chairman Wynne: Thank you, Al. I think you did cover many important highlights. I would now like to introduce our second summarizer, Dr. Gerald Handel, who has been asked to focus on areas neglected by the conference, as well as to contribute some ideas about future directions for family interaction research.

Dr. Handel: To be asked to conclude a densely packed two-day conference of 29 distinguished specialists in family interaction by identifying neglected areas is a challenging assignment, made more so by my not having seen any of the seven position papers in advance of their delivery. When the ancient Greeks wanted to know the future, they consulted an oracle, the most famous of which was the one at Delphi. Since I am asked to provide a prognosis as well as a diagnosis I feel as though I am being asked to serve as a Philadelphia oracle. I assume that we are all, to some extent, suffering, as Dr. Watzlawick has remarked, from "information overload." Therefore, I shall strive for the brevity my role requires but I hope to be less cryptic than the classical model.

As I try to organize my impressions of these 16 hours of talk, it seems to me that the conference has suffered from one fundamental and pervasive neglect—insufficient attention to conceptualization. A great deal of attention has been given to very specific and often minute questions of gathering and categorizing data, but these questions have not been related to questions of basic guiding concepts which should direct the gathering and analysis of one or another kind of data. We have not jointly addressed ourselves to the question: In what terms should a family be conceived? Some of the very basic issues were raised by Dr. Framo in his opening remarks, but the conference made little or no effort to confront the very searching questions he asked. To be sure, individual speakers occasionally touched on these matters in passing, but they never became the focus of concentrated discussion.

The conference has not addressed itself to the most fundamental question of all: What is family interaction and how shall we conceive of it? Both for research and for purposes of practicing and evaluating therapy, it makes some difference whether interaction is thought of as rates of participation in a discussion, or as a pattern of communication without regard to the component contributions of specifically identified family members or, as I would suggest, as the offering of selves in conjunctions and disjunctions of meaning. If we think of interaction as arising from selves we will be led to very different research procedures than if we think of it solely as a group phenomenon without regard to psychological characteristics of the individuals who compose the group. If, as I believe, interaction is a product of selves or perhaps more precisely selves in roles which are interrelated, then we are led to the conclusion that interaction can adequately be understood only if we also consider relationships. From this point of view, the title of the conference reflects inadequate conceptualization and should perhaps have been "Systematic Research on Family Relationships and Family Interaction." Dr.____told us in very personal terms about his family relationships. He talked, for example, about his relationship with his brother. Certainly one of the things that we should want to understand is, What is brotherhood? We have not had a new concept in this field since "sibling rivalry," and there is surely more to sibling relationships than that.

Another aspect of our conceptual task is to ask: What do people learn from interaction? We are attentive both in research and in clinical work to what children learn from their parents, but we do not pay much, if any, attention to what siblings learn from each other or what spouses learn from each other. And it is surely a reasonable hypothesis that what they learn from each other is a function of the type of relationship that they sustain.

Mentioning learning reminds us again of the problem of conceptualizing interaction. I am suggesting that we can and should study family interaction as learning. Prevailing views of family interaction, among researchers and clinicians, construe interaction as communication, as defensiveness, as power, but not very often as learning. Family interaction, being expressive of selves and of relationships, is also the confrontation of fantasies, the contention of definitions of reality, the affirmation of past history, the effort to define a future, and undoubtedly a great many other things that I have not thought of or observed. The essential point to be made here is that research on family interaction cannot take us very far if we do not give more attention than this conference has done to the task of systematically conceptualizing interaction. Attention to this task would seem to me to be one of the first orders of business for the future.

On this kind of foundation, it would seem to me that research should be directed to understanding the connections between family group phenomena and individual phenomena. Sociologists study power in families. What are the relationships between power in the family and the various members' sense of individual strength? Or, what do people imagine they are doing when they give or don't give support to another family member? Clinical workers are giving attention to how families engender defense mechanisms, security operations and symptoms in their members. How does a family engender interests? How does a family shape the use of the talents of its members?

An entirely different area that was mentioned only in passing by Dr. Wynne has to do with the relationships of psychophysiology to family interaction. What role, if any, does metabolism play in family interaction? Endocrine output? Neurochemistry? At some point in the future such issues will perhaps receive more concentrated attention, and we may live to see the day when sociologists join with biologists of various kinds in collaborative researches.

Not much attention has been paid here to family development. For all its difficulties and frustrations, systematic study of the family will, it seems to me, have to attempt longitudinal studies more than is now the case. This may call for new forms of collaboration among research institutions so that when families move from an area they will not become lost cases but may be kept as part of the research by collaborators at other institutions. Is it entirely fruitless to propose a research that begins with courting couples and follows them, for, say, a period of 10 years? I do not doubt that such research would be difficult to conduct, but some of the difficulties stem from the ways in which funding and career lines are institutionalized. Perhaps these are not insuperable.

No doubt many participants in the conference have an entirely different conception of future directions than those pointed to here. Perhaps we can all agree, however, that many more centers of family research are necessary than now exist.

Chairman Wynne: Before we conclude, I would like to express my personal appreciation, and I believe the appreciation of the entire group, to Dr. Framo and the other members of the Eastern Pennsylvania Psychiatric Institute staff who have helped to make this meeting possible. I think those of us who participated can only be dimly aware of the tremendous amount of devoted labor that they had to put in to bring this meeting about, and I want to express our collective appreciation for the opportunity to be here.

(Saturday Afternoon Session Adjourned)

Commentary and Observations

JAMES L. FRAMO

Scientific conferences have always met a need not serviced by other media of information exchange between professional workers. The primary method that investigators use to inform others about their work is publication in books or journals. Publications, however, have the disadvantage of being too slow to allow an interchange or questioning of views and, besides, open candidness in formal writings is often prevented by the restrictions of publication standards. Conferences allow immediate reactions, criticisms, and follow-up inquiries by colleagues in face-to-face confrontations. When professionals react to each other as human beings in a setting which encourages free interchange of views, they have a greater opportunity to discover new levels of communication, understanding, and discovery. Whenever people interact there will be, to be sure, communicational breakdowns and misunderstandings, but such is the nature of human relationships. Before discussing the subject matter of family interaction research, it would perhaps be appropriate to describe some of the interesting features of the group process of this particular conference.

As stated in the introductory chapter, it was difficult to predict how this group of family specialists would interact with each other. One identifiable piece of hidden orchestration was the system of family therapists, which, like a family, had its own history of loyalty bonds, caring, alliances, competitiveness, and jealousies. As in every group, this system had its own politics, and its members had jockeyed for position around the ideological issues of status, the various "schools" of family therapy, and the particularly loaded question of whether there should be a national organization of family therapists. It should be mentioned that differences between professional workers have a positive side; the history of science is full of examples of controversy advancing scientific discovery. Although very little of the workings of the private culture of the family therapists surfaced in the verbal exchanges, undoubtedly they had strong, if unnoticed, effects on the process of the conference. The family therapists of this conference, however, largely suppressed their disparities in the face of the challenge of the researchers who, although not organized as a system, nonetheless shared a quality of experience that differed greatly from that of the family therapists in dealing with the same subjects of study. Whereas the clinicians were used to taking responsibility for mitigating distress and consequently searched for human meaning and the substance of family life, the researchers were intent on creating order by organizing the data from family interaction that would form the basis of a science. Each group, initially, then, considered itself superior to the other. For instance, in one of the satellite conferences that took place during lunch, one of the family therapists remarked to a colleague, "Those researchers sure have a long way to go." Similarly, a researcher commented to a systematic investigator, "When are those clinicians going to straighten out their thinking?"

In the light of the foregoing sub-processes, it was not surprising that, following the initial phase of politeness and wariness, there occurred early in the conference a marked polarization of the "hard" and "soft" investigators. The dichotomy between the two groups, however, was not only inevitable but perhaps indispensable in those early and middle stages. The clinicians, having had lots of experience crossing freely through multiple and contradictory levels, were able to tolerate the ambiguity which existed among the issues of the conference, while the researchers necessarily had to maintain a controlled attitude. The early failures of the two groups to get together created tension at times, but the tension was constructive and was part of the effort, vital to the life of the conference, to reduce the disparity in experience. Although the clinicians and researchers were certainly not united at the end of the conference, there were several factors that helped diminish the distance between them. There were some participants, for example, who, not joining any particular faction, were able to stand at the interface and feel the intricacies and mystery of family process by looking both ways. The most powerful impact on the group process, and the one which freed the conference of its polarity, however, was the presentation by the anonymous author. This professional family therapist explored one of man's perpetual and universal dilemmas—how to deal with the "craziness" of one's own family without giving that family up. By sharing with colleagues a personal family chronicle, he moved the conference to an experiential dimension which cut right through the controversies, the issues, and the occasional pedanticism. Following this experience there was no more talk about "hard" and "soft" research.

Just as the researchers were moved by the immediacy of the experience of the anonymous paper and by the film of the family therapy session, so the ethnocentrism of the clinicians was jarred by the revelation that a considerable amount of thinking and work had already been done in the fields of family sociology and social and clinical psychology that was directly pertinent to family therapy—work that some of the family therapists had never heard of.

There were other aspects of the group process noted by the Editor that had nothing to do with the clinician-researcher dimension. These included phenomena which occur in all groups and which have been studied formally by social psychologists and group therapists, having to do with how group processes and individual behavior affect each other. For instance, during the course of the conference the group atmosphere at times was such that the participants found themselves saying things they didn't really believe. Certain built-in features of the structure of the conference, together with the nature of the participants, actuated and limited some conference behaviors. The formal sequence of position papers and the time limits of the discussion periods did not allow follow-up of a number of the fascinating and profound ideas that were set forth; perhaps conferences should be flexibly arranged so that the group is free to abandon its schedule and pursue a tangential course if it seems productive at the time (for example, it is interesting to speculate what would have come out of a concentrated focus on the implications of the anonymous paper for the rest of the conference). Often, because of lack of time, interruptions, and so forth, the participants felt they were speaking off the tops of their heads and dealing with topics superficially without getting across the real points they wanted to make, or they were hesitant to speak for fear of taking time from others. There were possibly other, more subtle influencing factors. Of all the professional groups with whom the Editor has been associated, the family therapy field has been the most free of interdisciplinary conflict, but it is possible that professional rank determined the quantity and quality of some of the contributions. Some of the participants may have felt intimidated by the presence of more famous professionals, whereas others, perhaps, needed to impress and demonstrate that they were a force to be reckoned with. Group-individual interaction effects may also have been manifested by: some participants addressing themselves to the stenotypist in order to be on record for future publication; by some pushing their own narrow preoccupations rather than attending to the matter at hand; by some practicing clever one-upmanship in order to deal with others' expertness; by fatigue and information overload; by the denial or exaggeration of differences; by prima donna-like behavior which all we professionals exhibit now and then in conferences, social gatherings, classrooms, and cocktail parties; and even by regressive phenomena which all humans are subject to when surrounded by others (one participant asked the Editor, as leader of the conference, to do something about the hard pillows at the hotel he was staying at).

What was extraordinary to the Editor, however, was not that the foregoing phenomena occurred, since they were expected, but that they were of minimal significance to the overall purposes of the conference. These successful, highly individualized participants, being truly professional, did what they were supposed to do and did not allow narcissism or personal matters to sabotage the meeting. In truth, overall, the conference was remarkably task-oriented as its members struggled to deal with singularly knotty matters. There were, moreover, numerous moments of genuine encounter when they did listen to one another and appreciated each other's viewpoints, however foreign these views may have been to their own experience. Carl Whitaker, immediately after the conference, wrote in a letter: "...I was disturbed by the mass of data but I suspect part of that is my clinical background and my inability to digest all the varying viewpoints because I'm really not familiar with the world of research. On the other hand, I took 20 pages of notes. I came up with a dozen ideas that to me were exciting relative to my own setting, and I came away with a tremendous respect for the guts of the research people in their insistence and push to accomplish something that,when it breaks through, is certainly going to redound to my increasing   knowledgeability and is certainly going to be profoundly useful in my own work and in the whole field of family understanding and family psychotherapy." Some of the researchers wrote that they had been touched on an experience level about family dynamics in such a way that they would have difficulty doing research on families in their old ways.

If final problems were not solved, if the conference did not meet all its goals, this stemmed more from the intrinsic complexity of the field than anything else. Perhaps the most important result of the conference was that the participants were forced to recognize more realistically what they could expect from one another, for there were over- and under-expectations in both directions. By the end of the conference there had developed an implicit agreement that systematic and therapeutic work with families was likely to proceed on a variety of levels, sometimes in complementary fashion, more often independent of each other. There was also a tacit and sober appreciation of the reality that these family researchers and clinicians needed to develop a more shared body of concepts before meeting with each other again. Any effort to develop a common language and set of concepts to unify research and clinical work with families would require systematic reasoning derived from shared experiences. This meeting did provide the opportunity for these investigators to meet each other in person and lay the groundwork for future collaborative efforts. As a result, a number of family therapy centers now include family researchers on their staffs, and vice versa, out of the recognition that each can enrich the work that the conference began.

Turning now to substantive matters, the kind of contextual research espoused in the field of family interaction study has its roots in general systems theory, the theoretical framework whose potential for understanding and dealing with modern man's technological, biological, behavioral, psychological, and social phenomena is only beginning to be realized (von Bertalanffy, 1968). Utilizing such principles as organized complexity, holistic functioning, interdependence of parts, open systems, information processing, feedback, transaction, homeostasis and heterostasis, goal-directedness, and progressive change, general systems theory, which cuts across all sciences and humanities, does not replace or refute previous scientific work, but enlarges, integrates, and reorients knowledge about the world and its inhabitants. General systems theory already has a short tradition in the behavioral and social sciences where its integrative and humanistic values portend revolutionary changes. The field of psychiatry, for instance, having moved from medical to diagnostic to dynamic to social psychiatric models, almost has to go in the direction of a systems approach if it is to become a viable and competent arena for the relief of human distress. A first-rate book on this topic, *General Systems Theory and Psychiatry* (Gray, Duhl, and Rizzo, 1969) has pointed the way, as has an excellent grass-roots treatise of the subject, *The Absurd Healer* (Dumont, 1968). The genius of Freud led to a highly sophisticated decoding of the intrapsychic world of the individual, but it will take the profound insights of a general systems theorist of the future to integrate the intrapsychic with the interpersonal, the personal with the social, the individual with the family or group, the family with society, and the society with culture.

A mature science aims toward the theoretical ideal of achieving a balanced integration of theory, research, and practice. In this sense, the science of family interaction research is a young one, since it is just stepping beyond the stage of hypothesis formation and beginning to collect empirical and experimental data. The relevance of the data to be collected is what this conference was all about, with emphasis on how the newly-developed depth knowledge about families could be extended into a humanistic, systematized discipline. Despite the necessary delay in publication of these proceedings, the ideas expressed herein have a timelessness which presaged some of the developments that have taken place in the field since the conference was held (see Bodin, 1968; Lennard & Bernstein, 1969; Mishler & Waxler, 1968; Straus, 1969; and Winter & Ferreira, 1969).

Man as a system is ecologically situated in many systems, the most important of which is the family. The family, however, is not just another system among a whole range of systems. Its unique and powerful effects, rooted in blood ties and tenaciously-held emotional bonds of love and hate, shape the fiber of people's beings in a way that no other social system can begin to realize. Family influence persists through space and time, kept alive by "programming" and family ghosts of the past, and lived through other people in the present; family primacy does not affect geography, as adults discover when they try to break off contact and put physical distance between themselves and their families of origin. The long arm of family loyalty can stretch beyond death and the grave, like the thin, steel wires embedded in the brains of laboratory animals who, on command, will feel rage or fear or love, and will behave accordingly. Peer groups, friendship networks, work settings, social class, race, age, sex, nationality, religion, or any other social or cultural system can only have glancing effects as they provide a porous framework for invisible family links and obligations. It is only under the rare condition of overpoweringly repressive political systems that allegiance to the state or a Cause can supersede family fealty—as when the Hitler Youth turned their parents over to the Gestapo. The suggestion that the family is the most important of all social systems can be easily demonstrated by asking what one's first thought would be if a disaster such as an atomic attack or earthquake were to occur; would it not be, "I must get home to my family"? It is the Editor's opinion that, despite recent sweeping social changes, writings about the death of the family, and the experiments with other forms of living arrangements, the family will always be with us.

The point, however, is not whether the family is important, because agreement here is assumed. The full and broad implications of the family systems approach, nonetheless, have only begun to be appreciated. It was not until family therapists brought whole families together and observed their interactions that they took the roofs off people's houses, so to speak, and found out what novelists and playwrights have known all along about family life. The transactions of family therapy sessions, when disassembled and described in some detail, graphically reveal that, despite the comfort of family love, the joy of family play, the gratification of family sacrifice, there occurs among people intimately related to one another a blind destructiveness unmatched in the entire spectrum of all human relationships. For instance, aside from the fact that unwanted children are often physically abused, killed, or neglected, the inadvertent psychological devastation of children is shocking to observe, especially since it happens in a child-oriented society where parents will make any sacrifice for their children. Parents tend to do to children what was once done to them, or, in their efforts to undo what was done to them, they will go to other extremes. Consequently, one sees children parentified, assigned irrational roles, exploited, scapegoated, shamed, overindulged and made helpless, teased, humilated, and seduced. And since children cannot leave parents who have an unhappy marriage or who will die or collapse without them, many remain bound as captive objects, unable to leave and form families of their own. It is painful to witness the magic of childhood being crushed in those growing years that could be so wondrous. How many thousands of children lie awake in terror over the turmoil in their homes? What is the extent of the despair, cynicism, and bitterness that people feel about the emptiness of their family relationships? How many husbands and wives, fathers and sons, mothers and daughters, and brothers and sisters do not know each other and are strangers in their own homes? To be sure, disappointment, unfairness, hypocrisy and deceit are part of the human lot and an inevitable piece of family life. But the real tragedy in all of this is that family problems, which carry over from one generation to the next, are preventable, since we have some of the conceptual and therapeutic tools which can alleviate much of the unnecessary suffering. The true "Society for the Prevention of Cruelty to Children" is treatment of the whole family. Disturbed family relationships do not just cause unhappiness; they can generate frank psychiatric symptoms, family breakups such as divorce, separation and desertion, exaggerated generation gaps, medical problems such as heart attacks, ulcers, and accidents, conflicts involving in-laws and aged parents, suicide and murder in the family, and so forth. Of even greater consequence, family problems become translated and reverberate into many of the social problems that beset the contemporary American society: crime and delinquency, drug addiction, school problems, alcoholism, homosexuality, high divorce rate, etc.

The Editor feels it necessary to conclude this book by suggesting to the National Institute of Mental Health and other federal social agencies that they do not know what opportunities for critically decisive help they are missing by not recognizing the contributions that family systems theory can make. It is curious that, while every society instinctively regards the integrity of the family as basic to its survival, health and social care delivery systems and federal programs often work at cross purposes and tend to fragment the unity of the family. For instance, separate programs for children, adolescents, adults, or the aged not only miss the essential point of the interrelationships of these age groups, but such programs promote division and alienation between members of the family.

Traditional mental health models, which postulate that "psychiatric illness" exists within an individual as a focal disorder and that treatment should be aimed at changing that person's attitudes and perceptions about his streasful situations, need to be altered to the view that all behavior is "normal" in the sense that it is adaptive to its context, and that efforts should be directed at analyzing and changing contexts. Evidence is accumulating that traditional mental health practices label and fix emotional problems in individuals by not getting at the real family problems. Furthermore, mental health professionals, by sticking to the "sickness-patient-diagnosis-treatment" dimension often unwittingly collude with the family extrusion processes that populate foster homes, mental hospitals, prisons, and institutions for delinquents, the aged, and disturbed children. Educative, social, psychiatric, and welfare services should be oriented around the family unit, with the improvement of the *quality* of relationships within the family as their primary goal. There should be a Family Bureau at the federal level which could, for example, advise legislators on how proposed bills on such matters as welfare, child care centers, economic policies, unemployment, drug problems, divorce laws, juvenile law, social security, etc., would affect the quality of family life. Since we have only begun to scratch the surface in our understanding of family processes and the enormous complexity of the relationship between the family and the wider society, it is further proposed that family centers be established on a nationwide scale, staffed by both family therapists and family researchers.

The family as an institution has survived many thousands of years as the most workable kind of living for human beings because, as the mediator of the culture in preparing the young for the next generation, it has served to digest social change as well as act as a bulwark against upheavals which have occurred through the centuries. The crises of our times should compel us to reach beyond the mere survival of the family to a higher realization of its potential, differentiated and together, separate and personal, with dignity and fulfillment.

REFERENCES

1. Bodin, A.M. Conjoint family assessment: An evolving field. In Paul McReynolds (Ed.) *Advances in psychological assessment.* Palo Alto, Calif.: Science & Behavior Books, 1968.

2. Dumont, M. *The absurd healer.* New York: Science House, 1968.

3. Gray, W., Duhl, F.J. & Rizzo, N.D. (Eds.) *General systems theory and psychiatry.* Boston: Little, Brown & Co., 1969.

4. Lennard, H.L. & Bernstein, A. *Patterns in human interaction: An introduction to clinical sociology.* San Francisco: Jossey-Bass. 1969.

5. Mishler, E.G. and Waxler, N.E. *Interaction in families.* New York: Wiley, 1968.

6. Straus, M.A. *Family measurement techniques: Abstracts of published instruments.* Minneapolis: Univ. of Minnesota Press, 1969.

7. von Bertalanffy, L. *General systems theory. Foundation, developments, applications.* New York: Braziller, 1968.

8. Winter, W.D. & Ferreira, A.J. *Research in family interaction.* Palo Alto, Calif.: Science & Behavior Books, 1969.